Identities in South Asia

This book examines how identities are formed and articulated in political, social and cultural contexts across South Asia. It is a comprehensive intervention on how, why and what identities have come to be, and takes a closer look at the complexities of their interactions.

Drawing on an interdisciplinary approach, combining methodologies from history, literary studies, politics and sociology, this book

- explores the multiple ways in which personal and collective identities manifest and engage, are challenged and resisted across time and space;
- highlights how the shared history of colonialism and partition, communal violence, bloodshed and pogrom are instrumental in understanding present-day developments in identity politics; and
- sheds light on a number of current themes such as borders and nations, race and ethnicity, identity politics and fundamentalism, language and regionalism, memory and community and resistance and assertion.

A key volume in South Asian Studies, this book will be of great interest to scholars and researchers of modern South Asian history, politics, sociology, literary studies and social exclusion.

Vivek Sachdeva is a Professor of English at the University School of Humanities and Social Sciences, Guru Gobind Singh Indraprastha University, New Delhi, India. His doctoral research work is on adaptations of novels into films from the narratological perspective from Panjab University, Chandigarh. His book, *Fiction to Film: Ruth*

Prawer Jhabvala's *The Householder and Heat and Dust*, has been released in 2017. Presently, he is working on Shyam Benegal's cinema studying the representation of India as a nation in post-colonial times. He is also a translator and has translated two books of Hindi poetry into English. Currently, he is translating Punjabi poetry.

Queeny Pradhan is a Professor of History at the University School of Law and Legal Studies, Guru Gobind Singh Indraprastha University, New Delhi, India. She teaches Indian History, Legal History and Women in History. She did her doctoral research from the Centre for Historical Studies, Jawaharlal Nehru University, New Delhi. She was a doctoral research scholar in Modern Indian History, Nehru Memorial Fund, Teen Murti and a postdoctoral fellow at the Indian Institute of Advanced Study, Shimla. Her book *Empire in the Hills: Simla, Darjeeling, Ootacamund and Mount Abu, 1820–1920* was released in 2017. She was the ICCR Chair of Modern Indian History at the University of Vienna, Austria in 2018.

Anu Venugopalan is a Professor of Physics at the University School of Basic and Applied Sciences, Guru Gobind Singh Indraprastha University, New Delhi, India. She did her doctoral research at the School of Physical Sciences, Jawaharlal Nehru University, New Delhi and has been a postdoctoral fellow at the Tata Institute of Fundamental Research, Mumbai and the Physical Research Laboratory, Ahmedabad. Her primary area of work includes the foundations of quantum mechanics, the quantum-classical connection, decoherence, confined quantum systems and quantum information.

Identities in South Asia

Conflicts and Assertions

Edited by Vivek Sachdeva,
Queeny Pradhan and
Anu Venugopalan

LONDON AND NEW YORK

First published 2019
by Routledge
2 Park Square, Milton Park, Abingdon, Oxon OX14 4RN

and by Routledge
52 Vanderbilt Avenue, New York, NY 10017

Routledge is an imprint of the Taylor & Francis Group, an informa business

© 2019 selection and editorial matter, Vivek Sachdeva, Queeny Pradhan and Anu Venugopalan; individual chapters, the contributors

The right of Vivek Sachdeva, Queeny Pradhan and Anu Venugopalan to be identified as the authors of the editorial material, and of the authors for their individual chapters, has been asserted in accordance with sections 77 and 78 of the Copyright, Designs and Patents Act 1988.

All rights reserved. No part of this book may be reprinted or reproduced or utilised in any form or by any electronic, mechanical, or other means, now known or hereafter invented, including photocopying and recording, or in any information storage or retrieval system, without permission in writing from the publishers.

Trademark notice: Product or corporate names may be trademarks or registered trademarks, and are used only for identification and explanation without intent to infringe.

British Library Cataloguing-in-Publication Data
A catalogue record for this book is available from the British Library

Library of Congress Cataloging-in-Publication Data
A catalog record for this book has been requested

ISBN: 978-0-815-36199-2 (hbk)
ISBN: 978-0-429-03195-3 (ebk)

Typeset in Sabon
by Apex CoVantage, LLC

Contents

List of tables	vii
List of contributors	viii
Acknowledgements	xii

Introduction 1
VIVEK SACHDEVA, QUEENY PRADHAN AND
ANU VENUGOPALAN

1 Identity assertions and context of conflicts in
   South Asia 16
   T. K. OOMMEN

2 Constitution and conflict: mono-ethnic federalism
   in a poly-ethnic Nepal 32
   MAHENDRA LAWOTI

3 Literature as cosmopolitics: beyond nations,
   borders and identities 61
   SIMI MALHOTRA

4 Ideology as identity: progressive Punjabi poetry of
   the 1970s and after 68
   AKSHAYA KUMAR

5 Flying high or lying low? The moral economy of young women in higher education in Punjab, India NAVTEJ K. PUREWAL AND MANPREET K. GILL	102
6 Dalit assertion and different shades of movements defining Dalits: from accorded nomenclature to asserted one VIVEK KUMAR	125
7 The question of loyalty: minorities and South Asian nationalisms TANWEER FAZAL	145
8 *Adivasi* struggles in Chhattisgarh: 'Jal, Jungle, Zameen' SUDHA BHARADWAJ	161
9 Was Bhagat Singh an internationalist? Resistance and identity in global age APARNA VAIDIK	175
10 The languages of the Indian-English writer ARUNI KASHYAP	198

Tables

1.1	Religion and language variations in South Asian countries	23
2.1	Population of identity groups in seven provinces and Nepal	39
2.2	Ethnic/caste distribution in 14 and 10 provinces federal models recommended by RSDSPC and SRC, respectively	43
5.1	Rank-wise per capita income and sex ratio across the states of India	105
5.2	Percentage of students by gender enrolled at undergraduate level in Punjab	111
5.3	Percentage of students by gender enrolled in selected subjects in Punjab	111
5.4	Sex ratio in the districts of Punjab	112
5.5	Sampling of the qualitative study	113

Contributors

Sudha Bharadwaj is a civil rights and trade unionist lawyer in Bilaspur, Chhattisgarh, who was trained in mathematics at IIT, Kanpur. She has been associated with the labour movement led by legendary labour leader Shankar Guha Niyogi for the past thirty years. Also, as a human rights lawyer, she is a part of the collective 'Janhit,' which provides group legal aid to communities fighting displacements. She is also associated with Chhattisgarh Mukti Morcha. She is the General Secretary of the Chhattisgarh branch of the People's Union for Civil Liberties, and she was elected as its national secretary from 2014 to 2016.

Tanweer Fazal is a Professor at the Centre for the Study of Social Systems, Jawaharlal Nehru University, New Delhi, India. His areas of interest and specialisation are sociology of nationalism, ethnic and minority studies and peace and conflict studies. He has extensively published on Muslim and Sikh identities, minority nationalism and minority rights. He has been on the Advisory Board of *South Asian History and Culture* and ex-officio Member, Planning Commission's Working Group on Empowerment of Minorities for the 11th Five Year Plan.

Manpreet K. Gill is a research scholar at the School of Oriental and African Studies, London.

Aruni Kashyap is Assistant Professor of English at University of Georgia, USA. He is a writer and translator who writes in Assamese and English. In 2009, he won the Charles Wallace India Trust Scholarship for Creative Writing to the University of Edinburgh. Aruni is a Master of Fine Arts in Creative Writing (Fiction) from the Minnesota State University, Mankato, from where he graduated in 2014. His first novel titled *The House with a Thousand Stories* was published in 2013. He also has short stories published in several literary journals in India and abroad. Aruni has also translated from Assamese and introduced celebrated Indian writer Indira Goswami's last work of fiction, *The Bronze Sword of Thengphakhri Tehsildar.*

Akshaya Kumar is a Professor at the Department of English and Cultural Studies, Panjab University, India. He completed his Ph.D. from M.D. University, Rohtak, and has more than 25 years of teaching experience. His areas of interest include Comparative Indian Literature, Post-colonial Literature and Contemporary Literary and Cultural Theory. An established published author, his most recent book was titled *Cultural Studies in India: Essays on History, Politics Literature.*

Vivek Kumar is a Professor at the Centre for the Study of Social Systems, School of Social Sciences, Jawaharlal Nehru University (JNU), New Delhi. An alumnus of JNU, he has ten years of teaching experience, which includes stints at Tata Institute of Social Sciences, Mumbai, as well as JNU. His area of interest includes methodology of social sciences, sociology of marginalised sections and sociology of Indian diaspora. He has been honoured with the Tree-Sararu Award and holds an international collaboration with Harvard and British Columbia. He is the author of *India's Roaring Revolution: Dalit Assertions and New Horizons,* which is also his most recent peer-reviewed book.

Mahendra Lawoti is a Professor in the Department of Political Science at Western Michigan University, USA. His research covers democratisation, political institutions, ethnic politics and socio-political mobilisations in Nepal and South Asia. He has authored, co-authored, edited and co-edited ten books and published numerous journal articles, book chapters and opinion pieces. His book *Towards a Democratic Nepal* (2005) was reprinted multiple times and translated into Nepali in 2007. His recent books include the co-edited volume *Nationalism and Ethnic Conflict in Nepal* and co-authored *Government and Politics in South Asia,* and *Pahichan and Sanghiyata* is forthcoming. He has published articles in *Asian Survey, Commonwealth and Comparative Politics, Democratization, Himalaya, Journal of Democracy* and other journals, as well as chapters in numerous books. Dr Lawoti has conducted fieldwork in Nepal, India and Sri Lanka and has lectured in various countries in Europe, East Asia, the Middle East, North America and South Asia.

Simi Malhotra is a Professor at Jamia Milia Islamia University, New Delhi, India. Her specialisation includes contemporary literary and cultural theory including post theoretical developments, with research guidance, teaching and publications primarily concerning the same, culture studies with special focus on postmodernism and the interface of the globalising media with politics, as also folk cultural forms, with doctoral research and most publications, as well as much of research guidance and teaching being in this area, Indian philosophies and aesthetic practices, with some publications in this area. Simi Malhotra has many publications. Her works include *Literary Theory: An Introductory Reader*, *Popular Culture Studies*, special issue of *Creative Forum: Journal of Literary and Critical Writings, Vol. 1* and many other notable works.

T. K. Oommen is an Indian sociologist, author, educationist and Professor Emeritus at the Centre for the Study of Social Systems, Jawaharlal Nehru University, New Delhi, India. Dr. Oommen obtained his B.A. in Economics from Kerala University, Thiruvananthapuram in 1957 and M.A. in Sociology from Pune University, India in 1960. He continued at Pune University for his doctoral research and obtained Ph.D. in 1965 on *Charisma, Stability and Change: An Analysis of Bhoodan-Gramdan Movement in India*. Dr. Oommenn has received various awards like Swami Pranavananda Award in Sociology, 1997 by the University Grants Commission, Philipose Mar Chrysostom Navathy Award for Excellence, 2007 and Padma Bhushan by the President of India in 2008. He is also the first person from Asia or Africa to be elected as the President of International Sociological Association (1990–94). His works include *Citizenship, Nationality and Ethnicity – Reconciling Competing Identities*, *Pluralism, Equality and Identity – Comparative Studies*, *Citizenship and National Identity – Between Colonialism and Globalism* and many other distinguished works.

Navtej K. Purewal is a Social Scientist who completed a B.A. in Political Science in 1991 from Vassar College, USA and did M.A. in South Asian Area Studies from the School of Oriental and African Studies (SOAS), UK in 1992. She went on to do her doctoral studies in Development Studies from Lancaster University, UK from where she received her Ph.D. in 1998. She refers to issues, debates and literature which cross both spatial and disciplinary boundaries. Her most recent areas of focus are in the sociology of religion and gender and culture in South Asia. Her works include *Son Preference: Sex Selection, Gender and Culture in South Asia* (Oxford Berg), *Living on the Margins: Poverty, Social Access and Shelter in South Asia* (Ashgate) and her publications include studies of diasporic Sikh shrines, Sikh-Muslim relations, access to housing for the rural poor, the impact of displacement and partition and gender and development. Presently, she is holding the office of Deputy Director, South Asia Institute, SOAS, London, UK.

Aparna Vaidik is Associate Professor of History at Ashoka University, India. She formerly taught at Georgetown University, USA, offering courses such as Nation and Nationalism, and Indian Ocean in Age of Empire. Aparna Vaidik taught at the University of Delhi, India for five years during and after her Ph.D. where she taught classical antiquity, the Russian Revolution, and the history of Modern China and Japan. Her first book was on the spatial and penal history of the Andaman Islands, *Imperial Andamans: Colonial Encounter and Island History* (2010). She has received several research grants from the Indian Council for Historical Research, Georgetown University, USA and the Charles Wallace Trust. Currently, she is working on the history of the Indian revolutionary movement in North India.

Acknowledgements

The book is a result of the help and support given by many people and organisations. The opportunity to work at the Centre for Human Values and Ethics, Guru Gobind Singh Indraprastha University, enabled us to conceive the conference on 'Identity Assertions and Conflicts in South Asia,' which was held on 2–4 November 2015. We thank the university for giving us financial assistance and a platform to bring together scholars from various disciplines to engage with a number of themes: borders and nations, gender, regionalism, race, ethnicity, identity politics and fundamentalism, memory and narrative, resistance, etc.

The conference was co-sponsored by the Indian Council of Social Science Research (ICSSR). ICSSR encourages interdisciplinary research in India by supporting workshops, seminars, conferences and publication of books and journals. Their assistance for this conference was invaluable. We also acknowledge the help given to us by the Indian Council for Cultural Relations (ICCR). The council is a pre-eminent institution engaged in cultural diplomacy and the sponsor of intellectual exchanges between India and partner countries.

The role of our contributors is no less. The paper presenters from different parts of the country and outside contributed in a meaningful manner through their insights. Some of their papers are a part of this book. Many scholars shared their research and arguments. We acknowledge Sekhar Bandyopadhyay, Anshu Malhotra, Nonica Datta, Hilal Ahmed, Ram Puniyani, Gauhar Raza, Ranjeeta Dutta, Gopalji Pradhan, Dilip Simeon, S.M. Patnaik, Imtiaz Ahmed and Dhananjay Singh for delivering their papers in the conference, though they are not part of this book for some or the other reason.

There are many individuals who stood by us at a time when we felt that it may be difficult for us to go ahead with the conference. Prof Raghu Ram, Dr Nimisha Sharma, Prof Rita Singh and Prof Vaishali Singh provided the necessary support, encouraging us to go forward.

We would also like to thank the support staff of the University School of Humanities and Social Sciences, the University School of Law and Legal Studies and the University School of Basic and Applied Sciences.

No less was the support and backup given by our students, who were the backbone of the conference with their enthusiasm and energy. The list is long, and we can only mention the efforts of few, but all the students associated with this work at multiple levels are gratefully acknowledged. We would like to specially mention Karan Gupta, Jagrit Ahuja, Sanjana Gahlot, Kirti Sachdeva, Sakshi Sundaram, Karandeep, Sivakumara, Arjun Sajeevan, Saloni, Sakshi Yadav, Samarth Bhargava, Pooja Sehrawat, Sukriti Deswal, Manali Dogra, Rashmi Sirohi, Jyotsna, Priya Sinha, Vinayak Pant, Swati Tripathi, Monisha Rachel Rao, Farheen, Sagarika and Nitish Rai Parwani.

The book has emerged out of this conference. We take this opportunity to thank all the contributors of the book for their cooperation for without their support this book would not have seen the light of the day.

Introduction

Vivek Sachdeva, Queeny Pradhan and Anu Venugopalan

The multidimensional issue of identity gives birth to numerous questions, especially in our contemporary times in a global perspective. What is an identity? What role does identity play in an individual's life while understanding his/her own self and his/her relations with the others? How are the categories of Self and Other formed? How do these categories determine the nature of a society? What are the individual and collective identifications with the place, name and race? Are individual sentiments subsumed in the collective identity of a nation-state? Is the idea of a nation concurrent with the idea of a homeland? As the issue is complex, there are no easy answers.

I

The definitions of individual, subject and identity occupy an important position in social sciences and cultural studies. Disciplines like literary studies, film studies and cultural studies draw heavily on theorisation of concepts like subjectivity and identity. Philosophical inquiries in psychoanalysis, feminism, Marxism, post-structuralism question the earlier way of dealing with the concept of subjectivity understanding the human subject in coherent, rational and unified terms. Ideas of individual, identity and subject (or subjectivity) are different, yet they have their points of convergence. First in this trio is the relation between 'individual' and 'subject.' In philosophical discourse, ranging from Socrates through Descartes, Kant and Hegel, there have been various attempts to define human subject. If the individual has been understood in relation to one's physical attribute, the subject was a thinking being. In the post-enlightenment age, the subject was coherent, transcendental and universal, be it Descartes's famous dictum 'I think, therefore I am' or Hegel's 'World Spirit.' It is our thoughts, actions and our being conscious of ourselves make us subject. In the Hegelian philosophical perspective, the sense of self is linked with being aware of the Other. Their philosophical ideas founded on the notion of coherent and rational self were able to take the human subject out from the domain of religion and myth in which the individual was always subjected to collective notions rooted in the religio-mythic way of thinking. Our being conscious of ourselves and consequently, conscious of others is crucial to give us one or the other kind of subjectivity.[1]

Renaissance marked the beginning point when the human subject was understood beyond collective doctrines of religion, guilds or tribes. During the seventeenth century in the West, importance was given to rationality while defining the human subject, and in the late eighteenth and early nineteenth centuries under the influence of German Transcendentalism, imagination became central. Later, ideas given by Marx and Freud gave blows to the transcendental understanding of subject. In classical Marxism, human consciousness is determined by the class one belongs to, not vice-versa. Class is the crucial determining factor for subjectivity. Besides, ideology also performs its function in making individuals subjects. Althusser also states the transformation of individuals into subjects as 'Ideology Interpellates Individuals as Subjects.' Post-structuralist theories, especially developed under the influence of Jacques Lacan, deliberated on disunified subjectivity and identity. The speaking subject 'I' was not necessarily the linguistic 'I.' This resulted in the body gaining centrality in identity discourse.

Besides changes in the philosophical world, there have been historical factors which changed the way human subject began to look at himself or herself and became conscious of his/her identity. Ever since the late eighteenth and early nineteenth century, especially in Europe, societies underwent a major shift. The French Revolution and publication of literature in vernacular by the printing press gave people linguistic and national identities. As compared to subjectivity, identity is limited and fixed in nature. Various identities, such as gender identity, ethnic identity, caste identity, national identity, are relational. In the contemporary times, societies are governed by the notions of identities people cherish. The idea of identity has occupied the imagination of modern (wo)man so much and it has become so central to modern man that, as Stuart Hall says, nothing can be imagined these days without identity and even the concept of identity cannot be thought of in old ways. Ever since the onset of modernity, identity and politics of/around identity have changed the narrative of the human self and man's relation with the world around him. The modern self of man is no longer transparent or transparent as once thought by philosophers until the end of the eighteenth century. 'I believe that what this decentring requires – as the evolution of Foucault's work shows – is not an abandonment or abolition of "the subject" but a reconceptualisation – thinking in its new displaced or decentered position within the paradigm'(Hall 1996: 2).[2]

Politics over and of identities has not been limited only to South Asia. It is a global phenomenon. Though the history of identity cannot be said to have begun in the twentieth century, the first half of the twentieth century can be seen as the age of identities – their assertions and conflict. In different parts of the world different shades of identity issues came to the fore. America witnessed American Civil Rights Movements, which raised the concern of the rights of the Black population in the USA, racial segregation and injustice during Apartheid in Africa, the Holocaust in Europe was another dark demonstration of racial hatred, and in India, the communal riots that followed India's independence were yet another deadly instance of identity politics leading to a human catastrophe. Rabindranath Tagore in one of his poems wishes for India where 'the head is held high' and people are not divided by 'narrow domestic walls.' Unfortunately, there have always been gaps between poetic ideals of one world human community and actual reality. The concept of 'human identity' that Bikhu Parekh[3] discusses in the introduction of his book on identity reads like yet more wishful thinking of an idealist (though it is much needed in our present times), as identity assertions and identity conflicts continue to afflict the society we are a part of. It was once believed that globalisation would offer the solution to the question of identities, at least national identity.

Worldwide developments in recent times have destabilised the discourse of globalisation, which complicated the idea of identities. The implosion of the world, while standing on the anvil of the right-wing nationalism, has brought the issue of identities to the forefront. Amongst multiple identities that individuals carry, religious and ethnic identities in different parts of the world are shrinking the space. The narrative of politics of identity is fast changing the nature of the entire world. It has given birth to a new set of problems; complicated the already existing ones and reconfigured human understanding of himself/herself in which the colour of the skin, caste one belongs to, territories and political borders, sexual preference of an individual everything is being re-imagined. In the shrinking world, people have once again become conscious of their religious, national and racial identities. Despite our common human identity, the world is divided into different groups on the basis of our racial, religious, ethnic, linguistic and national and caste identities. These multifarious identities define us, give us a sense of self and make us conscious of the 'Other.' In the dialectical relationship between the two, the Self is the result of the formation of the Other and vice-versa. The formation of the Self also results in the Otherisation of some other group of people. One's sense of identity defines how one situates oneself in the world and relates oneself with others. The structuration of human society on the lines of identities gives priority to the Self at the expense of the Other, for which discourse is constructed and imposed on a society. The politics over identities is as much a construct as the notion of identity is. Nevertheless, human beings identify with their social, cultural and religious identities so strongly that assertion and conflicts of identities have always resulted in violence as 'the politics of identity is shadowed by the politics of violence' (Parekh 2008: 26). The relationship between identities and violence is two-way traffic. Both feed each other. If the assertions of identities result in violence, acts of violence also facilitate the process of identity formation. This process theoretically stands close to what Judith Butler calls 'performativity' of identity. Performativity of identity in daily life also becomes a means of Otherisation in a society. In a racist and sexist society, the colour of the skin and performance of gender becomes the crucial aspect of identity assertions and Otherisation of the marginalised communities, and in countries like India, performance of caste and religious identities plays almost a similar role in marginalising other communities.

II

In the post-second World War period, a number of colonies became independent in Asia and Africa. South Asia also saw the emergence of modern nation-states. Unfortunately, the nature of independence through partition of India has led to endless tensions in the post-colonial era. It resulted in the creation of separate boundaries and selection of historical memory, hiving off the slices of history not suited to the building of modern nation-states. Identity politics explores the tensions between the nation-state and communal consciousness. As the partition took place along religious lines, religion has cast its shadow over other kinds of identity consciousness. There has been an 'Otherisation' by the dominant communities, leading to simmering discontent and tensions. The dominance of Punjab in the newly independent Pakistan led to the discontent in East Pakistan. Language also played a role in the emergence of Bangladesh in 1971. Communal riots, terrorism and fundamentalism have emerged as the common concerns for almost all the South Asian countries. The Tamil-Sinhalese conflict has been destabilising Sri Lanka. There are a number of religious and political conflicts in South Asia.

In more recent times South Asian Association for Regional Cooperation (SAARC) has been formed in 1985 which includes India, Pakistan, Sri Lanka, Maldives, Bangladesh, Bhutan, Nepal and Afghanistan. South Asia has a niggling history of conflicts, which ensued primarily from the time India and Pakistan emerged as separate nations in 1947. Fragmentation of Pakistan and emergence of Bangladesh in 1971 further aggravated the challenges. Peace has been eluding this region for long. India-Pakistan conflict is perennial, and a new dimension of fundamentalism and consciousness of narrow sectarian identities have intensified conflicts and tensions in South Asia reflecting a number of identity conflicts in South Asia. Ethnicity, gender, religion, region, boundaries, history, society and languages all are part of these many-sided identities.

The term South Asia as a region emerged in the colonial period when the British imperial officials came to identify South Asia with religion and caste. The Orientalists looked at ancient India to be rich in science and culture. The Hindu heritage was pre-Islamic, and hence the Orientalists asserted that Hindu and Muslims enjoyed distinct histories. Consequently, a construction of communities emerged, resulting in specific communal identities. The colonial rule in South Asia, in order to acquire knowledge to control and dominate the unknown colonised territory and its people, prepared meticulous written documents, classifying land and people in a manner that typecast groups and individuals and stereotypes were constructed. Colonised also starting looking from the lens of the colonial masters and the already existing fault lines and divides became borders of the communities, which no outsider could trespass. This insider and outsider divide ultimately resulted in partition in South Asia, a dismemberment not forgotten till date.

It has created identity politics in post-independent nation-states in its most virulent form. Fundamentalism and identity rhetoric dominate the politics and has come to power on this issue in India and elsewhere.

The states in Asia were heterogeneous, unlike the nation-states of the West which were monoracial. There have been tensions over language and linguistic identities in India after Hindi was declared the official language. In more recent decades there have been regional tensions in Maharashtra. Shiv Sena in the 1970s objected to the domination of the South Indians in the 1970s and in 2008, Maharashtra Navanirman Sena (MNS) took up the issue of Biharis and North Indians taking away the economic opportunities of the Maharashtrians. Two strands of nationalism co-exist in India – pan-Indian and regional nationalism. These strands were accommodated in the quasi-federal nature of the Indian Constitution. The re-organisation of Indian states along the linguistic lines in 1956 is also based on the accommodation of this principle.

The attempt of a modern state is to homogenise the diversity, but the nation is constitutive of the diversity of different communities. This basic contradiction between the nation and the state is usually overlooked when the two terms are joined as nation-state.[4] (Maneesha Tikekar: p. 51, agreeing with Ranabir Sammadar). Prof. T. K. Oommen makes a critical distinction between the moral entity and the legal entity. The nation and nationalism are the ethical moral components which are supreme when the nation is in the process of making but as the national movement culminates in the formation of the independent state the legal entity takes charge, saddling the people with new duties and responsibilities for constructing a nation-state. There has been a conscious invention of tradition by the various communities to consolidate themselves. In modern times the boundaries have become rigid and the fluid identities have become a thing of the past. The conscious mobilisation of each community on an imagined tradition of the past has created its unique and distinct identity, but simultaneously created the distance with the other communities.

III

These pressing issues are the subject matter of this volume which has resulted out of a conference held from 2 to 4 November 2015 on the identities and conflicts in South Asia. Many South Asian scholars from different disciplines of humanities and social sciences and universities participated in the conference. For the edited volume, the editors selected the ten articles of immediate relevance. There is no idealist intent in this book to find a romantic solution to the problem of identity; rather, the attempt is to understand how the issues of identity are complicating the problems of the world.

The first chapter in the volume is 'Identity assertions and context of conflicts in South Asia.' T. K. Oommen addresses the issue of identity, focusing on the seven polities of Bangladesh, Bhutan, India, Myanmar, Nepal, Pakistan and Sri Lanka. He analyses the complex nature of the emergence of multiple identities as individual identities and collectivities, their connection with primordialism and constructivism and the nature of hierarchies within identities. Identifying four primary issues that foment conflicts, namely, the role of the nation-state, identity and equity, identity as a source of inclusion and exclusion and the identity of dominated minorities as a source of insecurity for the 'nation,' he argues that conflicts specific to South Asia originate out of the intersectionality of stratified, heterogeneous, hierarchical and plural societies. Based on this argument, he reasons that South Asian states are not nation-states like those in Western Europe but should instead be designated as national states celebrating cultural diversity and equality between identity groups. Reconstructing South Asian polities on these principles is suggested as an effective means to decreasing conflicts emanating out of identity assertions in this region.

In the next chapter, 'Constitution and conflict: mono-ethnic federalism in a poly-ethnic Nepal,' Mahendra Lawoti draws attention to the recent political and constitutional development in Nepal. The promulgation of the new Constitution in September 2015 gave birth to the intense six-month long agitation by *Madhesi* and Tharu community in the Tarai region, which was followed by Magar and Limbu communities joining the protest. Mahendra Lawoti tries to understand the eruption of conflicts between *Madhesi* community and others in Nepal despite having accepted the federal system in the country. *Madhesis* and other indigenous national communities wanted their respective identities to be constitutionally recognised, provincial or sub-provisional autonomies to be granted. Fearing that it would result in the rise in provinces in the country which would have direct financial implications with a threat to harmony in the country, the demand was rejected by the dominated ethnic groups such as Bahun, Thakur, Chettri and Sanyasi. As federal structure gives more space to different ethnic or racial groups in a society, theoretically it is assumed that federal system would ensure lesser conflicts; whereas in reality, it has been observed that the federal system may have a lesser number of massive identity conflicts, but it does have a large number of small conflicts in the society. Lawoti lists down factors responsible for identity conflicts in a federal state. Lawoti has studied the patterns of conflicts in Nepal ever since the matter of drafting the Constitution came to the fore, though Lawoti opines the history of conflicts goes back to 1950s. The new mapping of provinces, borders and percentages of different communities in the proposed provinces, according to the author, has complicated the issue of identities in Nepal. There were apprehensions of the restructuring of provinces in Nepal would result in mono-ethnic federal state. Lawoti questions this.

The chapter by Simi Malhotra, 'Literature as cosmopolitics: beyond nations, borders and identities,' looks at identities from the concept of cosmopolitanism. She problematises identitarian 'here' and 'now' through cosmopolitanism. Simi has banked on Derrida's critique of Kant's theory of cosmopolitanism to initiate the debate. Kant, quite like Greek philosophers in ancient time, while defining cosmopolitanism attaches importance to the city/state a citizen belongs to. Kant agrees to grant the foreigners the right to visit, but to stay, which Derrida critiques. Kantian allegiance to the state is akin to the good citizen's loyalty to the polis or the city, which he is expected to protect first. Kantian understanding of hospitality also has its inherent contradiction which Derrida deconstructs. In Seyla Benhabib's argument, the extension of the idea of cosmopolitanism can be seen who also questions the nation-state driver cosmopolitanism and sees hope in people-driven hospitality. Problematising the relevance of the concept of nation in the context of South Asia, Simi quotes Tagore that the West was trying to change the non-nation people of South Asia into nation people, which would result in sectarianism in a country like India. Tagore finds a solution in 'hospitality and tolerance' of diversity as a solution to rising intolerance and fundamentalism in South Asia.

Akshaya Kumar, in his chapter, 'Ideology as identity: progressive Punjabi poetry of the 1970s and after,' gives a comprehensive survey of Punjabi poetry, especially in the post-colonial period. Redeeming poetry from the identitarian grid of ethnicity, race and gender, Akshaya Kumar is interested in reading poetry as the enunciation of ideology and ideology as a marker of identity. He studies the shifts that Punjabi poetry had undergone during the period of the 1970s through 1980s, a period during which politics in Punjab also witnessed a major paradigm shift. From the progressive thought in the 1960s to the rise of the Naxalite thought in the 1970s, the political discourse in the 1980s changed its course towards the Khalistan movement. In his chapter, Akshaya Kumar studies ideology and aesthetics of *jujharvadi* Punjabi poetry. In Punjabi poetry, Guru Gobind Singh emerges as a metaphor of struggle against oppression, a metaphor which acquires different connotations during the period of Sikh militancy. Akshaya Kumar is careful in highlighting the ideological differences between the two even though their metaphor is common. In the third section of his chapter, he studies *jujharvadi* poets who survived after the ideology of the Naxalite gave way to Khalistan movement in Punjab. In this section, he studies these poets' ideological confusion, ambivalent silences and continuation of radical strain sans critical introspection. Through a long silence of Paash, as the poet reflects in his diary; Amrit Chandan, who once thought handcuffs and chains to be instruments of music, is more reflective and in his poetry the legacy of Sufi and Bhakti poetry can be read; and Lal Singh Dil emerges as a disillusioned Naxal – these are the signifiers of ideological and aesthetic change in Punjabi poetry for Prof. Akshaya Kumar.

Navtej K. Purewal and Manpreet K. Gill in their chapter, 'Flying high or lying low? The moral economy of young women in higher education in Punjab, India' looks at the education of girls in Punjab and the 'objective logic' that only helps the patriarchy and parental position. The moral economy is based on the benefits and investments that educating a young woman would accrue. The scarcity of girls has led to moral policing of the girls. Where girls challenge patriarchy, the girls' aspirations of 'flying high' are curbed and they are told to 'lie low.' The girls are continually seen as *'paraya dhan'* and their constant comparison to *'chirhiyaa da Chamba'* or the flock of birds signified the objective of marriage as the ultimate goal for the girls. There is a bias for boys as the inheritors of property, while the girls will 'fly' to their marital homes. These aspirations are no longer local but global as the arranged marriages abroad are actively sought. The girls' education is also seen in this context. Despite such goals, the girls are trying to subvert the role identities defined by a masculine society.

Vivek Kumar's chapter, 'Dalit assertion and different shades of movements defining Dalits: from accorded nomenclature to asserted one,' tries to analyse two issues related to Dalits; one, whether they are involved in 'identity politics' or in 'entity assertion,' second, the nature and intensity of their 'entity assertion.' What form has is taken in contemporary Indian society? Sociological literature amply proves that the structural location of certain groups in the Indian society has produced approximately 260 million people who are popularly known as Dalits (Kumar 2014: Caste and Democracy in Indian Society: A Perspective from Below). They were not considered to be part of the larger Hindu society and therefore had no space either in the sacred texts or the *varna-ashrama-dharma* scheme. They were cumulatively excluded from every type of human rights – social, economic, political, educational, occupational, residential, religious, etc. The matters were made worse because of the long temporal history of exclusion, which is said to be a few millennia old and is un-alterable even when one has achieved political, economic, educational mobility. The impact of this cumulative exclusion for a few millennia is that society as a whole denied their existence as human beings. That is why they have asserted, since time immemorial, to have their presence registered in the people's conscience. This assertion has taken place with different nomenclatures like *Ashprishya*, *Dalits*, *Bahujans* and now *Moolnivasis*, which have wrongly conveyed their identities. This chapter will highlight how Dalits are not involved in identity politics – they are included in the assertion to get accepted as human entities, worthy of human rights. Moreover, this chapter will attempt to analyse why the Western theory of 'identity politics' is a misfit in capturing this process of 'entity assertion.'

The second aspect highlighted in Vivek Kumar's is the nature and intensity of the assertion of aforesaid excluded communities acquired in contemporary India. How have they responded in modern times to the nature of their exclusion? Is there only one monolithic way in which they have responded or are there multiple ways? The simple answer is that they have reacted in multiple ways. However, the moot question is what are these various ways and why have they acted in such a way? The chapter examines these multiple ways and their reasons. These aspects are discussed by first analysing the nature of seven modern institutions – judiciary, polity, bureaucracy, industry, university, civil society and media as an industry. Have these institutions become inclusive or have they remained exclusive like the traditional social institutions in ancient and medieval India. In analysing the facts about the different shades of an assertion of the Dalits this chapter will follow a historical and evolutionary perspective. The chapter relies on both primary and secondary sources of data. We have also changed the frame of reference for a better analysis of the assertion of Dalits. The chapter highlights a few epistemological issues regarding their exclusion which will help us to define the category and its contours.

Tanweer Fazal's chapter, 'The question of loyalty: minorities and South Asian nationalisms,' describes the poly-ethnic Constitution of most South Asian states notwithstanding, the desire to fashion a state anchored in a homogenous people or a nation has proved irresistible to state functionaries and sections of the national elite. Assumedly, such a hegemonic construction of nationalism comes to be fiercely contested by minority groups resolute on preserving the pristine purity of their cultural inheritance leading to, at times, violent upsurges. Theorists have therefore come to suggest a persisting strain in the relationship of minority groups with discourses of nationalism. In the dominant nationalist constructs, therefore, the loyalty of minority groups comes under a cloud of suspicion. On the contrary, this chapter takes a nuanced view of the tenuous relationship between minority groups and national identity and examines the multifarious ways in which minority groups negotiate their terms of co-existence, accommodation and adaptation with several other competing identities within the framework of nation-states. It takes into account the structural variation in the nature and composition of minority groups to make sense of this vexed relationship. Therefore, the chapter distinguishes between three different strains of minority communities each specific regarding its composition and the politics that follow. One, cultural enclaves with real or fictitious association with a homeland often defined as a nation, nationality or sub-nation. Two, territorially dispersed but culturally or religiously distinct identities. Three, the indigenous communities or tribes. The chapter argues for a fresh theorisation of the relationship between minority identities and nationalism in South Asia.

Sudha Bharadwaj, a qualified lawyer and an activist, who has constantly worked for the rights of the tribal people in India, critiques the model of nation-state, an institution of modernity, from the point of view of *Adivasis* in Chattisgarh. Sudha Bhardwaj historicises the conflicts between the *Adivasis* and institutions of modernity, which dates back to the British rule in India. In postcolonial India, through the constitutional process, attempts had been made to protect the land of the *Advasis*. Most of the tribes of Chattisgarh, recognised by the British government, had been placed under the Schedule Five. However, there are gaps between the legislation and its execution in a state like Chattisgarh, where the office of the chief minister was held by a non-*adivasi* political leader. *Adivasis* have been a victim of bureaucracy and apathetic attitude of those in the power for the marginalised communities like tribals. Their lands and other natural resources, which they had been using without ownership, as understood under modernity, are taken over by companies with capitalist interests in the mineral-rich land. Constant exploitation and denial of justice have resulted in the rise of Naxalites in the region, which has further resulted in strong militarisation of the area. Constant developmentalism, as understood within the frame of capitalist ideology, and militarisation of the area has put these marginalised communities in eternal conflict with the modern nation-state. The state and its institutions such as legal, judicial or parliamentary have failed to provide justice to these people. From the vantage point of *Adivasi* identity, Sudha Bhardwaj raises few questions in front of the modern nation-state which works as an institution for and of the capitalist nation-state.

Aparna Vaidik in her chapter 'Was Bhagat Singh an internationalist? Resistance and identity in global age' questions the simple usage of categories like 'nationalist' and 'internationalist.' These categories seem more like the historians' constructs, with little to do with the actual happenings in the past. She argues that the Indian revolutionaries from the start in the 1890s were making national and international networks. She sees the connection between the Indian revolutionaries and the international ones, especially the Russian revolutionaries. Her chapter cites many instances of similarities between the revolutionary acts in Europe and the acts of the Indian revolutionaries. There were certain common strands amongst the Indian revolutionaries: young university students who were fiercely anti-colonial. They were politically aware and worked towards generating awareness amongst the masses about the evils of imperialism. Their court trials also aimed at creating publicity about the nature of colonial rule in India. Her chapter draws attention to the differences within the ideological position and strategy of Marx and Bakunin regarding revolution and the role of peasants. According to her, reading played an important role in creating a revolutionary consciousness. It was part of the middle-class phenomenon in the twentieth century.

Aruni Kashyap's chapter 'The languages of the Indian-English writer' problematises the way regional and linguistic identities operate in India. As an Indian writer in English, the question of implied reader becomes crucial for him. His argument hints at the bias amongst readers and critics that Indian-English writers would generally write for readers based in Delhi or any other metropolitan city, not for and about the region one belongs to. Association of the language of the colonial masters with the urban readers of metropolitan cities, Aruni has brought on the surface the typecast in the minds of Indian reader. His attempt in this chapter has been to dehegemonise English language by taking the language of the elites to the common man of Assam and its landscape. By writing Assamese novel in English, Aruni is deconstructing the power associated by regions, territories and language in India. He consciously and constantly asserts his north-east identity while writing in English.

The theme of identity assertions is significant at a time when the world in increasingly witnessing everyday bloodshed and violence over identities and homelands. Indeed, the space for open discussion and debate on this crucial issue seems not just imperative but an absolute necessity. South Asia shares a common history, culture and the legacy of colonialism. Post-colonial South Asia has to confront the challenges of modernity, in the midst of virulent fundamentalism. The modern state system has many pressure groups, with a varying degree of influence on state politics. Many South Asian states are facing problems from different fundamental groups posing a threat of subversion within. Such destabilising forces are affecting the entire region, straining the socio-political fabric of these countries. Cultural diversity, heterogeneity and peaceful coexistence are deeply rooted in the South Asian tradition and culture, based on the spirit of syncretism and eclecticism. It becomes pertinent to have a better and deeper understanding of these issues. The contributions in this volume have attempted to cover a wide range of themes of identity assertions and conflicts in South Asia.

Various themes discussed in this book underline the new markers of identity in more contemporary times in South Asia. The book contributes to the identity studies by giving fresh perspectives and a rethink on the existing issues of identity discourse. The role of the Constitution in the contouring of identities emerges as an important point. How the seven-province model provides the mono-federal model in Nepal, to make the Khas Aryas dominant, subsuming the diversity of Nepal. The politics of language and the dominance and hegemony of certain language(s) has been another dimension of marginalising not only the regional languages but also the sub-cultures and groups within the nation-states. This creates another issue of identity formation in South Asia and elsewhere. *Adivasis* are a vulnerable section of the nation-states and their interests are generally 'betrayed' in the broader concerns of a state. *Adivasis* are dismissed under the pressures of the corporate conglomerates. Historically too individuals like Bhagat Singh attempts to transcend the narrow sectarian, caste and regional identities to provide a new blueprint of a nation-state. The dilemma and challenges of minorities in plural and multicultural democracies is another dimension of the identity politics that has been raised in this volume. Gender identity is not a new concern in identity studies, but there is a new way of looking at the issue of gender identity through education. An important argument is how education can be both regressive and subversive. Patriarchy sees education as an upwardly mobile movement in the marriage market of the girls, while the girls and women of the families of Punjabi diaspora use education to subvert the stereotypes. Understanding the concept of cosmopolitics through Kant is an interesting approach to the issue of identarianism and identity. Comparing Kant's views with Tagore and a look at the non-nation people provides new insights into the issue of identities.

An important point made by Oommen is that the perception of difference is not a source of conflict, but the idea of superior and inferior is a cause of conflicts. Similarly, the privileged and the oppressed is another identity category which is applicable between the Hindu upper castes and the Dalits. The case of Sindhis in Pakistan and the Sindhis in India as mentioned by Oommen is an example of a culturally dispersed minority whose cultural identity is in peril of perishing. The way out is, as proposed by Oommen, 'consociational democracy,' which will not only acknowledge primordial identities but give representation to different ethnic, linguistic, regional aspirations. One would have to look at this model carefully before proceeding further. Another dimension of identity and identitarian tendency formation has been discussed through the study of progressive Punjabi poetry, which within a decade slips into 'primordial religious' identity. The story of Dalit identity through the various movements in contemporary India presents the political will of the Dalits to fight their own battles within the democratic frames. It is significant that the Dalit women and the

Introduction 15

Dalit diaspora have also been playing a role in such 'entity assertions.' Another important point that emerges in the chapters in this volume is that the minority question is not a national issue in South Asia. It transcends borders. The loyalty of the minorities is constantly questioned. A common colonial experience of the South Asian nation-states has played a role in socially classifying groups and people as minority and majority. Tribals have been also been included in this kind of classification.

This book is an attempt to broaden the discourse of identity studies through multiple ranges of readings.

Notes

1 The argument is derived from Peter V. Zima, *Subjectivity and Identity: Between Modernity and Post Modernity*, London, New Delhi, New York and Sydney: Bloomsbury, 2015.
2 Stuart Hall, and Paul du Gay (Ed.), *Questions of Cultural Identity*, London: Sage, 1996.
3 Bhikhu Parekh, *A New Politics of Identity: Political Principles for an Interdependent World*, Hampshire: Palgrave Macmillan, 2008.
4 Tikekar, Maneesha. "Nation, State and Identity Conflicts in South Asia." In *South and Central Asia: Building Linkages* (Collection of papers presented at an international seminar organised jointly by the Institute of Regional Studies & Konrad-Adenauer-Stiftung in Islamabad on 20–21 Oct 2008), Published by Aziz-ul-Haque, Institute of Regional Studies (IRS), Islamabad, 2009.

References

Hall, Stuart, and Paul du Gay, ed. 1996. *Questions of Cultural Identity*. London: Sage.
Parekh, Bhikhu. 2008. *A New Politics of Identity: Political Principles for an Interdependent World*. Hampshire: Palgrave Macmillan.
Tikekar, Maneesha. 2009. "Nation, State and Identity Conflicts in South Asia." In *South and Central Asia: Building Linkages* (Collection of papers presented at an international seminar organised jointly by the Institute of Regional Studies & Konrad-Adenauer-Stiftung in Islamabad on 20–21 Oct 2008), Published by Aziz-ul-Haque, Institute of Regional Studies (IRS), Islamabad.
Zima, Peter V. 2015. *Subjectivity and Identity: Between Modernity and Post Modernity*. London, New Delhi, New York and Sydney: Bloomsbury.

Chapter 1

Identity assertions and context of conflicts in South Asia

T. K. Oommen

South Asia is a familiar academic construction in the context of the area studies programme of both the First World – North America and West Europe – as well as the Second World, the erstwhile socialist countries of the Soviet Union and East Europe. However, its genealogy can be traced to the colonial period as a part of the wider notion of the Orient. Its first incarnation was as a part of Near (the Middle East), Far (China) and Middle (South Asia) Orient. In its second embodiment, South Asia was a part of the Third World along with Africa and Latin America. During the Cold War era it was perceived as traditional, under-developed, over-populated, irrational and politically chaotic (Pletsch 1981: 565–90).

If the colonial mission was to civilise the Orient, the Cold War project was to modernise the Third World (Oommen 2000: 153–70). With the onset of globalisation, South Asia became a part of the One World schema, and the states of the region aspired to build modern nation-states, following the model of West Europe, an untenable proposition given the empirical realities prevailing here. Identity assertions of South Asian states, both across and within them, are persisting sources of conflicts and I propose to unfold most of them, in the course of this chapter. As a prelude to this exercise, I shall provide the requisite conceptual clarifications on identity in Section I, followed by an empirical analysis of South Asia in Section II. Section III concludes the argument proposed in this chapter.

I

Identity is a contested concept and often a stigmatised one. There is no agreement even about the nature of identity. Some argue that identities are primordial, that is fixed and given forever but others insist that they are constructed. The primordialists say that identity is a latent phenomenon present universally, which is invoked by deprived communities/groups at an opportune moment when they experience an erosion of existing privileges or when they attempt to overcome long-standing denials of privileges. That is the moment for identity assertions crystallises when communities/groups experience downward mobility as well as those who aspire upward mobility struggle for it, according to primordialists (see Balibar and Wallerstein 1991). In contrast, the constructivists argue that identity is ephemeral and it is invariably the products of constructions in particular historical contexts (Hobsbawm and Ranger 1983). An example will help clarify the matter. It is true that the Hindu identity of South Asia is one constructed by outsiders. But what is important is not who invented it and when but why this identity stuck while other identities, for example, barbarians, did not. I suggest that the identity of Hindu fulfilled an emotional need, struck a familiar chord, denoted a common homeland, a shared religion and even a civilisation. This was not true of the barbarian; another identity label invoked to refer to Indians which was instantly rejected. That is, some of the constructed identities become acceptable precisely because they contained a primordial element which is often construed as 'sacred' by the collective in question. Therefore, the imagined dichotomy between primordialism and constructivism is not neat and tidy (see Oommen 1997).

Further, identities fall on a fixity-flexibility continuum: identities based on race or gender are relatively stable; those based on religion (one can convert), language (one may forget one's mother tongue and learn a new language) are flexible, and identities based on class and citizenship are fluid. The debate is also anchored to the facile assumption that modernisation leads to the eclipse of traditional identities and the emergence and acceptance of new ones. This assumed displacement syndrome is far from observed reality. In the process of social transformation, some identities are retained, some are re-invented, others are newly created, while still others are rejected. The empirical process is far more complicated than conceptual simplicity implies.

Identities relate to individuals and collectivities. The latter encapsulates group/community/national and civilisation identities. Individual identities are role-related, based on kinship (e.g. daughter, father, mother-in-law) occupational (teacher, plumber, politician), ideological (anarchist, socialist, democrat) and may be better referred to as role-set. While all individuals have role-sets, some have a limited and others have an expanded role-set. If individuals have role-sets, collectivities have identity sets based on solidarity or hostility. Whether it is 'we' Indians, Hindus, Students, Tamils or whatever, each of these imply a 'they' with differing identity. Differences need not imply inferiority or superiority, but often they are perceived to be so. Thus collective identities carry with them seeds of conflicts particularly when collectivities do not recognise the other's identities simply as different but as inferior or superior. Thus identity coupled with perceived inferiority or superiority is the source of conflicts.

Identity set implies multiple identities, and there is a tendency to hierarchise identities creating a vexatious problem. For example, if an Indian citizen claims that she is an Indian first and a Bengali, only second, everybody applauds her. But if somebody were to say that 'I am a Muslim first' almost everybody would disapprove his assertion. This is a wrong way of situating identity because it tends to hierarchise identities. Identities are contextual, citizenship identity is relevant in matters relating to the state (voting, paying tax, etc.), cultural identities are connected in social matters (worship or eating the kind of food one likes or putting on the dress one prefers), occupational identity is relevant in the context of work and so on. Ignoring this tendency is to construe a master identity and subordinate all other identities to that master identity. In turn, a hierarchy of loyalty is conceived leading to many conflicts. However, if one shifts from vertical to horizontal identities, the assumed conflicts will be seen to become irrelevant. A Muslim, for example, may identify with and be loyal to Ummah, the brotherhood of fellow believers all over the world, which necessarily transcends his/her citizenship identity. To put it pithily, there is no hierarchy of identities but only contexts of identity.

Identities are sources of both privileges and deprivations. Contrast the upper-caste/-class urban Hindu male with the lower-class Dalit rural Muslim female. If the first identity-set facilitates cumulative domination, the second set leads to cumulative oppression. In between, there are identity sets which occasions dispersed domination as in the case of an upper-caste male below the poverty line and a Dalit female who is a heavy political weight. Another context of identity assertion manifests in the case of minorities – religious and linguistic. It is necessary to distinguish between national minorities which have historical claims to a territory, who can sustain their cultural identity (as in the case of Sindhis in Pakistan) and ethnic minorities who are territorially dispersed (such as Sindhis in India) and do not have the resources to sustain their cultural identity (the Indian Sindhis have practically lost their mother tongue). A comparison of territorially dispersed ethnic minorities and territorially concentrated national minorities in South Asia is telling. The national minorities may have their provincial states and can demand even sovereign states, but ethnic minorities do not have the requisite resources even to demand representation in polity and government. The nature of their identity assertions and the conflicts they engender vastly vary across national and ethnic minorities.

Identities also vary in their power of assertion. The cumulatively dominant identity groups tend to assert their hegemonic identity and may have the resources to interrogate the state. In contrast, the cumulatively dominated identity groups often struggle to create new identities which are emancipatory in tenor. These two types of identities – hegemonic and emancipatory – are qualitatively different. If the hegemonic identity groups tend to perpetuate their domination, emancipatory identity groups often demand their equality as citizens. The natures of conflicts created by these groups are qualitatively different; if the hegemonic groups indulge in undemocratic conflicts, emancipatory groups foment democratic conflicts.

Finally, boundaries of identity groups are often hazy, fuzzy, shifting and contested. Even if we assume that female and male are neat and tidy gender groups, how about the third gender consisting of lesbian, gay, bisexual, and transgender (LGBT) people? Religious identities are said to be rigid, but syncretism often renders them nebulous. A person who grew up away from her ancestral motherland often forgets her mother tongue. It is true that identities are invented and nurtured, but they are usually forgotten and relegated to the background. Identities are subjected to pluralisation and hybridisation. Even as some identities disappear, new ones emerge. Indeed humans are identity seeking creatures (Oommen 2005: 149–70).

In spite of this universal quest, some of the identities are undervalued, stigmatised and even viewed as dangerous while others are privileged, viewed as safe, indeed celebrated. This raises issues relating to identity and security. I shall list just four of them which foment conflicts. First, the institution of nation-state indulges in simplicity, merging, unifying and homogenising identities. This is often taken as a pre-requisite for pursuing state policies. Consider the identities constructed by the Indian state – Scheduled Castes, Scheduled Tribes, Other Backward Classes – and religious minorities each of which bunches together numerous identity groups. In contrast to the homogenising tendency of the state people are a. incessantly in search of their specific roots and b. create new identities in staking claims for new entitlements. Arzal Muslims, Dalit Christians and Urdu speakers afford examples of this. Thus the internal differentiation which state regimes often ignore comes alive in the context of availing benefits from the state.

Second is the issue of identity and equity. It is widely held that traditional identities will melt away in the cauldron of modernisation and culturally homogeneous societies will gradually emerge. This facile assumption has come to nought. What often happens in modernising societies is that the newly inducted value of equality becomes anchorages for creating and asserting new identities. Thus four processes – homogenisation, pluralisation, traditionalisation and hybridisation – conjointly emerge (see Oommen 2005: 149–70). Third, identity becomes a source of inclusion as well as exclusion. Those who belong to one's identity group are favoured, and the outsiders are discriminated. This tendency is common particularly under conditions of material scarcity. When economic development accelerates in such polities, the tendency accelerates leading to nepotism and corruption often manifesting in conflicts.

The perspective about identity varies across the dominant majority and the dominated minority. A section of the majority tends to think that recognising and nurturing the identities associated with minorities, particularly religious minorities, (in the case of South Asia) is a security risk for the nation. This perception is created and nurtured by religious majorities and militant groups associated with them. If they capture political authority, this perception gets reinforcement even through state machinery. The usual tendency on the part of the minorities which are perceived as security risks to the 'nation' is to distance itself from the state, leading to their collective alienation. On the other hand, the dominated minority often tends to think that the perception that it is a security risk is a manufactured one to deny them social justice. Thus, security and justice come to be juxtaposed as contesting values in the context of identity assertions. Those who surrender their identity stand an excellent chance to secure justice while those who assert identity may become an endangered species. This is a vexatious issue.

The four issues I have raised, namely, abbreviation and even abrogation of identities versus elaboration of identities, the tendency for group identity and equality pulling in opposite directions, identity as the basis of social inclusion and discrimination and identity of dominated minorities as a source of insecurity for the 'nation' in the perception of the dominant majority are all seminal sources of conflict in all polities. In Section II I propose to examine these issues concerning South Asia.

II

South Asia is often conceptualised as a civilisational region, and it consists of nine polities, but I leave out two of them – Afghanistan and Maldives – and focus on the remaining seven: Bangladesh, Bhutan, India, Myanmar, Nepal, Pakistan and Sri Lanka.[1] Societies, more appropriately polities, can be classified into four – stratified, heterogeneous, hierarchical and plural, based on their internal social milieu. All societies are stratified, and identity assertions and conflicts emanating out of them are shared by all of them. However, thanks to intersectionality some conflicts can be specific to South Asia, such as the conflicts arising out of the intertwining between caste and patriarchy.

In the contemporary world, most societies are heterogeneous. The sources of heterogeneity are two, race and culture; the two predominant elements of culture being religion and language. Heterogeneity is not specific to South Asia. The phenomenon which generates conflicts based on identity peculiar to South Asia is a hierarchy, based on caste. While the theological principles anchored to caste are specific to India and Nepal, the two Hindu majority polities of South Asia, caste influences everyday life of other countries of South Asia also. There is a fourth factor which engenders conflicts in South Asian polities because they are 'plural societies' as Furnivall (1948) invoked the term. The classic description of plural society based on the colonial situation reads,

> Each group holds by its own religion, its own culture, its own ideas and ways. As individuals, they meet but only in the market place. . . . There is a plural society, with different sections of the community hiring side by side but separately within the

same political unit. . . . Nationalism within a plural society is itself a disruptive force, tending to shatter and not to consolidate the social order.

(Furnivall 1939: 468)

In this rendition in plural societies, the co-existence of different segments, usually of racial collectivities, one native and the other alien, is the function of force imposed by the colonial power. South Asian polities are all post-colonial, and yet the distinction between 'insiders' and 'outsiders' not in the literal sense but the symbolic sense is deeply entrenched. If hierarchy based on caste institutionalises inequality, plurality based on insider-outsider dichotomy (Oommen 1986: 53–74) problematises identity. The theatre of conflicts in South Asian polities lies at the confluence between hierarchy and plurality, that is, inequality and externality. The insider-outsider polarisation in South Asian polities is to be discerned primarily regarding religious and language, often as a combination of the two. What I shall focus on this theme is understanding identity assertions and conflicts. An understanding of the religious and language groups in South Asian polities and the status accorded to them by the state is helpful to discern the contexts of conflicts (Table 1.1).

The South Asian countries may be divided into three based on their dominant religious collectivities: Hindu (India and Nepal), Muslim (Bangladesh and Pakistan) and Buddhist (Bhutan, Burma and Sri Lanka). The political divide between Hindu and Islamic polities came into being during the colonial regime. The language was the basis of state formulation of Bangladesh, although its dominant identity changed from language to religion. Thus the presence of non-Bengali Muslims whose language is Hindi (Bihari Muslims) created identity conflicts. Further even the aspiration of Bengali Hindu and Chakma Buddhists could not be adequately accommodated. The tribal population of Bangladesh is distributed into several religious groups, but the Chakma and Marwasi are predominantly Buddhists inhabiting the Chittagong Hill Tracts (CHT) bordering India. Thus although Bangladesh temporarily rejected religion as the basis of state formation after wresting freedom from the co-religionists of Pakistan, it reclaimed its religious identity to gain authenticity as a 'nation-state.'

In Pakistan, the saliency of religion was explicit right from the beginning, and religious minorities such as Hindus and Christians

Table 1.1 Religion and language variations in South Asian countries

Country		
Bangladesh	Religion	86% (Muslims); 12.1% Hindus; 1.5% Others; Islam (state religion)
	Language	95% Bengali (official language)
Bhutan	Religion	70% Buddhists; 25% Hindus; Buddhism (state religion)
	Language	70% Dozongkhsa (official language); 25% Nepali
India	Religion	82% Hindus; 12.12% Muslims; 2.34, Christians; 1.94 Sikhs (No official/national religion)
	Language	40.22% Hindi; 8.3% Bengali; 7.8% Telugu; 7.45% Marathi; 6.32% Tamil; 5.18% Urdu
Myanmar	Religion	87% Buddhists; 5.6% Christians; 3.6% Muslims; 2.6% Animists; Buddhism (state religion)
	Language	Over 80% Burmese (official language); rest are small tribal languages
Nepal	Religion	89.5% Hindus; 5.3% Buddhists; 2.7 Muslims; Hinduism (state religion)
	Language	58.4% Nepali (official language); 11.1% Maithili; 7.6% Bhojpuri
Pakistan	Religion	97% Muslims; 2% Hindus; Islam (state religion)
	Language	48.2% Punjabi; 13.1% Pushto; 11.8% Sindhi; 9.8% Saraiki; 7.6% Urdu (official language)
Sri Lanka	Religion	69.8% Buddhists; 15.17% Hindus; 7.36% Muslims; Buddhism (national religion)
	Language	70% Sinhala (official language); 15% Tamil (second official language)

Source: *The Europe World Year Book*, 2000, Europa Publications, London

felt alienated. But even Muslim protestant sects such as Ahmedias were labelled as heretics and declared non-Muslims. The Muslim refugee migrants from India to Pakistan (Mohajirs) are also treated as outsiders, and their nativity claims within the territory of Pakistan contested. Curiously the mother tongue of Mohajirs is Urdu which is also the official language of Pakistan. Thus both in Bangladesh and in Pakistan, the rupture between insiders and outsiders are clear and vivid. Here the insider-outsider dichotomy is not a matter of physical belonging but that of their symbolic acceptance as insiders (Fazal 2000: 175-99).

The rupture between insiders and outsiders is more accentuated in Sri Lanka. While the original inhabitants of the Island state, the Veddas, are marginalised and have become a microscopic minority, the contending groups – Sinhala Buddhists, Tamil Hindus and Tamil Muslims (referred to as Moors) -are all migrants from India. This shared ancestral homeland does not dilute the religious, linguistic identity conflicts between Tamil Hindus (who migrated from Tamil Nadu) and Sinhala Buddhists whose origin can be traced to Bihar and Orissa. Tamils are also divided based on religion – Hinduism and Islam. While religious groups such as Hindu and Buddhists have territorial anchorages, Muslims and particularly Christians in Sri Lanka are territorially dispersed and are drawn from both linguistic groups – Sinhalese and Tamils. Thus insiders are not natives, but the dominant group and outsiders are not immigrants but the dominated groups.

The case of India is admittedly more complicated not only because of its huge size but also because of its staggering diversity. It is true that 82% of Indians are Hindus but the 13%-14% Muslims counts 140 Million, the second biggest Muslim country in the world. Christians constitute barely 3% but count 25-30 million. The Sikhs, the third biggest religious minority, the youngest of Indic religious, counting 18-20 million claims a specific language (Punjabi; written in Gurumukhi script) and a homeland, the Indian Punjab. The Buddhists and Jains are less than 1% each and do not have a common language or territory. Migrant religions such as Jews, Zoroastrians and Baha'is are tiny and do not pose any serious conflicts.

In the understanding of the Rashtriya Swayamsevak Sangh (RSS), the Hindu militant association, all the religious groups of Indic origin are Hindus and hence insiders, that is Hindus, Jains, Buddhists, Sikhs and all those tribals who follow animism and naturism are Hindus. The Indian state has also accepted this perception. Thus the tribals that have not converted to Islam and Christianity were counted as Hindus since the 1951 Census of India. Similarly, Buddhists, Jains and Sikhs are defined as Hindus in the Hindu Code Bill, promulgated in 1956. The insider-outsider divide in India is between those who belong to religions which originated in India and Muslims and Christians who are perceived to be products of conquest and colonialism, respectively. But the fact is that pre-conquest Islam and pre-colonial Christianity were present in India and the overwhelming majority of Indians who profess Islam and Christianity are converts from local castes and tribes. However, the moment they embrace these religions, they are perceived as cultural outsiders although they are political insiders, that is citizens, by a section of Hindus (owing allegiance to RSS) and by the Indian state through some of its legislation and policies.

The Hindu majority Nepal is less complex in that 90% are Hindus, and although there are numerous languages, nearly 60% are Nepali speaking. The identity assertions are predominantly based on castes and tribes, ecology and valley dwellers and Madhesis who speak Maithili (11%) and Bhojpuri (8%), languages which are also spoken in areas contiguous to the Indian Territory. While these languages are accorded constitutional recognition in Nepal, they are treated as mere dialects of Hindi in India. Similarly, both Bhutan (70%) and Myanmar (87%) are predominantly Buddhist countries, and inter-religious conflicts are less virulent.

The general point that emerges is that identity assertions in post-colonial South Asia are mainly based on religion, and the fact that religious identity is often bolstered by linguistic identity invariably reinforces the insider-outsider wedge. This is evident from the following points:

1   The tendency to identify specific languages with particular religions: Sanskrit with Aryan Hinduism, Tamil with Dravidian Hinduism, Urdu with both North Indian and Pakistan Islam, Hindi with North Indian Hinduism, Pali with Buddhism, Punjabi written in Gurumukhi with Sikhism, Bengali with Bangladeshis who are also Muslims, etc. The linking of religion with language leads to the crystallisation of a series of complex and competing identities manifesting in conflicts.
2   This results in some of the religious-linguistic groups staking their claim on the specific territory as their exclusive homeland, often ignoring the equally legitimate claims of other groups (religion is largely de-territorialised, but the language is localised). The claims of Sikhs in Punjab (ignoring Punjabi Hindus and Punjabi Muslims), Muslims in Kashmir Valley, Tamil Hindus in Jaffna, Sindhi Muslims in Pakistan and Chakma Buddhists in Bangladesh foment conflicts because they are invariably defined as 'anti-state.' But these are essentially 'national' claims that are claims of territorially anchored linguistic collectivities. The

confusion arises out of the conflation between state and nation. At any rate, state policy towards these religious-linguistic collectivities are coercive, even oppressive. But the state policy would draw its legitimacy from the majority of the population belonging to the dominant religious-linguistic collectivity.

3 For South Asian states the cut-off points of history vary, notwithstanding their common civilisational history, depending on which religious collectivity constitutes their dominant population. Pursuantly, 'national' reconstruction is neither a New Beginning nor a New Revolution but the re-conquest or the re-discovery of an appropriate past depending on who constitutes the national mainstream, i.e. the hegemonic religious collectivity. Thus for North India and Nepal, the re-conquest dated back to the era of the Aryan Hindu advent some 3,500 years ago. But this is contested by the Dravidian Hindus of South India, particularly Tamil nationals. For Sri Lanka, Burma and Bhutan the three Buddhists majority states of South Asia, the nodal points of history vary depending on the time at which the dominant form of Buddhism became its national religion. For Sri Lanka this nodal point is around the third century BC; for Bhutan, it is the seventh century CE, and for Burma, it is eleventh century CE when Theravada Buddhism got firmly entrenched there. For Bangladesh and Pakistan, the cut-off point of history is the medieval period, when Muslim rule was firmly established in the Indian Subcontinent. The differing layer of history invoked by the different South Asian states for national reconstruction influence their policies towards religious collectivities including religious denominations. These policies, in turn, legitimise the cognition about insiders and outsiders.

I have noted earlier that South Asian countries are mainly populated by people of three religions – Hinduism, Islam and Buddhism – but one cannot find any pattern of state policy based on religious composition (Oommen 1990: 17–33). Pakistan and Bangladesh are the two Muslim majority states of South Asia under consideration, excluding Afghanistan and Maldives. Pakistan is an Islamic state, in that, it is a state with Islamic laws that but not a theocratic state because the ordained priests (Ulema) are not given the responsibility for governing the state although their opinion is often sought in the formulation, interpretation and application of state laws. The state in Pakistan is, however, expected to enable the Muslims to order their lives 'in accord with the teaching and requirements of Islam set out in Holy Quran and Sunnah.' The first constitution of Pakistan promulgated in 1956 explicitly referred to it as the Islamic Republic. Although this was omitted from the 1962 Constitution, the 1973 Constitution declared Islam as the state religion and prescribed that a. the president and the prime minister ought to be Muslims and b. that all laws should be brought in conformity with the values of Islam. In 1981, President Zia Ul-Haq stated that the purpose of the state of Pakistan is to promote the ideology of Islam and subsequent governments reiterated this position. Consequently, not only religious minorities such as Hindus, Sikhs and Christians but Islamic sects like Ahmedias are also marginalised. The fact that Urdu came to be associated with Muslims in the Indian subcontinent. Although it is the mother tongue of only a small percent of the population, it is adopted as the official language in Pakistan, which further complicates matters. Thus the dominant identity of Pakistan is based on Islam and Urdu (Oommen 1990: 17–33).

Bangladesh emerged in 1972 to safeguard the interests of a linguistic category and hence the Bengali-speaking Hindus, Christians and Buddhists, were promised equality and liberty. In fact, the 1972 Constitution of Bangladesh declared itself as a Socialist and Secular state. But from 1975 the military regime took definite steps towards Islamisation and in 1988 Islam was declared as the state religion of Bangladesh. Although Bangladesh started as a secular state, it adopted an Islamic ethos. Coupled with the fact that 95% of its population is Bengali speaking, the predominant identity of Bangladesh is Bengali – Muslim identity.

The three Buddhist majority states of South Asia also vary about the official status accorded to religion. Buddhism is the official religion in Bhutan right from the beginning. In Burma, Buddhism became the state religion in 1961, but this recognition was withdrawn in 1962. However, Buddhism was declared as the national religion subsequently. If Burma wavered in the matter of having an official religion, in post-colonial Sri Lanka no explicit recognition was given to Buddhism, but it is the official religion for all practical purposes. The mainstream national identity in Sri Lanka is Sinhala-Buddhist. The general point is that irrespective of the nature of political authority, the monarchy in Bhutan, a military dictatorship in Burma (until recently) and democracy in Sri Lanka – Buddhism is the dominating religion. While in Sri Lanka there are two official languages – Sinhala and Tamil – in

Bhutan and Burma the language of the majority linguistic groups is the official language.

The two Hindu majority states of South Asia vary in according official status to the majority religion. Nepal was a Hindu State ruled by monarchy until recently, but the dominant ethos is that of Hinduism even in present democratic Nepal, and the dominant language is Nepali. Nepal had four constitutions since 1948, but the 2015 Constitution declared Nepal as a federal republic. The Terai region with 51% population has only 62 out of 165 seats – i.e. 37%. The identity assertions in Nepal are based on region and caste groups. In the case of India, there is no official religion, and 22 languages are accorded official status. But that does not mean that the dominant religious majority does not assert its hegemony and the most populous linguistic group – the Hindi speakers – do not insist on their superiority. Here again, the combination of 83% Hindus and 38% Hindi speakers assert their superior and distinct identity giving birth to community-based conflicts. But India (along with Nepal) is not only a plural society wherein the insiders and outsiders (i.e. those who follow alien religions) are polarised, but is also a hierarchical society wherein acute conflicts exist even amongst insiders, that is between caste groups, particularly those above the poverty line and those below it. This lethal combination of plurality and hierarchy makes India a theatre of numerous types of identity assertions and consequent conflicts.

III

I want to conclude this chapter by suggesting that the fundamental problem that besets South Asia is the disjunction between empirical reality and the model of nation-building they have adopted from West Europe. Nations and States always existed, but their linking is a recent phenomenon, approximately 370 years. The problem started in 1648 with the conclusion of the Treaty of Westphalia which linked nations and states, giving birth to the institution of the nation-state. The nation-state endeavours to create uniform, homogeneous citizenship. That is, the nation-state is a culture destroying the institution, save the culture of the majority, religious or linguistic, often a combination of the two. In contrast, nations, big and small, are culture affirming, that is, identity asserting entities. Nations are incessantly in search of roots. Therefore, when several nations are yoked together in one state, conflicts are inevitable. Nation-states are graveyards of identities. When Western nation-states were constituted, they destroyed all identities except those based on class, gender and age. Later, after the turbulence of migration, racial identity also assumed some salience. But the social reality of South Asian states is radically different-they are heterogeneous based on religion and language. Unless identities based on these factors are recognised and legitimised, conflicts will persist. As of now, these identity groups are perceived as cultural outsiders to the polity as a whole or in part of it, although they are political insiders. But all political insiders are not treated on equal ground, thanks to a hierarchy anchored to the caste system. That is, South Asian polities are at once plural and hierarchical, drastically different from West European nation-states. Therefore, the institution of the nation-state is utterly unsuitable to South Asia.

The second dimension of disjunction concerns the autonomy of individuals and group identity. The Enlightenment Project which celebrated its triumph in inventing the universal man/women who by definition transcend all primordial ties – religion, language, nationality, etc. – is the second problem. The Enlightenment Project got initiated one and a half centuries after the Treaty of Westphalia. When anti-Jewish riots broke out in 1789 in Alsace in France, the Count of Claremont-Tonnerre declared: 'The Jews should be denied everything as a nation, but granted everything as individuals.' This was based on the perception that Jews have allegiance to one another, that would endanger their terminal loyalty to France as citizens. The Enlightenment Project endorsed the universality of human individuals but completely denied specificity of group identities. Nation-States uphold the individual's freedom but deny group identities, particularly of minority groups.

Neither the institution of the Nation-State as conceived through the Treaty of Westphalia, which pursues cultural homogenisation, nor the Enlightenment Project, which denies group identity within nation-states, suit the empirical reality of South Asia. Group identity assertions are built into the empirical realities of South Asian polities. Therefore I have argued that South Asian states are not nation-states but should be designated as national states which should acknowledge and celebrates cultural diversity and equality between identity groups (Oommen 2009:22–43). If we do not reconstruct South Asian polities based on these principles, conflicts emanating out of identity assertions will persist.

What is the way out? I venture to suggest that consociational democracy which provides representation to primordial identities is the way out.[2] This system existed long ago under the millet system of the Ottoman Empire and now exists in Belgium. Given the territorial anchorage of democracy (based on constituencies), spatially dispersed groups and communities-religious, linguistic, tribal and caste – will not have the possibility of getting adequate and appropriate representations in legislative bodies at different levels. To cope with this problem, consociational democracy will go a long way in blunting identity assertions and conflicts geared to them.

Notes

1 Afghanistan is left out because of non-availability of data, and in the Maldives, the contexts of conflicts are not based on identities of groups but based on personality clashes.
2 For details, please see Lijphart (1980).

References

Balibar, Etienne, and Immanuel Wallerstein. 1991. *Race, Nation, Class: Ambiguous Identities*. London: Verso.

Fazal, Tanweer. 2000. "Religion and Language in the Formation of Nationhood in Pakistan and Bangladesh." In *Nation and National Identity in South Asia*, edited by S. L. Sharma and T. K. Oommen, 175–99. Hyderabad: Orient Longman.

Furnivall, J.S. 1939. *Netherland India*. Cambridge: Cambridge University Press.

———. 1948. *Colonial Policy and Practice: A Comparative Study of Burma and Netherlands India*. Cambridge: Cambridge University Press.

Hobsbawm, E., and T. Ranger, eds. 1983. *The Invention of Tradition*. Cambridge: Cambridge University Press.

Lijphart, Arend. 1980. *Democracy in Plural Societies: A Comparative Exploration*. New Haven: Yale University Press.

Oommen, T.K. 1986. "Insiders and Outsiders in India: Primordial Collectivism in Nation Building." *International Sociology* 1(1):53–74.

———. 1990. "State and Religion in Multi-Religious Nation-States: The Case of South Asia." *South Asian Journal* 4(1): 17–33.

———. 1997. *Citizenship, Nationality and Ethnicity*. Cambridge: Polity Press.

———. 2000. "Changing Modes of Conceptualizing the World: Implications for Social Research." In *Methodology in Social Research: Dilemmas and Perspectives*, edited by P. N. Mukherjee, 153–70. New Delhi: Sage Publications.

———. 2005. "Challenges of Modernity in an Age of Globalization." In *Comparing Modernities: Pluralism Versus Homogeneity*, edited by Eliezer Ben Rafael, and Yitzhak Stanberg, 149–69. Leiden: E.J. Brill.

———. 2009. "Political Federalism, Community Identity and Cultural Pluralism." In *Federal Power Sharing: Accommodating Indian Diversity*, edited by Akhtar Majeed, 22–43. New Delhi: Mank Publications.

Pletsch, C.E. 1981. "The Three Worlds or the Division of Scientific Labour, circa 1950–75." *Comparative Studies in Society and History* 23:569–90.

Chapter 2

Constitution and conflict
Mono-ethnic federalism in a poly-ethnic Nepal

Mahendra Lawoti[1]

Introduction: federal contestations

Scholars and practitioners often recommend federalism to prevent and manage conflicts, but its adoption has exacerbated ethnic conflict in Nepal. This chapter seeks to answer why this happened. The new Constitution promulgated in September 2015 and the federal model it adopted invited an intense six-month-long movement (shutdowns of highways, towns, educational institutions, etc.) in the Tarai/Madhesh (Southern Plains) by the Madhesi and Tharu, including a blockade with implicit support of the Indian government. Nearly five dozen people, including security personnel, died and much more were hurt during the movement. A widespread shortage of fuel, cooking gas and other essential consumer items throughout the county made lives of millions of people difficult, negatively affected the economy and delayed reconstruction work in the earthquake hit areas.

The hill indigenous nationalities, particularly Magar and Limbu, also launched protests against the federal model and other constitutional articles. Women, Dalit, indigenous Nationalities and Madhesi allege that many discriminatory provisions exist in the new Constitution and that the 2015 Constitution is regressive because it took away much equality enhancing rights awarded by the Interim Constitution of 2007 (Hachhethu 2015; Limbu et al. 2016).

The federal model was the most contentious issue during the tenure of the first and second Constituent Assembly (CA). The inability to reach a consensus over the federal model led to the dissolution of the first CA (2008–12) while hurriedly finalising a federal model without building consensus, which was the norm in first CA, in the second CA invited the longest movement in the country's history. The contestation is primarily centred around the issues of provincial borders and the names of the provinces. The Madhesi and indigenous nationalities want autonomy to self-govern and recognition of their identities at provincial and sub-provincial levels. This would require Nepal to create 10–14 provinces that transform major ethnic groups into pluralities in their homeland and name those provinces and sub-provinces with cultural markers and symbols of the marginalised ethnic groups as in India, Spain and elsewhere.

The dominant ethnic group (Khas Arya: Bahun, Thakuri, Chhettri and Sanyasi) and the major political parties its members lead and control reject such a federal model, arguing that having too many provinces would be costly, invite violent ethnic conflicts and could even disintegrate the country. They prefer a federal model with five to eight provinces. They finally imposed a federal model with seven provinces arguing that it would facilitate development. The marginalised Madhesi and indigenous groups allege that seven-province federal model does only not recognise their identities or deny autonomy to them, but it facilitates the continued domination of the Khas Arya ethnic group in most of the provinces by making it a majority or a large plurality.

Despite the protests and the six-month-long street movement, the ruling Khas Arya leaders have refused to accommodate the core issues of recognition of identities and autonomy. They amended the Constitution to partially address the demands relating to the electoral method and proportionality but only agreed to form a political mechanism to look into the contested issue of provinces' border demarcation. The Madhesi and indigenous groups continued their protests but redirected the activities of the toned down movement to Kathmandu.

After briefly reviewing the literature on federalism and conflicts in the next section, I will look at how the adopted federal model deals with autonomy and identity recognition of various ethnic groups. Then, I will analyse why the Madhesi, whose demands were partially met, launched an intense six months long movement while the indigenous hill groups, whose demands for autonomy and recognition were flatly rejected have not been able to do so despite attempts. Then the chapter will try to gauge whether Nepal may witness protests and conflicts in the future.

Federalism, violent conflicts and disintegration

Federalism and the break-up of countries

The debate about federalism in Nepal has revolved around which type of federal structure prevents and manages conflict and separatism and fosters stability and economic development. Since different federal countries have different federal structures, the critical question is what type of federal structure would be suitable for different countries.

Federalism has managed and prevented conflicts and undermined separatism in many culturally diverse democracies by providing autonomy to territorially concentrated minorities and sharing power amongst different groups (Bermeo 2004; Elazar 1987; Gurr 1993; Lijphart 1977; Stepan 2001). However, some "federal" countries have disintegrated, either peacefully or after going through violent conflict. Such incidents have reinforced the fear amongst some that group autonomy could be slippery.

The USSR, Yugoslavia, Czechoslovakia, Pakistan and Ethiopia are one set of "federal" countries that disintegrated. The break-up of the USSR and Yugoslavia caught global attention and scholars who studied them have argued that federalism is responsible for the break-up (Cornell 2002; Roeder 2009). However, many scholars do not consider the aforementioned former communist regimes or non-communist dictatorship as federal countries despite the designation (Anderson 2014; Hale 2004; Kavalski and Zolkos 2008; Leff 1999). Federalism requires a clear separation of power between the centre and provinces, constitutionally and in practice, and that is possible only in democracy. The centre controlled the provinces in these non-democratic countries, engendering dissatisfaction in the provinces. The regional groups rebelled and declared independence when the political opportunity became available after democracy was introduced (Suny 1991). The "federal" structure provided provincial-level political bases to launch the challenges successfully (Cornell 2002; Leff 1999: 210–11).

Other non-communist federal countries like British West Indies (1958–62), British Central African Federation (1953–63), Mali Federation (1959–60) and Malaysia-Singapore (1963–65) have also disintegrated. These "federalism" lasted for a short period. Institutions need time to have an impact (Lijphart 1999). One cannot blame federalism for the break-up of the shortly lived countries as its political impacts were yet to manifest.[2] Others have argued that without a capable centre and a federal identity, among other things that take time to build, federalism cannot be sustained (Kavalski and Zolkos 2008).

In another set of countries like Burma (1948–62), Cameroon (1961–1972), Congo (June 1960–September 1960), Ethiopia (1952–62), Indonesia (1949–60) and Libya (1951–63) unitary structure replaced federalism. Bermeo (2004) argues that the imposition of federalism by outside forces (Britain, Britain, Belgium, UN Resolution, Netherlands and Allies/UN, respectively) led to their failure. Outside forces had also imposed the short-lived federalism (British West Indies, British Central African Federation, Mali Federation and the Malaysia-Singapore) discussed earlier (French pressure for Mali federation, British in rest of the three) (Bermeo 2004). The absence of consent of different groups to establish federalism led to their inability to remain together. For federalism to sustain, local should demand it and countries should adopt it with the consent of different groups. Further, all the aforementioned non-communist federal countries were either not democratic or had been ruled by the non-democratic regime before breaking up (Center for Systemic Peace 2016). Watts (2005) argues that "genuine" democratic federations have not yet failed. Stepan (2001) likewise claims that all democracies with territorially mobilised groups have federalism. Thus, only non-democratic and imposed "federations" have failed or broken up.

Federalism and violent conflicts

Democratic federal countries may not disintegrate but still could face conflicts. Federal countries have witnessed less number of intense violent conflicts but a higher number of less intense conflicts compared to unitary states (Gurr 1993; Saideman et al. 2002; Toft and Saideman 2010) but a popular misperception associates federalism with violent conflict. This myth needs to be demystified. Countries that witnessed large-scale deaths in ethnic conflicts were largely unitary state at the time of conflict: Rwanda (900,000), Somalia (550,000), Sudan (2,300,000, two conflicts), Burundi (200,000), China/Tibet (1,200,000), Indonesia/West Papua (100,000), Indonesia/East Timor (600,000), Iraq/Kurds (180,000), the Philippines/Muslim (150,000). Federal countries that witnessed more than 100,000 deaths are Nigeria/Biafra (800,000),

Pakistan/Bangladesh (500,000), Yugoslavia (260,000) and Russia/Chechnya (200,000) (Scaruffi 2009).[3] Pakistan and Yugoslavia were non-democratic "federalism" while Nigeria and Russia were/are core ethno-federalist states (see the following).

Scholars have been identified several factors as contributors to the conflict in federal countries. One, federal democracies encounter a higher number of less intensive disputes and protests because people use their right to dissent, organise and protests (Gurr 1993; Saideman et al. 2002). Since the number of governments is higher and closer to the people in federal countries than in unitary states, the cost of organising and engaging in peaceful protests is lower, and hence we witness a higher number of low-intensity conflicts. However, when provinces address some of the demands in federal democracies partially or completely in conflict, intensity reduces or conflict ends. Protests and movements are part and parcel of democracy, and contribute to making the government responsive toward its citizens, including towards the marginalised groups. It reduces alienation and strengthens democracies. This is a positive aspect of the conflict. The violent conflicts discussed next often lead to negative consequences.

Two, when territorially concentrated groups' demand for autonomy is denied, the countries often witness violent conflict. The state, often controlled by the dominant group, may attempt to repress the movement demanding autonomy. The dominant group may also engage in a backlash against what it considers threatening activities of the minorities. On the other hand, the minorities may engage in violent activities if they believe that peaceful movements have not yielded autonomy. The conflict in Sudan before its break-up and adoption of federalism and the conflict in Sri Lanka are some examples.

Three, violent conflicts amongst and between identity groups have occurred over recognition of identities or the lack of it. 'The instances of failed federations indicate the limits of thinking about federalism primarily as a principle for the distribution of power across territorial subdivisions . . . failure is indicated by the lack of consideration for management of identities'(Kavalski and Zolkos 2008: 163). On the other hand, in addition to creating territorial units to empower and facilitate self-governance, many federal countries like India, Canada, Ethiopia, Belgium, Malaysia, Nigeria, Russia and Spain adopted ethnic group names or named the provinces in minority languages to manage the diverse population.

Four, Lemco (1991) and Adeney (2006) found federal countries with less number of provinces were unstable (operationalised as secession by Lemco and disintegration of countries, end of federalism or end of the federal regime by Adeney). According to Lemco, no federal country with 2 to 5 provinces was stable while countries with 6 to 11 provinces were stable less than 40%, while countries with 12 and more provinces were stable more than 60% of the time. Adeney (2006) found that countries with twoto7 provinces failed more than 65%, while countries with 8to12 provinces failed 20% and countries with more than 13 provinces failed 13%. Horowitz (1985), Manor (1998), McGarry and O'Leary (2009), Filippov, Ordeshook and Olga Shvetsova (2004) and Hale (2004) concur that smaller number of provinces increase the possibility of instability. I have come across no studies that argue that a fewer number of provinces provide a higher degree of stability.

Depending on how political leadership creates borders, an ethnic group could become a majority, plurality or minority. That will determine whether ethnic members are likely to become advantaged, disadvantaged or not directly affected (Horowitz 1985). Adeney (2006: 172) similarly argues that 'the greater the number of units in the federation, the lower the potential for a unit to be excluded from a coalition.' Inclusion reduces dissatisfaction and alienation. Less number of provinces may result in the creation of borders that deny self-governance to smaller ethnic groups. Denial of self-governance arrangement has often led to violent conflicts.

Five, Hale (2004) and Adeney (2006) argue a core ethnic region in ethno-federal states increases the likelihood of state collapse (defined as state break-up and large-scale civil war) while ethno-federal countries without a core ethnic region did not collapse.[4] Extreme disparities in population, size or wealth of constituent federal units contribute to stress and conflicts (Watts 2005). A group dominating the polity often imposes policies it deems good on rest of the groups in the polity. Such policies often favour their group while disadvantaging others, inviting protests and rebellion. A core ethnic province can emerge in countries that are mostly bipolar societies or in multi-ethnic societies with a majority group where provinces are constructed without breaking the large ethnic group. On the other hand, societies having a large number of ethnic groups with no single group forming a majority is considered to be less conflict-prone (Bangura 2006; Bates 2000).[5]

Six, some federal countries may witness conflicts due to demand more rights and power. Bakke and Wibbels (2006: 37) argue that 'the interaction of high interregional inequality and ethnic concentration increases the likelihood of ethnic conflict.' Others have argued that asymmetrical federalism might better serve culturally diverse countries with different contexts and groups (Kavalski and Zolkos 2008: 9). Canada and India have awarded different groups and provinces with different types of power.

Seven, countries have witnessed violent conflict when rights and power awarded to provinces were challenged, eroded or taken away. Kashmir in India has seen a rise in violent conflict, including a separatist movement,[6] largely due to frequent central interventions in provincial politics and taking away power awarded to the only Muslim dominated province in the country (Adeney 2006).

This brief literature review points out that design of federalism matters in managing or exacerbating ethnic conflicts as well as disintegration or consolidation of countries. In the next section, I will examine how the seven-province model in Nepal treats different ethnic groups with regard to recognition and autonomy.

Mono-ethnic federalism in a poly-ethnic society

The competing claims over federal models in Nepal have primarily revolved around the recognition of identity and self-governance rights to marginalised ethnic groups or their denial. The marginalised groups have strongly demanded naming provinces and sub-provincial units in ways that reflect their groups and their cultures, largely because state symbolism have pervasively pandered to the dominant Khas Arya practices, rituals and symbols. Likewise, they are demanding demarcation of provincial and sub-provincial units in ways that would allow them to influence provincial and sub-provincial policies to compensate for their inability to influence policy making at the federal level due to their countrywide permanent minority position (Lawoti 2005). The new Constitution has largely rejected both demands. The 2015 Constitution (Constituent Assembly 2015) adopted federalism but a model that enables the Khas Arya ethnic group ("upper" caste hill Hindus – 31.25% population) to decisively dominate six of the seven provinces (Table 2.1) as well as federal politics at the centre. The Khas Arya's majority in only two provinces and only plurality in four provinces and at

Table 2.1 Population of identity groups in seven provinces and Nepal

Prov. (pop.)	Largest identity group		Second-largest group		Third-largest group		Fourth-largest group		Fifth-largest group	
	Group	Pop. (%)	Group	Pop. (%)	Group	Pop. (%)	Group	Pop. (%)	Group	Pop. (%)
1	Khas Arya	1,262,544 (27.84)	Rai Kirant	578,404 (12.83)	MCM	503,586 (11.11)	TaraiIN	500,246 (11.03)	Limbu	364,830 (8.05)
2	MCM	3,425,258 (63.38)	Madhesi Dalit	829,606 (15.35)	TaraiIN	480,490 (8.89)	Hill IN	286,158 (5.3)	Khas Arya	264,009 (4.89)
3	Khas Arya	2,050,844 (37.09)	Tamang	1,129,323 (20.42)	Non-Tamang-Newar-hill IN	1,049,4903 (18.98)	Newar	935,312 (16.92)	Hill Dalit	291,620 (5.27)
4	Khas Arya	756,228 (38.6)	Magar	362,256 (18.5)	Dalit Hill	349,269 (17.83)	Gurung	218,971 (11.18)	Non GuMaIN	125,320 (6.4)
5	Khas Arya	1,383,232 (29.51)	MCM	989,498 (21.11)	Magar	729,102 (15.56)	Tharu	705,709 (15.06)	Hill Dalit	482,696 (10.3)
6	Khas Arya	953,153 (61.25)	Hill Dalit	355,659 (22.85)	Magar	183,283 (11.78)	Non-Magar hill IN	38,554 (2.48)	Tarai IN	7,864 (0.50)
7	Khas Arya	1,532,141 (60.02)	Tharu	439,267 (17.21)	Hill Dalit	330,241 (12.94)	Hill IN	82,377 (3.23)	MCM	50,512 (1.98)
Nepal	Khas Arya	31.25	MCM	15.03	Magar	7.12	Tharu	6.56	Tamang	5.81

Self-tabulation from Ethnic and Caste Groups, Census 2011, Nepal.

Source: Department of Sociology and Anthropology (2014)

the centre may deceive non-electoral politics specialists. The plural political party or group, especially if there are no close competitors, wins much more seats than its vote/population share in electoral politics. The electoral methods, by design, especially the First Past the Post (FPTP) method but to some extent, even the Proportional Representative (PR) electoral method as well, help to create artificial majorities (Lijphart 1999). The consistent capture of majority seats by Khas Arya, despite being only a plurality, under FPTP electoral method in all six general elections in Nepal demonstrates this tendency,[7] even though other factors also contributed to the outcome.

Khas Arya (an ethnic group that speaks the same language and shares the 'upper' caste hill Hindu culture) is nearly four times larger than the second largest ethnic group (Magar – 7.12%) and two times larger than the regional identity group (comprising of Madhesi non-Dalit caste group,15.03%).[8] In such a context, is the domination of the Khas Arya in most provinces a foregone conclusion? The answer is no. The alternative federal models make this clear. The Restructuring of the State and Distribution of State Power Committee (RSDSPC), with a majority, and the State Restructuring Commission (SRC), with a two-thirds majority, recommended 14 and 10 provinces federal models, respectively, in the first CA. Many experts proposed ten or more provinces (see Tamang 2005). These models demarcated provincial borders to facilitate Madhesi and indigenous groups to become the majority, plurality or competitive to the plural group in their native homeland. Madhesi becomes a majority in one province in both models. Limbu, Rai, Tamang, Tharu, Sherpa and Magar become plural groups in the SRC or RSDSPC or both models. Newar, Magar and Gurung become competitive second largest groups in one or both models. Additionally, 10–14 provinces would facilitate the election of a higher number of marginalised group members compared to the seven-province model. The federal polity would become relatively inclusive as well.

Notes: 1. I calculated the population percentage from the total population of districts. This does not add up to 100% due to "Other" Dalit, "Other Janajati," etc., categories that have not been lumped in sub-categories. 2. Rai Kirant consists of Aathpariya, Bantawa, Chamling, Khaling, Kulung, Loharung, Mewahang Bala, Nacchiring, Rai, Sampang and Thulung, Yamphu. During the 2011 census, many members of linguistic communities that earlier identified as Rai began to disavow the identity. Many other members of such groups, however, identify as Rai. All of them identify as Kiranti. 3. The Tarai indigenous nationalities (Tarai IN) from Jhapa, Sunsari and Morang districts in South-East Nepal have demanded a separate state. 4. MCM = Madhesi non-Dalit Caste and Muslims; MCMD (Madhesi Caste + Muslim + Madhesi Dalit) = 78.73%; MC (Madhesi non-Dalit Caste) = 51.8; Muslims = 11.58%.

Further, the competitive second largest group (Newa, Gurung and Magar) in the 10–14 provinces model could benefit from electoral politics in their respective native provinces due to their more cohesive identity than that of Khas Arya thatis comprised of four castes. This could allow the groups, compared to the Khas Arya, to win more seats than their vote share. Even if the groups are not able to obtain advantages of plurality, the 10–14 provinces could blunt the advantages that could go to the plural Khas Arya ethnic group due to the small margin between the plural and second largest groups. In the seven-province model, the Khas Arya would have decisive domination as no ethnic group's population is close to it.

When many more groups have chances of forming a majority or plurality in provincial legislatures in the 10–14 provinces model, the ensuing dynamics will benefit other groups as well. It would produce a more competitive political environment that could increase the bargaining power of smaller identity groups. The inability of Khas Arya to enjoy hegemonic domination would benefit even caste groups like the Dalit and the religious minority like Muslims because the chances of provincial governments led by and dominated by the more orthodox Hindu Khas Arya will decrease. The emerging identity-coalitional politics in such provinces would increase their chances of being influential coalitional partners or supporters in provincial politics. Likewise, the 10-province federal model has a provision for non-territorial mechanisms for Dalit while the seven-province model has not.

Numerous smaller marginalised groups will face similar or worse consequences in the seven-province model, primarily in two ways. First, the Constitution eliminated the sub-provincial autonomy and recognition awarded to 22 indigenous groups and Protected Area to numerous minorities (provisioned by SRC and RSDSPC federal models). Tamuwan, Limbuwan, Sherpa province, for example, would have each accommodated and recognised around a dozen smaller indigenous groups.[9] Second, compared to the 10–14 provinces models, the decidedly smaller identity groups' population proportion would be smaller significantly in the seven-province model.

For example, Lepcha would have only 0.08% population in Province One instead of around 0.2% in Limbuwan (Eastern province) of 10–14 provinces model (Table 2.2).

The new Constitution has awarded the right to name the provinces to the provincial assembly. This is effectively a rejection of identity of marginalised groups. In six of the seven provinces, as pointed out earlier, the dominant group is a majority or a large plurality. Except in Province Two, the marginalised native groups may not be able to name the provinces that reflect their group or culture. In fact, in most or all the six provinces, the Khas Arya could impose the names that reflect and convey their ethnic group, its language and culture. Naming the provinces with terms like "Sagarmatha," the highest mountain in the world, supposedly a "neutral" term but it is from the dominant language. Chomolungma is the name of Everest in native language of the Himalayan region.

The seven-province federal model is thus a mono-ethnic federal model. This was attained by gerrymandering to make the marginalised groups non-competitive and less significant minorities. These features will increase the likelihood of the Khas Arya winning majority seats in six out of seven provincial assemblies and the federal parliament. The enhanced political representation granted by the electoral dynamics will enable the Khas Arya to continue to dominate the non-political arenas as well. Further, while the Constitution has not recognised the identities of marginalised groups at the provincial and sub-provincial level, it has reinforced the identity of the Khas Arya. The Constitution defines the term Khas Arya multiple times in the Constitution, providing it with constitutional status, while not extending similar recognition of non-other groups (Limbu et al. 2016). The seven-province federal model would thus facilitate the continuation of symbolic and substantive hegemonic domination of Khas Arya in the new federal republic Nepal. However, the marginalised groups are likely to continue challenging the mono-ethnic hegemonic domination and it may result in violent ethnic conflict.

Federation and conflicts in Nepal

As mentioned earlier, the new Constitution invited long protest movements at the time of its finalisation and promulgation. However, movements are difficult to sustain over a long period as the collective action problem literature points out (Olson 1971).

Table 2.2 Ethnic/caste distribution in 14 and 10 provinces federal models recommended by RSDSPC and SRC, respectively

#	Name of province	14 provinces model		10 provinces model	
		First-largest group (population %)	Second-largest group (population %)	First-largest group (population %)	Second-largest group (population %)
1	Limbuwan	**1 Khas Arya (28)**	Limbu (27)	**Limbu (27)**	Khas Arya (27)
2	Kirat	**Rai (34)**	Khas Arya (29)	Rai (35)	Khas Arya (27)
3	Sherpa	Sherpa (36)	Khas Arya (14)	X	X
4	Mithila-Bhojpura-Koch Madhesh	Madhesi (72)	Khas Arya (12)	Madhesi (72)	Khas Arya (13)
5	Sunkoshi	2 Khas Arya (37)	Tamang (14)	X	X
6	Tamsaling	**Tamang (44)**	Khas Arya (29)	Tamang (35)	Khas Arya (30)
7	Newa	**3 Khas Arya (38)**	Newa (36)	**1 Khas Arya (37)**	Newa (36)
8	Narayani	4 Khas Arya (43)	Magar (10)	2 Khas Arya (45)	Magar (11)
9	Tamuwan	**5 Khas Arya (35)**	Gurung (32)	**3 Khas Arya (33)**	Gurung (32)
10	Magarat	6 Khas Arya (40)	Magar (34)	**Magar (35)**	Khas Arya (35)
11	Lumbini-Awadh-Tharuwan	**7 Khas Arya (27)**	Tharu (26)	**Tharu (27)**	Khas Arya (25)
12	Jadan	8 Khas Arya (55)	Sherpa (19)	X	X
13	Karnali	9 Khas Arya (62)	Dalit (19)	4 Khas Arya (60)	Dalit (19)
14	Khaptad	10 Khas Arya (75)	Dalit (20)		

Source: Hachhethu (2014: 51); numbered Khas Arya counts the provinces it dominates; bold indicate the competitive plural groups

The government and top leaders of the major parties appear to be counting on the inability of the marginalised groups to sustain strong movements for considerable periods. Their strategy appears to be working but the question is would the marginalised groups be able to relaunch their movements in the coming years? What do the development of contentious politics in the country (see Lawoti 2007) and literature on autonomy movements indicate?

The amendment of the Constitution, which partially addressed the representation question, may have reduced the rationale for movement in some people's eyes. Further, India appears to be backtracking from its strong support of Madhesi movement, beginning from the lifting up of the blockade. These developments appear to make the Madhesi movement weaker due to loss of internal and external support base. However, the Madhesi movement continued onto the elections, even though in less intense scale, and obtained electoral victories in the local, provincial, federal elections. Some argue that the participation in the election may have begun the process of mainstreaming the political parties of the marginalised groups but Madhesi and indigenous leaders declare that they are preparing and waiting for the right opportunity to relaunch effective movements. Madhesi and indigenous organisations have begun to form alliances in preparation for that.

Historical analysis of marginalised groups' movements in Nepal and global trends suggest that Nepal may again witness intense movements of the marginalised groups. The literature on autonomy movements points out that subsequent movement often builds on previous ones (Gurr 1993). The formal demand for autonomy and recognition of identity is an old issue in Nepal, at least from the early 1950s, and it has only been growing ever since (see Lawoti 2007 for earlier conflicts and rebellions). Even when the marginalised groups were not able to launch effective movements for a long time, they continued to raise the issues, develop the network and establish organisations. The movements expanded and were able to gain some concessions when the political opportunity became available (Lawoti 2015). This suggests that unless the state addresses the underlying issues and causes, even though the intensity of movements may go through troughs, subsequent mobilisation may become intense when political opportunities become available.

The Khas Arya leaders prevented the formation of a single province in Madhesh, a major demand of Madhesi parties that could have established an approximate core ethnic province. With around half of the population of the country, such a province would have dominated the central polity. Imbalanced federalism often invites conflict (Adeney 2006; Hale 2004; Horowitz 1985). The Khas Arya leadership may have prevented the threat of conflict from one angle but they went on to invite it from another angle. They established mono-ethnic federalism, which facilitates hegemonic domination of their group. Unlike a province with a demographic strength that may deter challenges for some time (see O'Leary 2001), the establishment of hegemonic domination by a group without popular majority may increase the confidence of and incite the opposition with collective demographic strength to launch movements sooner.

The seven-province mono-ethnic federalism denied autonomy to indigenous groups and truncated the Madhesi concentrated area. A large number of scholarship have shown that when the state denies demands of territorially concentrated groups for recognition of identity and autonomy through federalism, the minorities launch movements to attain them, including violent ones (Gurr 1993; Horowitz 1985; Stepan 2001; Bermeo 2004; Lijphart 1977). The denial of autonomy and recognition of territorially concentrated marginalised groups by the Constitution and the seven-province model may continuously invite autonomy movement and conflict, even though usually at a low-intensity level. Unlike the dominant group created bogey of the impossibility of empowering a large number of groups by federalism, such a situation is favourable for devising institutions that prevent domination by any group (Bates 2000; Bangura 2006) but the leaders not only squandered away the opportunity, they might have also created conditions that intensify conflicts sooner.

The seven-province federal model demonstrates additional conflict-inviting tendencies. Studies point out that federations with fewer numbers of provinces have been more unstable around the world (Adeney 2006; Hale 2004; Horowitz 1985; Lemco 1991: McGarry and O'Leary 2009; Watts 2005). More than two-thirds of the federations in the world, including poor ones, have more than eight provinces. Thus, despite the claims by the dominant group leaders and the major media outlets, which the dominant group controls, that larger number of provinces would be less viable, the global experience demonstrates the opposite – federations with a fewer number of provinces have been more unstable. One cause for the instability is that the seven provinces are inadequate to meet the aspirations for autonomy of many marginalised groups, as discussed earlier. Another problem could be the supply side inefficiencies created by lumping different groups with dissimilar cultures and aspirations and different ecological zones with diverse environment and contexts that result in the varying needs by the seven-province model (Sharma 2007). Economists argue that it is easier and more efficient to provide services in more homogenous provinces (cultural, geographically).

Many in Nepal often assume that larger geographic and population sizes of the provinces would facilitate development by enabling a broader market for goods and services. However, what such Nepali critics forget is that political leadership in the US and elsewhere invented and adopted federalism in the first place to expand markets (Riker 1964; Ziblatt 2004). Thus, the argument that the creation of territorially smaller provinces in federal Nepal would constrain the market demonstrates ignorance of basic objective and rationale for establishing federalism – that of expanding market. If an important aim of establishing "coming together" federalism was to expand the market by uniting countries, it is inconceivable that the central leaders, who have a significant role in design and implementation of "holding together" federalism, would create provincial borders that constrain the market. Thus, Nepal would continue to operate as a common market under federalism, and, in fact, more effectively so, as described next.

The logic of market-preserving federalism, which says that economic growth is attained from competition amongst provinces because competition promotes efficiency in investment and production (Weingast 1995), points out that seven-province model would facilitate less competition compared to 10–14 provinces model. Hence, the seven-province federalism would contribute less in economic development. This exposes the fallacy of popular perception in Nepal that a large number of provinces would be costlier and problematic. Though intuitive, this perception is largely an uninformed opinion, bereft of knowledge of political economy theories. According to the logic of market-preserving federalism theory, a higher number of provinces would generate more economic growth, and not only meet costs associated with a greater number of provinces (of course, not ad infinitum) but also produce a higher net economic benefit.

Third, the powerlessness of provinces may also contribute to generating conflicts and separatist movements. The powerlessness of "national" provinces in the USSR, Yugoslavia and Pakistan bred dissatisfaction and alienation along national lines that ultimately boiled over and led to conflict and disintegration (Bakke and Wibbels 2006; McGarry and O'Leary 2009; Suny 1991). What is important to remember here is that the "national" borders became problematic because the central state deprived the national community of essential power. National communities in democratic federal states where the provinces enjoyed substantial power have not disintegrated. The literature that criticises federalism and autonomy arrangements (Cornell 2002; Roeder 2009), in fact, base their arguments on case studies of sham federalism like the USSR and Yugoslavia that had not empowered provinces (Anderson 2014). The new Constitution in Nepal has adopted federalism but concentrated power in the centre and severely weakened the provinces by denying many necessary rights (Limbu et al. 2016). This has already generated conflict between the provinces and the centre, and if provinces are not empowered, they may become further alienated. The issue is not that we should weaken the federal institutions but, following the subsidiary principle, give each level of government power that is necessary for fulfilling their functions.

Fourth, scholars have argued that self-government is not enough for the success of federalism, as the institution is about both self-rule and shared rule (Anderson 2016; Lijphart 1977; McGarry and O'Leary 2009). Shared rule requires consociational mechanisms: cross-community executive powersharing, proportional representation of group throughout the state sector, ethnic autonomy in culture and formal or informal minority-veto rights (Lijphart 1977; McGarry and O'Leary 2009). The new Constitution has provision for proportional representation, but it is less inclusive compared to the 2007 Interim Constitution because it added Khas Arya as a beneficiary. Likewise, the exception to the Equality Rights (Article 18) states that special provisions could be made for 'socially and culturally marginalized groups,' but it lists 22 categories, including poor Khas Arya, peasants, labourers, youth, children, senior citizens, under which most Nepalis will fall, effectively making the provision useless. There is no provision of minority-veto rights, and as discussed earlier, the leaders deliberately denied autonomy to indigenous groups. The cross-community executive power sharing is also weak. Though the cabinet includes some ministers from marginalised groups, Khas Arya has over-representation (55%; nearly double its population of 31%). What is interesting is the overwhelming representation of Bahun in the cabinet and other influential sectors of the state (and society). Its population is 12.2%, but they occupy nearly four times more cabinet posts (46%). Only one Dalit (13% population) is a cabinet minister while indigenous groups have 18% representation (30%–35% population) but only from the Magar ethnic group. What is perhaps more revealing about the lack of power sharing is that the Khas Arya occupy all the top positions of the seven most important offices in the country (president, prime minister, chief justice, army chief, police chief, speaker of the Lower House and speaker of the Upper House).[10] Among the Khas Arya, Bahun occupy 71% of those positions, pointing out to the increasing concentration and consolidation of power by the Bahun after 1990 (Chemjong 2018; Lawoti 2010).[11] These trends are also indicative of the absence of informal power-sharing norms in the country. Bahun domination is prevalent in the bureaucracy, as well as, ironically, in civil society organisations like the media and major human rights groups.

Fifth, no genuine federal countries that are democracies have destabilised. Many scholars do not consider non-democratic federalism as genuine (Anderson 2016; Stepan 2001; Watts 2005). "Federalism" in non-democratic countries failed because, among other things, free, substantive and genuine negotiations and bargaining among different sides at the time of establishment as well as over the years did not occur. Consent of different sides is necessary for sustaining federalism (Bermeo 2004; Kavalski and Zolkos 2008; Lemco 1991). In Nepal, the ruling parties claim that 90% of CA members signed the constitution that adopted the seven-province federal model, but they forget to mention that some Madhesi and indigenous political parties opposed and boycotted the process and the establishment deployed the military during the promulgation of the new Constitution. Sri Lanka's similar experience that led to the ethnic civil war could be sobering. The political front of Tamil minority did not participate in the 1972 and 1978 constitution-making process and/or their promulgation because the new constitutions rejected autonomy and federalism, amongst other problems. An overwhelmingly large majority of the Sinhalese Buddhist Parliament members supported and endorsed the promulgation of constitutions that favoured their language, culture and religion and rejected the Tamil demands. This precipitated a violent ethnic conflict soon after in the 1980s that lasted for three decades and resulted in around 100,000 deaths.

The Khas Arya leaders openly and severely abused and manipulated the democratic process during the second CA. They first prevented the first CA, where minority groups empowering federalists had a two-thirds majority, from finalising a decision on the federal model in the name of consensus building. Eventually, when it appeared that the first CA would have to take the issue to the full house and decide the matter through voting, they had the CA full house meeting postponed around a dozen times so that its term would expire. They dissolved the CA at the last minute. When the Khas Arya led major parties obtained a majority in the second CA, they undermined the democratic process to ram through the federal model they preferred. They not only conveniently forgot the need for consensus, for which they repeatedly insisted upon during the first CA, but even abdicated the multiple agreements the state had signed with marginalised groups' movements to recognise identities and provide autonomy, which were then enshrined through amendments in the Interim Constitution 2007 (Bhattachan 2014; Government of Nepal 2007; Lawoti 2016; Limbu et al. 2016). The Khas Arya leaders prohibited indigenous and Madhesi CA members from forming a caucus while middle ranked Khas Arya leaders openly formed a cross-party front and lobbied and pressured the top leaders to reject minority empowering federalism and establish a mono-ethnic federalism.

Despite electing the CA, in reality, around a dozen old male Khas Arya leaders negotiated the contested issues, prepared drafts of the agreed upon points and finalised the Constitution during the second CA. Public input was limited to a few hours' interaction in the Khas-Nepali language for two days in district headquarters during the rainy season when public participation is low because of weather and agricultural activities in a predominantly agricultural country. Nepal has never held any general election during the rainy season for that reason. Kantipur daily reported that even the sitting president's brothers, who are Madhesi, did not understand the draft of the Constitution written in the Khas-Nepali language, indicating that the document would have been incomprehensible to millions of others whose native language is not Khas-Nepali even if the documents had been available. The Nepali Congress (NC) and CPN-UML leaders issued illegal whips informally banning registration of amendments and they forced the few courageous CA members who had defied and registered amendments to withdraw them by threatening expulsion from the parties. In the final phase of the second CA, the political leadership discouraged even substantive discussion and deliberation on various articles of the Constitution, including on the federal model. The second CA passed hundreds of articles of the Constitution in a couple of days, demonstrating an absence of genuine deliberation.

Scholars have called such elite-driven and controlled "participatory" processes, the objective of which is to legitimise the maintenance and protection of elite interest and power, as tokenistic and manipulative participation (Arnstein 1969; Chambers 2005; Hart 1992). The abuse and manipulation of the democratic constitution-making process and its outcomes in Nepal have angered, frustrated and alienated a large number of the population. For the alienated groups, the current Constitution and model of federalism are not legitimate. Like the non-democratic federalism and absence of democratic deliberations leading to instability in many countries, the manipulation of democratic process has generated distrust and dissatisfaction and has already generated conflicts, and will probably continue to do so in the future.

The Constitution and the seven-province federal model have some positive elements but many conflict – inviting tendencies and indicating an unstable future for Nepal. The positive elements, such as ending the monarchy, do not undermine or diffuse problems generated by the federal model. All the possible problematic dynamics may not manifest simultaneously, but even if some do, Nepal would become unstable. What is dreadful even to think is what might happen if all or most of the possible problems coincide at the same time, as when crises occur?

The earlier discussion suggests that the polity needs to carry out substantive reform with regard to a number of provinces and powers to them. However, an arduous process for changing the borders of existing provinces may further push the country towards conflict. Articles 274:4–7 of the Constitution requires multiple majorities and supermajorities (1. majority in the concerned provinces, 2. support by a majority of the seven provinces and 3. a two-thirds majority in federal parliament) to approve changes in numbers and borders of provinces. In the absence of peaceful ways to demand and settle issues of forming new provinces, groups aspiring for a new province or changes in the borders will have to rely on non-systemic activities to get their demands fulfilled. The almost impossible amendment procedure is an invitation for conflict.

Will the movements of the marginalised groups, if they intensify, foster separatist movements, especially if they are unable to get concessions? The literature suggests that separatist movements may face challenges due to development of a federal identity (Kavalski and Zolkos 2008), which exists to some extent in Nepal due to more than 200 years of statehood. The problem lies in the way the Nepali identity was framed and defined and perceived by different groups. It could widen the differences amongst Nepalis with the rise in political awareness of inequality and discrimination, and more so when the resulting rising aspirations remain unmet. In a situation where "federalism" is not working, going back to the unitary structure may not be an option. Anderson (2016) points out that in countries with high ethnic diversity like the USSR and Yugoslavia, going back to a unitary structure was not an option because the leaders adopted "federalism" since the unitary structure was not an option in the first place. Diverse countries that adopted federalism after the failure of unitary structure disintegrated after federalism also failed. Likewise, the failure of "federalism" in Nepal could lead to disintegration, as going back to the failed unitary structure would not be an option in a diverse country like Nepal.

The rise of multiple separatist organisations in the Madhesh after the turn of the century is an indicator of more alienated people becoming aware of the discourse and the available alternatives. Even though the violent separatist movements are less active than before, observers of Madhesh point out that there is considerable attraction amongst the youth towards Dr. CK Raut, who is championing a free Madhesh through non-violent means. The repeated discourse of violence, Apter (1997) argues, makes the act more acceptable once it takes place. The delay or the denial of demand for genuine autonomy and proper recognition, repression of movements by the state, derision of Madhesi by the hill leaders, public and media, inability to deliver by the weak provincial government, and the continued spread of separatist discourse by multiple organisations may likely increase acceptance of separatism by more people in the Madhesh.

Mobilisation capacity and conflict possibilities

A puzzle in the eyes of some is why the Madhesi mobilised extensively even after the group received some concessions while the indigenous groups, whose major demands the state rejected, were not able to do so? Social movement and nationalist mobilisation literature point out various factors that affect mobilisation, such as territorial concentration, socio-political awareness, cohesive identity, relative deprivation, resource mobilisation, political opportunity, the framing of issues and (the lack of) co-optation (Gurr1993; Horowitz 1985; McAdam, Tarrow and Tilly 2001; Van Cott 2005). My comparative analyses of Dalit, indigenous nationalities, Madhesi and Limbu movements has shown that many of the aforementioned variables matter for identity mobilisation, but a longer history of relatively independent socio-political movement explains the ability of the Madhesi to launch intense movements earlier than other groups in Nepal (Lawoti 2012).

The inability of the indigenous nationalities to launch intense protest movements against the new Constitution shows that having grievances is not sufficient, especially in a patronage-based polity like Nepal. The ruling parties and their Khas Aria leaders interfere and undermine movements of the marginalised groups through co-optation, promise of reward or through threats, as well as repression when the movements appear threatening to the dominant group interests. For example, the state rounded up around two dozen Tharu leaders not affiliated with major political parties after unknown people killed eight police officers in a rally. They are still in prison even after three years while their case is sub judice and stalled, and the Tharu movement that was gaining momentum screeched to a halt due to the absence of leaders. Meanwhile, as a strategy to salvage its discredited image amongst the Tharu, the then NCP-UML rewarded its Tharu leaders, who had followed the party's instruction and criticised the Tharu movement, to middle ranks in the party organisation.

To launch sustained movements, the Nepali experience shows that the marginalised groups have to meet at least two related conditions. First, the leaders should be independent of the major political parties led by the Khas Arya to avoid interference and co-optation. The movements launched by the ethnic associations of the indigenous nationalities and their federation, Nepal Federation of Indigenous Nationalities (NEFIN), have not been successful to force the state in conceding to their major demands partly because of interference from the senior Khas Arya leaders of the major political parties. Many leaders of the ethnic associations belong to major political parties and they have not been able to act beyond their political parties' interests and influence of the top party leaders. The greed and the fear factor have also affected the movements. Some of the ethnic leaders are afraid that their top leaders would be displeased and penalise them, such as depriving them of getting the nomination to compete for the party in the elections or wanting to please the leaders in the hope of getting rewards.[12] Marginalised group-specific political parties and their leaders are independent of the influence of the Khas Arya led major parties and they could provide a more autonomous. I will discuss this in detail next.

Second, the organisations leading the movements have to be capable of fielding a large number of cadres on the streets for a considerable period. The ethnic associations may not be able to do so for a couple of reasons. These associations do not have full-time cadres. They also do not offer lifelong career opportunities for members. They also have limited capacity to reward and penalise members. Group-specific or political parties that prioritise the issues of the marginalised groups are necessary to overcome these challenges.

However, the size of the parties has to reach a critical level to be capable of launching and sustaining long and effective movements. This requires time and experience. Existence and operation over a long period appear to be necessary for increasing political awareness, support base and expanding organisation by recruiting political cadres and leaders. On the other hand, an absence of relatively large group-specific political party means that the politically inclined members of the groups often end up aligning with and supporting the major political parties led by Khas Arya that promote the leaders' ethnic agendas.

Amongst the different marginalised groups, the Madhesi have a longer history of the establishment of a political party, and hence they enjoy a relatively independent socio-political movement that expanded over the years to command sizable support base, launch effective movements and win elections. While the Dalit, indigenous and Madhesi groups started identity movements in late 1940, the socio-politically aware members of Dalit and indigenous groups largely formed non-governmental organisations (NGOs) and ethnic associations, respectively, for a long time while the Madhesi established a political party, the Nepal Tarai Congress (NTC), in 1951. Amongst other issues, it demanded federalism. The NTC participated in the Madhesi movement against the imposition of Khas-Nepali as the language of instruction in schools during the mid-1950s (Gaige 1975) there is no record of ethnic associations of indigenous groups opposing it. The party won around 2% of the popular votes in the 1959 general election even though it did not win a single parliamentary seat. The NTC became inactive after the monarch co-opted its leader during the Panchayat regime

(1960–90) but it had generated considerable political awareness amongst the Madhesi while it was active. The Madhesi political movement re-emerged during the mid-1980s when Gajendra Narayan Singh formed the Nepal Sadhvawana Parishad, which transformed in 1990 into a political party, the Nepal Sadhvawana Party (NSP). The NSP received double more percent of votes than NTC and won some parliamentary seats in the three elections during the 1990s but was not able to launch and sustain an effective movement. However, the NSP further expanded political awareness and fostered growth of organisations and networks in the Madhesh. The Madhesi eventually launched effective movements in 2007 and 2008 on the foundation of political awareness, network and organisations engendered by earlier political activities. They forced the state to accept federalism, carry electoral reforms and expand affirmative action policies. The Madhesi parties went on to obtain more than 11% of votes in the 2008 and 2013 elections (Lawoti 2013) and formed a government in Province Two after the 2017 elections.

The indigenous nationalities established political parties only in 1989 and 1990 and the Dalit during the mid-1990s (Lawoti 2012). The indigenous parties won only around 1% of votes during the 1990s. More indigenous group-specific parties emerged after the 2006 regime transition. They collectively obtained around 2% and 4% of popular votes in the 2008 and 2013 elections, respectively. They won some seats in both elections from the proportional representation category but have not won any seat yet from the FPTP method. Though the indigenous groups went on to launch many movements during the transition period and some sustained ones attained some concessions, the movements overall did not enjoy widespread popular participation like in the Madhesh. The comparison of Madhesi and indigenous experience suggests that group-specific political parties with a 4% support base may not be able to launch and sustain long popular movements but they could become capable of doing so when their support base expands to obtain around 10% of popular votes.[13] However, the 10% support base may be less applicable to the indigenous specific political parties because the ethnic associations and their supporters may complement and fill the gap of insufficient political cadres during the movements.

The Tharu, Limbu, Tamang, Rai and Newar have established group-specific political parties while Magars lead and support a more broad-based party raising the issues of marginalised groups, the Nepal Janamukti Party. Indigenous leaders formed the Federal Socialist Party to represent the indigenous groups, but it united with Madhesi Jana Adhikar Forum to consolidate strength and offer an alternative to the existing major parties. The indigenous parties have a much shorter history and are smaller than the Madhesi. They have contributed less in spreading awareness and have less capability to get support, votes and seats in elections, and field cadres to the streets and attract people during the street movements. The smaller support base due to shorter history appears to be the major reason for their inability to launch effective movements.

The experience of the Madhesi movement and political parties shows that it takes time to expand, grow and become effective to launch intense and effective movements. This suggests that with the passage of time the movements of the indigenous groups could become more effective after expansion and capacity development of group-and-agenda specific political parties. If the Madhesi that received partial political concessions in the federal structure were unhappy enough to launch and sustain long movements, the indigenous groups, who did not receive any major concessions, have stronger reasons to do so. What this means is that Nepal may continue to witness mobilisation, movements, conflicts and instability in the future.

Conclusion

This study has shown that any type of federalism does not work in diverse societies. Federal structures that do not recognise identities, provide autonomy and empower marginalised groups, in fact, may invite conflict. The Khas Arya leaders and media personnel unleashed a campaign of denigration and spread misinformation that identity-based federalism would incite violent ethnic conflict in Nepal but ironically it looks like they may have contributed in inviting and exacerbating ethnic conflicts (street protests, violent ethnic conflicts, expansion in separatist movements) by adopting, supporting and defending the seven-province mono-ethnic federal model.

To empathise with the leaders involved in the federalisation process, the issue of federalism is complex in very diverse countries like Nepal. The three federal models, for example, do not accommodate the interests of migrant groups. While many groups are territorially concentrated, members of homeland groups as well as others have migrated to the homeland of other groups, or are territorially dispersed (Sharma 2008). Federalism and associated institutions should accommodate the aspirations, fears and needs of different identity groups to be accepted, win support and undermine resistance from different segments of the society to maintain a lasting peace.

When excluded identity groups aspire for autonomy and empowerment, denial is not a solution unless the aim is to repress, which is not a long-term solution, and it may, in fact, exacerbate the problem. Nepal's complex context suggests it needs to innovate additional accommodative mechanisms. It could mean providing autonomy and recognition to not only territorially concentrated groups (provincial and sub-provincial) but even awarding cultural and other rights to territorially dispersed groups, including to migrant groups if they so desire. The provision of both individual and group rights through asymmetrical federalism, non-territorial federalism, sub-provincial autonomy, protection of human rights and so on may result in overlap of rights across geographic territories. This may look messy and not look easy to implement, but federations like India and Belgium have shown that it is possible. Without addressing aspirations and needs of different groups and managing the fear of others in innovative ways, and extending equality and equity based on the principle of justice, considerable conflicts, big and small as well as long and short, may continue to bog down the country.

Notes

1 Abi Narayan Chamlagai assisted in this research in aggregating ethnic/caste data. The chapter was finalised in July 2016, and analyses cover issues and events before that. Some updates were incorporated in early September 2018.
2 Unitary states like Indonesia (2000), Sudan (2013) and Somalia (1991, but no international recognition to Somaliland) have broken up.
3 The number of the bracket is an approximate death toll from Scaruffi's list.
4 Countries with a core ethnic region that witnessed large-scale civil war are the USSR, Nigerian 1st Republic, Pakistan, and Yugoslavia (Hale 2004).
5 O'Leary (2001) argues that Staatsvolk, a national or ethnic people, who are demographically and electorally dominant – though not necessarily an absolute majority of the population. This argument goes against Hale's core ethnic group argument. Hale's argument appears more plausible on empirical examination.
6 Unitary countries like the UK (Scotland), France (Corsica), Burma (Karenni), Turkey (Kurds), Iraq (Kurds), the Philippines (Mindanao),

Angola (Cabinda), Senegal (Casemance), Sri Lanka (Tamil), China (Tibet and Xinjiang) are also facing secessionist movements.
7 The artificial majority of the Nepali Congress, which only won a plurality (not majority) of votes, in the three majoritarian Parliament also demonstrates this tendency. The party won 67.89%, 53.66% and 55.12% of parliamentary seats, respectively, in 1959, 1991 and 1999 with 37.2%, 37.75% and 36.14% of popular votes.
8 Madhesi is a loose regional identity formation to which Muslims and Madhesi Dalit also identify with.
9 The proposed Madhesh region for Madhesi accommodates 49 caste groups. Thus, the argument by anti-identity federalists that aspirations and identity of 125 ethnic/caste groups in Nepal cannot be practically accommodated and recognised either demonstrates ignorance or is part of fear mongering.
10 The data is from early September 2018.
11 The Thakuri/Chhetri were also dominant and Newar enjoyed overrepresentation in the bureaucracy and polity before 1990.
12 My argument is not that ethnic associations are not necessary for the success of movements. They have been leading the cultural revival, which is the cultural capital. Culturally aware people join street movements when the movements reach a certain height. Cultural capital is a necessary condition for building political capital. My argument is only that as long as the leaders of the associations cannot remain autonomous from Khas Arya leaders of the major parties, they may not be able to lead an effective movement.
13 Some might argue that the 2007 and 2008 Madhesi movement contributed to the growth of the Madhesi parties. It is partly true, but we should not forget that the Madhesi Jana Adhikar Forum, which led the movement, had developed organisation and network across the Tarai districts before the movement. This organisation, which transformed into a party and its network, led the 2007 movement. More important, the fact that the Madhesi people came to the streets in larger number suggests that political awareness had already spread considerably in the community. The previous political parties and their activities had contributed toward it.

References

Adeney, Katharine. 2006. *Federalism and Ethnic Conflict Regulation in India and Pakistan*. New York: Palgrave Macmillan.
Anderson, Liam. 2014. "Ethnofederalism: The Worst Form of Institutional Agreement. . .?" *International Security* 39(1): 165–204.
———. 2016. "Ethnofederalism and the Management of Ethnic Conflict: Assessing the Alternatives." *Publius* 46(1): 1–24.
Apter, David. 1997. *Political Violence in Analytic Perspective*. In *the Legitimization of Violence*, edited by D. Apter. New York: New York University Press, (1–32).
Arnstein, Sherry A. 1969. "A Ladder of Citizen Participation." *Journal of the American Institute of Planners* 35 (4):216–24.
Bakke, Kristin M., and Erik Wibbels.2006. "Diversity, Disparity, and Civil Conflict in the Federal States." *World Politics* 59 (October):1–50.

Bangura, Yusuf, ed. 2006. *Ethnic Inequalities and Public Sector Governance*. New York: Palgrave Macmillan.
Bates, Robert H. 2000. "Ethnicity and Development in Africa: A Reappraisal." *The American Economic Review* 90 (2):131–34.
Bermeo, Nancy. 2004. "Conclusion: The Merits of Federalism." In *Federalism and Territorial Cleavages*, edited by U. M. Amoretti and N. Bermeo. Baltimore: John Hopkins.
Bhattachan, Krishna B. 2015. "Dohora Mapdanda (Double Standard)." www.esamata.com, 2014. [cited 2015]. http://esamata.com/np/2014/double-standard/.
Center for Systemic Peace. 2016. "Polity IV: Regime Authority Characteristics and Transition." Datasets: Center for Systemic Peace.
Chambers, Robert. 2005. *Ideas for Development*. London: Routledge.
Chemjong, Dambar. 2018. "Jatiya Rajyasattako Etihasiki." *Kantipur Daily*, June 24.
Constituent Assembly. 2015. *Nepalko Sambidhan*. Kathmandu: Constituent Assembly Secretariat. Department of Sociology and Anthropology. 2014. Ethnic and Caste Data, 2011 census, district and VDC: Tribhuvan University.
Cornell, Svante E. 2002. "Autonomy as a Source of Conflict: Caucasian Conflicts in a Theoretical Perspective." *World Politics* 54:245–76.
Elazar, Daniel J. 1987. *Exploring Federalism*. Tuscaloosa: The University of Alabama Press.
Filippov, Mikhail, Peter C. Ordeshook, and Olga Shvetsova. 2004. *Designing Federalism: A Theory of Self-Sustainable Federal Institutions*. Cambridge: Cambridge University Press.
Gaige, Frederick H. 1975. *Regionalism and National Unity in Nepal*. New Delhi: Vikas.
The Government of Nepal. 2007. *Nepalko Antarim Sambidhan (Interim Constitution of Nepal)*. Kathmandu: Government of Nepal.
Gurr, Ted Robert. 1993. *Minorities at Risk? A Global View of Ethnopolitical Conflicts*. Washington, DC: United States Institute of Peace Press.
Hachhethu, Krishna. 2014. "Balancing Identity and Viability: Restructuring Nepal into a Viable Federal State." In *The Federal Debate in Nepal*, edited by B. Karki and R. Edrisinha. Kathmandu: Support to Participatory Constitution Building in Nepal.
———. 2015. "The New Constitution and Identity Politics in Nepal." Paper read at *9th South Asia Conference on Culture as a Factor in Regional Cooperation in South Asia*, November 26–27, New Delhi.
Hale, Henry. 2004. "Divided We Stand: Institutional Sources of Ethnofederal State Survival and Collapse." *World Politics* 56 (January):165–93.
Hart, Rogers A. 1992. *Children's Participation: From Tokenism to Citizenship*. Florence: UNICEF.
Horowitz, Donald. 1985. *Ethnic Groups in Conflict*. Berkeley: University of California Press.

Kavalski, Emilian, and Magdalena Zolkos, eds. 2008. *Defunct Federalisms: Critical Perspectives on Federal Failure*. Burlington: Ashgate.

Lawoti, Mahendra. 2005. *Towards a Democratic Nepal: Inclusive Political Institutions for a Multicultural Society*. New Delhi, London, and Thousand Oaks: Sage Publications.

———, ed. 2007. *Contentious Politics and Democratization in Nepal*. New Delhi: Sage Publications.

———. 2010. "Informal Institutions and Exclusion in Democratic Nepal." *Himalaya* 28(1–2): 17–32.

———. 2012. "Dynamics of Mobilization: Varied Trajectories of Dalit, Indigenous Nationalities, and Madhesi Movements." *Nationalism and Ethnic Conflict*, edited by M. Lawoti and S. I. Hangen. London: Routledge.

———. 2013. *Pahichanbadidalkobistar (Expansion of Identity-Based Parties)*. Kantipur, December 13, 7.

———. 2015. "Competing Nationhood and Constitutional Instability: Representation, Regime and Resistance in Nepal." In *Unstable Constitutionalism: Law and Politics in South Asia*, edited by M. Tushnet and M. Kholsa. New York: Cambridge University Press.

———. 2016. "Prolonged Transition and Setback in Reforms: Timing, Sequencing and Contestations Over Reforms in Post-Conflict Reforms in Nepal." In *Building Sustainable Peace: Timing and Sequencing of Post-Conflict Reconstruction and Peacebuilding*, edited by A. Langer and K. G. Brown. Oxford: Oxford University Press.

Leff, Carol Skalnik. 1999. "Democratization and Disintegration in the Multinational States: The Breakup of the Communist Federations." *World Politics* 51 (2):205–35.

Lemco, Jonathan. 1991. *Political Stability in Federal Governments*. New York: Praeger.

Lijphart, Arend. 1977. *Democracy in Plural Societies: A Comparative Exploration*. New Haven and London: Yale University Press.

———. 1999. *Patterns of Democracy: Government Forms and Performance in Thirty-Six Countries*. New Haven and London: Yale University Press.

Limbu, Shankar, Bhim Rai, Dinesh Kumar Ghale, Nanda Kandangwa, Tankabbahadur Rai, and Ramhari Shrestha. 2016. *Aadibasi Janajati Adhikarko Sandharvama 'Nepalko Sambidhan' ko Addhyantatha Bishleshan*. Kathmandu: LAHURNIP.

Manor, James. 1998. "Making Federalism Work." *Journal of Democracy* 9 (3):21–35.

McAdam, Doug, Sidney Tarrow, and Charles Tilly. 2001. *Dynamics of Contention*. Cambridge: Cambridge University Press.

McGarry, John, and Brendan O'Leary. 2009. "Must Pluri-National Federations Fail?" *Ethnopolitics* 8(1): 5–25.

O'Leary, Brendan. 2001. "An Iron Law of Nationalism and Federation? A (neo-Diceyian) Theory of the Necessity of a Federal Staatsvolk, and of Consociational Rescue." *Nation and Nationalism* 7 (3): 273–96.

Olson, Mancur. 1971. *The Logic of Collective Action: Public Goods and the Theory of Groups*. Revised ed. Cambridge: Harvard University Press.

Riker, William H. 1964. *Federalism: Origin, Operation, Significance*. Boston: Little, Brown, and Co.

Roeder, Philip G. 2009. "Ethnofederalism and the Mismanagement of Conflicting Nationalism." *Regional and Federal Studies* 19(2): 203–19.

Saideman, Stephen M., David Lanoue, Michael Campenni, and Samuel Stanton. 2002. "Democratization, Political Institutions, and Ethnic Conflict: A Pooled Time-Series Analysis, 1985–1998." *Comparative Political Studies* 35 (1):103–29.

Scaruffi, Piero. 2016. *War and Casualties of the 20th and 21st Centuries 2009*. [cited June 20, 2016]. www.scaruffi.com/politics/massacre.html.

Sharma, Pitamber. 2008. *Unravelling the Mosaic: Spatial Aspects of Ethnicity in Nepal*. Kathmandu: Himal Books.

Sharma, Vijaya R. 2007. "Comparative Study of Federation Proposals for Nepal." *Liberal Democracy Nepal Bulletin* 2 (2):34.

Stepan, Alfred. 2001. "Federalism and Democracy: Beyond the US Model." In *The Global Divergence of Democracy*, edited by L. Diamond and M. F. Plattner. Baltimore and London: The John Hopkins University Press.

Suny, Ronald Grigor. 1991. "The Soviet South: Nationalism and the Outside World." In *The Rise of Nations in the Soviet Union*, edited by M. Mandelbaum. New York: A Council of Foreign Relations Book.

Tamang, Sitaram, ed. 2005. *Nepalko Sandarvama Rajyako Punsanrachana*. Kathmandu: Samana Prakashan.

Toft, Monica Duffy, and Stephen M. Saideman. 2010. "Self-Determination Movements and Their Outcomes." In *Peace and Conflict*, edited by J. J. Hewitt, J. Wilkenfeld, and T. R. Gurr. Boulder: Paradigm Publishers.

Van Cott, Donna Lee. 2005. *From Movements to Parties in Latin America: The Evolution of Ethnic Politics*. Cambridge: Cambridge University Press.

Watts, Ronald. 2005. *Models of Power Sharing*. Washington, DC: National Democratic Institute.

Weingast, Barry R. 1995. "The Economic Role of Political Institutions: Market-Preserving Federalism and Economic Development." *The Journal of Law, Economics, & Organization* 7 (1):1–31.

Ziblatt, Daniel. 2004. "Rethinking the Origins of Federalism: Puzzle, Theory and Evidence from Nineteenth-Century Europe." *World Politics* 57 (October):70–98.

Chapter 3

Literature as cosmopolitics
Beyond nations, borders and identities

Simi Malhotra

Introduction

These are indeed troubled times. All around us sectarian identity assertions of different forms are raising their ugly heads and challenging the very foundations of 'being human' as we would have understood it to be down millennia. Coming from the discipline of literary studies wherein attempts have been made both by deployments of certain kinds of literary and cultural articulations, and claims of doing identity politics of race, class, gender, etc., by what would have commonsensically concatenated itself as 'literary theory.' Notwithstanding, the mandate of doing literature and culture in general and writing, in particular, can be seen as an ethical means of leading one beyond the cesspool of the identitarian 'here and now,' to the promise of a cosmopolitical democracy to come. The keywords here are thus, to begin with, cosmopolitanism and writing. But because the conference also seeks to focus specifically on South Asia, I, after having demonstrated what a potential cosmopolitics may have to do with writing, will specifically home in with an illustration of the same from South Asia.

To elaborate the argument, I present to you how Kant's formative definition of cosmopolitanism, and hospitality as required therein, relied heavily on the agency of the nation. Derrida critiqued this privileged role given to the nation and instead crediting the agency of hospitality and forgiveness to iterative quasi-linguistic acts primarily operable in non-national spaces like 'cities of refuge,' and drawing inspiration from pre-national formulations of both Hebraic and Hellenic spiritual heritage. While this would also take me through Seyla Benhabib's attempt to forge 'another' kind of cosmopolitanism, that not only eschews the parochial sectarianism of the nation but also steers clear from a vague and potentially dilettante cosmopolitanism. What would be truly cosmopolitical, its assertion of culture as a tool towards democracy to come will finally find echoes in remembering of Tagore's prophetic critique of the nation, thus making us home in, as said earlier, into what could be the way out of identitarianism for us in South Asian cultural praxis.

Contemporary attempts to understand cosmopolitanism often trace their roots to Kant's 1795 essay "Perpetual Peace." In "Perpetual Peace" Kant argues that with increasing trade, travel and commercial relationships among Nation-states, soon war would have become a thing of the past because the need for economic growth will require Nations to be hospitable to each other, leading to a certain kind of mutual tolerance and cosmopolitanism. Hospitality becomes a key term for Kant in this regard, and he defines hospitality thus:

> Hospitality means the right of a stranger not to be treated as an enemy when he arrives in the land of another. One may refuse to receive him when this can be done without causing his destruction; but so long as he peacefully occupies his place, one may not treat him with hostility. It is not the right to be a permanent visitor that one may demand. A special contract of beneficence would be needed to give an outsider a right to become a fellow inhabitant for a certain length of time. It is only the right of temporary sojourn, a right to associate, which all men have. They have it by their common possession of the surface of the earth, where, as a globe, they cannot infinitely disperse and hence must finally tolerate the presence of each other.
>
> (105–6)

There are few points to be noted here. First of all, as one can see, prima facie it is clear from the definition that while indeed under the covenant of perpetual peace that nation-states would probably arrive at, the outsider would be tolerated and not meted out with hostility, but he would be only given temporary visitation rights and not permanent resident rights. This suggests possible limitations in Kant's definition of hospitality. Apart from the prima facie restriction that emerges from the quote itself, Derrida points out how on several other grounds, Kant's notion of cosmopolitanism is not the beginning of cosmopolitan thought but rather a break in an already existing chain of true cosmopolitics, because Kant makes hospitality conditional. To quote Derrida from a 1997 interview with Bennington, wherein he points out the limitation of Kant's notion of hospitality and cosmopolitanism:

> There is a tradition of cosmopolitanism, and if we had time we could study this tradition, which comes to us from, on the one hand, Greek thought with the Stoics, who have a concept of the 'citizen of the world.' There is St. Paul in the Christian tradition, with a call for a citizen of the world as, precisely, a brother. St. Paul says that we are all brothers, that is sons of God, so we are not foreigners, we belong to the world as citizens of the world; and it is this tradition that we could follow up until Kant for instance, in whose concept of cosmopolitanism we find the conditions for hospitality. But in the Kant's concept of the cosmopolitical, there are some conditions. First, you should, of course, welcome the stranger, the foreigner, to the extent that he is a citizen of another country, that you grant him the right to visit and not to stay. There are some other conditions that I can't summarise here quickly, but this concept of the cosmopolitical which is very novel, very worthy of respect (and I think cosmopolitanism is an excellent idea), is a limited concept.

Over and above the prima facie observation that is made on the basis of the earlier quote from Kant – that the Kantian notion of hospitality allows only temporary visitation rights and not permanent residence to the outsider – Derrida raises a couple of more points about the limitations of the Kantian notion of cosmopolitanism: That Kant comes more as a break in the long tradition of hospitality where Derrida shows that rather than, as Kant presumes that hospitality is a result of nation-states trying to arrive at perpetual peace amongst themselves, hospitality is a much older concept coming from the Greek Cynics and Stoics on the one hand and the Biblical Abrahamic and Pauline tradition on the other, from when nation-states did not even exist. For Derrida, Kant's notion of hospitality and cosmopolitanism is very conditional and limited. Furthermore, as Derrida points out, the Kantian notion of hospitality seems to be more of a privilege that the local community may choose to dole out to the outsider. The agency of the Kantian kind of hospitality, as further buttressed by the state and the police permitting it, thus lies with the machinery of the nation-state.

In fact, when Derrida, adopting many of Kantian ideas, publishes his seminal work on the subject, i.e. *Cosmopolitanism and Forgiveness* (2003), in which he argues that it is not the nation-states but cities, which historically, often falling outside the purview of the official nation-state machinery, have been the real sites of a future-oriented hospitality. They are currently demographically constituted through the 1990s to 2000s to the present times, as 'cities of refuge.' These points made by Derrida, in problematising a Nation-state driven cosmopolitanism, get further highlighted by Seyla Benhabib in her 2006 book 'Another Cosmopolitanism,' where she shows that in the Kantian kind of state-sponsored cosmopolitanism, the mechanism of its implementation still depends on the rulers themselves. To quote Benhabib, 'Cosmopolitan citizens still needed their individual republics to be citizens at all' (24) and the onus of according refuge or asylum still lies with the sovereign. In fact, Benhabib quotes Derrida to show that in such a conditional cosmopolitanism apparent hospitality is but normatively juridico-political where, and I quote Derrida, 'Limits are set, boundaries are established and protected with violence; asylees are turned away; refugees are denied entry and aid; citizens are denaturalized' (Derrida in Benhabib 2006: 157). Benhabib, instead, taking recourse to Derrida again, suggests how, as different from such nation-occasioned instances of hospitality, one has to rather look at "new forms" (74) of political agency and subjectivity. Following Derrida's notion of writing as 'iteration,' what Benhabib calls "democratic iterations" (48), the linguistic and cultural repetitions by the people themselves, which thus transform, in their constant invocation and revocation, the established view. For Benhabib people by engaging in these iterative acts of reappropriating and reinterpreting rules become thus not just the subject of but the authors of the laws. As Benhabib says, 'The democratic people can reconstitute itself through such acts of democratic iteration so as to enable the extension of democratic voice. Aliens can become residents, and residents can become citizens. Democracies require porous borders' (68).

For Benhabib, the influence of cosmopolitanism should not be seen as a threat to democratic sovereignty; rather, it promises 'the emergence of new political configurations and new forms of agency, inspired by the interdependence.' (74) As Benhabib elaborates, following Derrida, that only when one inculcates hospitality that is not nation-driven but rather people-driven, in iterative quasi-linguistic acts, that one can have a cosmopolitics oriented towards a democracy to come.

Derrida talks about the two strategies through which this cosmopolitics would work, namely hospitality and forgiveness, as what linguists would call 'speech acts.' Thus, further underscoring the literary-linguistic modes of the cosmopolitical itself, Derrida reiterates, especially in the second lecture on forgiveness, that the Nation or a public institution has neither the right nor the power to forgive and can at best bring about, through the political performance of the 'theatre of forgiveness' a 'therapy of reconciliation.' Pure forgiveness engages only two singularities, the victim and the perpetrator and their mutual discursive interactions.

So, as we have discussed so far, for a true cosmopolitics that can redeem one from sectarian identitarian politics, rather than a vague cosmopolitanism, one needs to move beyond the nation as the defining marker and instead rely on cultural acts akin to writing. This is precisely what Tagore highlights in his collection of essays titled *Nationalism* (1917), and I would end my presentation by putting before you some choicest quotes from Tagore's volume where he shows how South Asia has to eschew the notions of nation and nationalism, and foreground instead its cultural roots, to free itself from a potential lapse into parochial sectarianism. Interestingly, Tagore practically begins his first essay in the volume, i.e. 'Nationalism in the West,' by saying, 'Neither the colourless vagueness of cosmopolitanism nor the fierce self-idolatry of nation-worship is the goal of human history.' Thus, right at the beginning, as we established in our argument so far, Tagore equidistances himself from vague cosmopolitanism and parochial Nationalism. Let us then try to see what Tagore's view of the nation is. In the third essay, 'Nationalism in India,' he says,

> I am not against one nation in particular, but against the general idea of all nations. What is the Nation?
>
> It is the aspect of a whole people as an organised power. This organisation incessantly keeps up the insistence of the population on becoming strong and efficient. But this strenuous effort after strength and efficiency drains man's energy from his higher nature where he is self-sacrificing and creative.

Obviously, as Tagore establishes, some peoples of the world, who are nations, try to convert even other peoples of the world, like

South Asians in Tagore's immediate context of the description, who are not nations, into nations. For Tagore rather than falling in for the lure of this sectarian claiming unto oneself the identity of a nation, peoples of such non-nations should resist the same. Calling the nation a machine, Tagore, in a direct critique of Kant's thesis in "Perpetual Peace," shows how the so-called agreement between nations, far from bringing a cosmopolitanism of hospitality and peace, would only result in further marginalisation of the non-nation peoples. I quote Tagore from 'Nationalism in the West':

> You say, these machines will come into an agreement, for their mutual protection, based upon a conspiracy of fear. But will this federation of steam-boilers supply you with a soul, a soul which has her conscience and her God? What is to happen to that larger part of the world, where fear will have no hand in restraining you? Whatever safety they now enjoy, those countries of no nation, from the unbridled license of forge and hammer and turn-screw, results from the mutual jealousy of the powers. But when, instead of being numerous separate machines, they become riveted into one organised gregariousness of gluttony, commercial and political. What remotest chance of hope will remain for those others, who have lived and suffered, have loved and worshipped, have thought deeply and worked with meekness, but whose only crime has been that they have not organised?

Instead of talking of nationalism (and like sectarianisms) as the ideal that Tagore's India, i.e. today's South Asia, should espouse, Tagore makes hospitality and tolerance of diversity as the prime goal that India has had and should continue to cherish. Tagore, in 'Nationalism in India,' says,

> India is too vast in its area and too diverse in its races. It is many countries packed in one geographical receptacle. [. . .] Be it said to the credit of India that this diversity was not her creation; she has had to accept it as a fact from the beginning of her history. In America and Australia, Europe has simplified her problem by almost exterminating the original population. Even in the present age, this spirit of extermination is making itself manifest, by inhospitably shutting out aliens, through those who themselves were aliens in the lands they now occupy. But

India tolerated difference of races from the first, and that spirit of toleration has acted all through her history.

There could not be a better note to end this chapter than this last quote of Tagore which rings for today's troubled sectarian times, where intolerance and fundamentalisms threaten the very foundation of who we South Asians have prided ourselves in having been and ought to continue to be. I rest my case in only praying that a truly non-identitarian and cosmopolitical pursuit of literature and culture can show us the way out of the parochial sectarian and identitarian rut that plagues our society today.

References

Benhabib, Seyla. *Another Cosmopolitanism*. New York: Oxford University Press, 2006.

Bennington, Geoffrey. 1997. *Politics and Friendship. A Discussion with Jacques Derrida*. Centre for Modern French Thought, University of Sussex. December 1. www.livingphilosophy.org/Derrida-politics-friendship.htm. Accessed on 1 November 2015.

Kant, Immanuel. 1970, 2003. "Perpetual Peace" (1795). In *Kant: Political Writings*, edited by Hans Reiss, trans. H. B. Nisbet. Cambridge: Cambridge University Press.

Tagore, Rabindranath. 1917."Nationalism." www.tagoreweb.in/Render/ShowBook.aspx?ct=Essays&bi=72EE92F5-BE50-40D7-8E6E-0F7410664DA3. 1 November 2015.

Chapter 4

Ideology as identity
Progressive Punjabi poetry of the 1970s and after[1]

Akshaya Kumar

All kinds of denominations – religious as well as secular, temporal as well as spatial, ethnic as well as linguistic – are summoned to lend precise identity markers to people, places and literary articulations. Literature, for instance, hardly exists as literature. Invariably, it is either pigeonholed in some category of culture already in circulation or is arrested in some new-fangled frame. It is either divided into eras and ages, whose temporal spans are determined somewhat arbitrarily by some self-styled authoritative literary historians or is seen regarding its national or provincial address it presumably is written from. As a result of this over-riding anxiety to pin down literature to a definitive identity-driven matrix, the critical industry has generated a number of labels – ranging from 'minority literature' to 'mainstream literature,' 'black literature' to 'ethnic literature,' 'regional literature' to 'vernacular writing' so on and so forth. All literature, notwithstanding its emancipatory potential, is therefore pre-fixed in the settled identitarian grids of culture.

Amongst various secular categories that are often invoked to redeem literature from its original trappings, the most conspicuous is the category of ideology.[2] As a category of analysis, ideology does suffer substantial semantic promiscuity. In the limited context of the chapter, it stands for a shared creed of ideas that human beings arrive at and which are subsequently reified coherently to understand, explain and approach the complexities of lived reality. At any point in time, many ideologies co-exist and compete for domination. The present chapter, however, foregrounds the ideology of the 'left' that hinges largely around the ideas propounded by Marx and Engles, and later on, supplemented by the ideas given by Lenin, Mao and other thinker-activists of the same creed.[3] This ideology gained currency largely after the Russian Revolution of 1917, and it peaked during the Cold War. There was a 'red scare,' and America had to devise 'policy of containment' to check the expansion of communism all across the globe.[4] Nations, peoples and literature across the globe were approached mainly through the prism of their ideological tilt; other identity markers consequently were relatively relegated to the background.

Even across the range of Indian language-literatures the ideology of the left, with its different shades, exercised enormous influence. With the arrival of All India Progressive Writers Association (AIPWA) at Lucknow in 1936, ideology emerges as a palpable frame of reference.[5] Within the broader rubric of Indian literature, each language literature gravitated towards this kind of ideological appropriation. Hindi, Telugu, Urdu, Kannada, Bengali, Marathi, Malayalam, Punjabi and other languages produced their ideology-driven literature under the umbrella of *pragativadi* or progressive literature. Across different languages, almost simultaneously, Marxist literature made its strong presence under different region-specific names. In Hindi it acquired different shades as it moved from being *pragtivadi* to *janvadi*; in Punjabi it began with moderate progressive orientations and then took the aggressive form of *jujharvadi*, in Urdu, it worked under the title of *tarraqi-pasand* literature; in Telugu, it moved from *abhyudya* to more aggressive *virasam* brand of poetry.

In the chapter, an attempt has been made to assess the ideological quotient of the so-called progressive Punjabi poetry, right from its somewhat moderate rise in the 1960s to its sudden decline in 1980s and after. A range of critical questions are asked in the process about its latter-day ideological conundrums and departures, and, more importantly, its somewhat atavistic re-lapse into quasi-religious rhetoric.[6] By foregrounding progressive Punjabi poetry of the 1970s, the chapter argues that for a while the discourse of ideology outwardly does seem to provide a rallying point, but the primordial religious identities always lurk beneath and strike back to regain primacy.[7] This poetry draws inspiration from ideology overtly and loudly, but within less than a decade the discourse of theology takes over sometimes with necessary camouflage and sometimes in somewhat common terms towards identitarian ends.[8] Even an expansive definition of ideology as theorised by latter-day New Left thinkers – Raymond Williams, in particular, – might well fail to accommodate the religious proclivities of the *jujharvadi* poets during 1980s.[9] The growth and the decline of progressive sentiment in modern Punjabi poetry is mapped to understand the limits of ideology as a marker of identity in the South Asian context.

I

Punjabi progressive poetry has undergone a checkered past, marked by its formidable presence, its sudden eclipse, its aggressive resurrection and, finally, its equally devastating rejection – all of this happens within less than 20 years. As early as 1963, Sant Singh Sekhon used a rather strong and somewhat cataclysmic expression "post-progressive" (to be precise and exact *Uttar-Pragativadi*) in the context of Punjabi poetry (*"Uttar-Pragativadi Punjabi Sahit," Alochana*, 4–9).[10] In his intervention, he identified some innate tendencies of Punjabi poetry during late 1950s such as its 'self-glorifying nationalism'(5) and 'backward-looking idealism'(7), and its 'bourgeoisie romanticism'(5) and 'sophisticated aestheticism'(8). This phase saw the rise of a range of poets who were experimental, idealists, romantic, cerebral and psychological.[11] Sekhon would attribute a number of deep-seated historical reasons for the sudden decline of progressive sentiment in modern Punjabi poetry. He observed,

> Perhaps, there was the rise of Nehruism in the country, and the partial success of five year plans and general acceptance of Nehruvian policy of non-alignment had weakened the revolutionary fervour of the youth so much that abandoning all other aims, they had started to worship their physical attributes.
> (6)

Other more precise reasons included the multiple divisions of communist movement in Punjab, the nominal presence of Punjabi writers and artists in IPTA (Indian People's Theatre Association) and PWA (Progressive Writers Association) in 1960s, and the petty bourgeoisie character of middle-class Punjabi poets and their limited experience of reality at the ground level.

(a)

But in the late 1960s and early 1970s, the scene changed quite dramatically, both locally and globally, precipitating a revival of progressive sentiment in a much more combative form. Economically, the Green Revolution did increase the per capita income of Punjab, but socially it ended up accentuating inequalities.[12] The delay in the implementation of land reforms added to the unrest. Nationwide, due to tense centre-state relations, regional murmurings had started acquiring high decibel levels. Telangana agitation had grown violent, and in an incident of indiscriminate police firing in 1969, it consumed the life of 369 students. Naxalbari uprising in 1967 followed by the setting up of the Communist Party of India (Marxist-Leninist) in 1969 had brought Calcutta to a boil.[13] Dalits of Maharashtra galvanised themselves to form Dalit Panthers along the lines of Black Panthers of America.[14] Internationally, the student movements all across the US due to antiwar sentiments and other civil rights movements like feminism and gay rights had fostered a mood of volatility and unease all around.[15] The May 1968 protests of students all across the world and the Tet offensive during the Vietnam War provided new causes for the emergence of militant poetry.

Against the backdrop of this build-up, a host of young Punjabi poets descended on the scene with an unprecedented revolutionary intent, questioning the armchair progressivism of their predecessors or senior poets. Profoundly dissatisfied and disenchanted with the rather shallow and soft expression and experience of preceding generation of progressive poets like Mohan Singh, Baba Balwant, Takhat Singh, Sant Singh Sekhon, Santokh Singh Dheer, S.S. Meesha, Amrita Pritam and others, the new Punjabi poets inaugurated a virulent form of insurgent progressivism, termed as *jujharvad*. The generation of progressive poets of the late 1950s and 1960s did articulate socialist anxieties. For instance, in his oft-quoted poem "Taj Mahal," Mohan Singh fired a rhetorical salvo at the feudal structure of the medieval past: 'Is that really a thing of beauty/ or just an illusion/ sustained by the tears of/ thousands of hapless workers?'(*Prof. Mohan Singh Rachanavali*, 67). Takhat Singh brought out the poignancy of alienation of a worker who cannot consume the products that he makes: 'If you long to live more/ keep working tirelessly./ Dare not touch the fruit/ of the tree that you plant./ Dare not wear the cloth/ that you spin with your own hands./ Dare not eat even a seed of the grain/ that have sown.' (*"Vasiyat," Vangaar*, 60). Sant Singh Sekhon also declared his commitment to progressive concerns: 'I can sing about the rosiness of cheeks. . ./but something pierced through me/I will sing songs of sorrow/ of the dust of lost tracks/till people fight out/ this sense of loss' (*"Mera Geet," Kaav Doot*, 9). But never did these poets raise their pitch to a level of combative vengefulness.

Taking on the mild-mannered progressives of Mohan Singh-Amrita Pritam period, Pash, an iconic young poet bellowed: 'Today the time has come/ that we recognise our relationship with ourselves/ and fight the battle of ideas/ outside our mosquito nets' (*"Vela Aa Giya," Sampoorn Pash-Kavi*, 55). He dismissed his poet-predecessors as "paper-tigers": 'You are a broken basket/not capable of carrying anything/ you just keep showing off an airgun/ you cannot kill anyone'(*"Kaagazi Sheraan de Naam," Sampoorn Pash-Kavi*, 62). Merely espousing the cause of the downtrodden was not enough, he declared: 'Take out machine-guns waving in the air/ now the nectar of lecture would not do' (*"Shraddhanjali" Sampoorn Pash-Kavi*, 60). Darshan Khatkar, another bellicose voice, ranted thus: 'We shall not bow our heads/ begging for life crawling in the squalor/ raising our heads we shall wink at the lightning'(*"Sangi Sathi," Sangi Sathi*, 9). Sant Ram Udasi, invoking those who had sacrificed their lives for the cause of a possible revolution, pledged, 'We will join you soon/ We shall not let burning pyre go cold/ We shall keep it alive by sacrificing ourselves/ We shall not let the movements for justice become widowed' (*"Ek Shraddhanjali – Ek Lalkar," Udasi: Jeevan te Smuchi Rachna*, 145). Udasi wanted his "pair of bulls to go full-throttled," "to sow weapons" in the field (*"Haliyan-Paliyan da Geet," Udasi: Jeevan te Smuchi Rachna*, 119). Lal Singh Dil found in 'arrow' the perfect measure to cover the distance between the powerless 'us' and the powerful 'them'(*"Doori," Naglok*, 33).

A host of other compatriots of Pash, particularly Sant Sandhu regretted the passivity of his predecessors: 'I don't have the leisure to read elegies/ I have some unfulfilled tasks of previous births/ Bed and sofa appear to me full of thorns'(*"Raat," Sis Tali Te*, 37). Harbhajan Halwaravi, another contemporary, addressed them as 'lion[s] of circus' who 'mistake the imprisonment of cage with the freedom of sky': 'He [the encaged lion] treats lions outside the cage/ as naïve animals/ . . . he believes that all the lions/ would be brought to the zoo, all decked up/ and the obdurate ones would be killed' (*"Circus da Sher," Paun Udaas Hai* 1981: 45–6). Fatehjeet clamoured for direct action:

> I know/ they will talk about revolution/ While taking recourse to Marx, Lenin and Mao,/ they shall not hesitate anywhere./

Without suffering even a slight pinch of a thorn/ they shall claim to hold an elephant inside a tiny box/ claims and only claims, they shall make.
("Hakikataan," Kachi Mitti de Baune, 77)

Even poets who were not as aggressive turned to 'the rhetoric of martyrdom' in the wake of Naxalite movement in Punjab. Jagtar, known primarily as a leading Punjabi *ghazalgo,* broke into free verse.[16] And in his collection *Lahoo de Naksh*, which he wrote in the thick of *jujharvadi* Punjabi movement, he acquired unprecedented flamboyance: 'Take me away from court/ To place of execution/ So that earth becomes pregnant by/ Taking my blood in its womb' (*'Niyanshala vich Liyanda Giya Doshi,'Lahoo de Naksh*, 18). He would almost snub: 'If you have to remain circumscribed/ in the orbits drawn by your compass/ then we depart./ We do not believe in behaving like a milestone planted in the earth' (*'Faisla,'Lahoo de Naksh*, 37). He despised the word "sympathy" hitherto used for the poor by the condescending elders: 'But none among us walks on the crutches of sympathy,/ The very word "sympathy" for us/ is like the broken sandals of our granddad' (*'Niyanshala vich Liyanda Giya Doshi,'Lahoo de Naksh*, 16). Surjit Patar, young as he was in the late 1970s, demonstrated rare impetuousness. Even he made grandiose claims of being the harbinger of new dawns: 'This small bit of passion of the heart that I have/ evinces a sensation, fierce/ Don't let it extinguish, my dear friends/ Who knows it might bring the dawn tomorrow' (*Hava vich Likhe Haraf*, 42). His otherwise very moderate idiom attained vehemence as grim and sombre semiotics of 'blood,' 'fire,' 'murder' and 'death' took over his poetic unconscious: 'False colours would strike the headlines in the newspapers/ no one would publish a story about the spill of your blood' (*Hava vich Likhe Haraf*, 52). He resented attempts of hiding behind the aesthetics of indirection: 'say wound a wound, do not declare it a flower/ remove misery, just do not write a verse on it' (*Hava vich Likhe Haraf*, 56).

(b)

As mentioned earlier, while some native observers attributed local reasons such as the marginalisation of low and middle-level peasantry during and after Green Revolution in particular for the rise of radical Punjabi poetry, other critics would cite volatile international setting. Aijaz Ahmad, however, underlined the rich international intertextuality of emerging progressive urge in the 1960s thus:

> Politically, the movement was something of a junction for three progressive movements of the period: the Bolshevik lineage of socialism, the transcontinental anti-fascist front, and anti-colonial/anti-imperialist struggles across the tri-continent of Asia, Africa and Latin America – the so-called 'third world.' And, connected with these, the much broader struggle for universal emancipation, or what I simply call 'democratisation,' by which I mean such things as the struggle for women's emancipation, the demand for equal rights of electoral representation, or struggles against racism and caste oppression.
> (Ahmad 2011: 29–30)

The rise of adventurists like Charu Majumdar, Kanu Sanyal and radical Maoists like Nagi Reddy at the national level also contributed tangibly to the charged up atmosphere. The *jujharvadis* evinced enormous open-mindedness to incorporate all kinds of instances of oppression anywhere in the world within their poetic ambit. The militant resistance, particularly the one offered by the underdogs of the world, was their staple source of inspiration. This kind of internationalism is ingrained in Punjabi unconscious, for right from Ghadar movement to latter-day separatist movements, the Punjabis do tend to establish international linkages to sustain their local struggles.

Vietnam which was a ready metaphor of protracted resistance against American imperialism in the '70s, for instance, happened to be a constant presence in *jujharvadi* poetry. Amarjit Chandan wrote, 'He is coming, He will come; He shall have pistol in his hand/ which he describes is an instrument of sweet melodies./ The exiled voices shall get their homeland in/ not one, not two, in lot many Vietnams!' ('*Auh,'Kuan Nahin Chahega* 10). In fact, he went on to publish poems about Vietnam in Punjabi translation under the title *Mera Naam, Tera Naam Vietnam* (1969). Later on, in the mid-80s, surprisingly enough, he tended to distance himself from his invocation of Vietnam in his poetry thus: 'I sloganeered in favour of Vietnam, published poems in Punjabi translation on and around Vietnam, but I could not write a poem about Vietnam. It could not become my experience' ('*Guachiyaan Hoyiaan Chitthiya an,'Kavitavaan*,16).[17] Lal Singh Dil, who was a frontline Naxalite, juxtaposed the role of combative old men in war-torn Vietnam with that of the passive and complicit Gandhi back in India and Punjab particular thus:

> There the weak-legged oldies
> Barely go away from their villages
> Shoo away the falling bomb
> With their spin of the sticks
> That it bursts back into the enemy camp
> Here Gandhis do not have the freedom
> To walk to the enemy camp
> Doling out advice on Bhagat Singh's hanging.
> ('*Vietnam*,'*Naglok*, 57)

Gandhian socialism, with its emphasis on non-violence and non-possession, had no place in the poetry of '70s, often termed as *jujharvadi* Punjabi poetry. Till date in Punjab, Gandhi is held responsible for the hanging of Bhagat Singh.[18]

Sant Ram Udasi, another major *jujharvadi*, was a singer-poet of the masses. He had the capacity to spellbound rural audiences with his passionate singing of radical songs and poems. For him, Vietnam was Punjab under siege, and every Vietnami was Sikh fighting for his motherland:

> 'Death' to the tyrants;
> And shield to the poor,
> This is the strength of a true Sikh.
> Your Sikh always fights for truth
> Even if he fights in Vietnam.
> ('Guru Gobind Singh
> Ji de Naan,' Udasi: Jeevan te
> Smuchi Rachna, 173)

He believed that it was Gobind who was fighting there, and it was Gobind who would fight here too: 'After being free from Vietnam and Cambodia/ Gobind comes back to fight in India'(173). There is a visible shift from socialist realism to radical realism, that is, instead of approaching reality in reified doctrinal terms or through set ready-made ideologised paradigms, the emphasis is now on engaging with life directly at the level of experience. Writing back to his senior comrades, reminding them of their slightly effete and bookish brand of socialism, Pash would say,

> You who write letters to beloveds
> Refrain from committing paper-abortion
> Though impotent is the point of your pen,
> You who, with a look at stars, teach
> How revolution to cause!
> Know thyself before teaching
> That revolution when it comes
> Will also show you the stars.
> ('An Open Letter,' *Reckoning with Dark Times*, trans. Tejwant, 16)

This is how young poet took on Amrita Pritam's rather melancholic and diseased progressivism in the last part of the poem:

> As a thorny cactus today
> The corpse of Waris Shah has grown
> On society's body-politic.
> Tell it that beyond the name of Waris Shah now
> It is the age of Vietnam
> Each Khera is the battlefield
> Where war is waged for our rights now.
> ('An Open Letter,' *Reckoning with Dark Times*, trans. Tejwant, 16)

This was an explicit rejection of Amrita Pritam's plaintive lyricism couched as it was in mystical allusions/ illusions of the medieval past.[19] Ironically a local icon of composite Punjabi culture, namely a Sufi poet Waris Shah became a cultural liability for the young *jujharvadis*, and Vietnam, a distant land, turned out to be their preferred address to access their native Punjab.

Amarjit Chandan, whose grandfather was Ghadarite, and who himself was a close associate of Pash, Dil and Udasi, wrote with the ruthlessness of an uncompromising revolutionary. In his slim volume of poetry entitled *Kaun Nahin Chahega* (1975) brought out in the thick of Naxalite unrest, he asked with a death-defying vehemence:

> How long will you keep vomiting in the tear-gas?
> How long the unholy colonial boots

Trample over your books?
Rise and tell the loyal lathis:
Till the alphabets of blood are true,
Till the ink of our rights is pure
There is no difference between a pen and a bayonet
and the noose of the hanging rope is never widowed
('Kadon Tak,'Kaun Nahi Chahega, 5)

Blood, bullet and bomb lent a certain piquancy to his idiom: '/ When a reference was made to sprinkle blood on the picture of a martyr/ one friend got up,/ waved the pistol and fired in the air' ('*Ek Din,'Kaun Nahin Chahega*, 14–15). At the level of aesthetics, the contemporary trends of anti-poetry and absurd literature did inseminate the waywardness of youthful protest.[20] In the late 1960s, a movement of anti- or non-poetry and ridiculous poetry had started in which poets across Indian languages deliberately used savage imagery and uncouth idiom to create the touch of the raw and unsavoury real.

(c)

On the whole, at one visible level, the *jujharvadis* thus emerged as poets-in-arms. As they wrote and reacted against state-oppression, they were repeatedly incarcerated and subjected to third-degree torture by the state. All progressive poets, without exception, went to jail and they wrote from their prison cells. They produced a rich corpus of what is in Punjabi called as *bandi-kaav* (prison-poetry). In their poetry, there was hardly a gap between stage poetry and the so-called artistic poetry. Also, there was a propensity to privilege country-life over city life. All the leading poets of this movement starting from Pash, Sant Ram Udasi to Lal Singh Dil and others happened to be not just poet-activists but warrier-poets who led the campaign on the field from the front. Regarding its ideological propensities, the jujharvadi poetry was often approached as a radical extension or a robust form of progressive poetry. Therefore Kesar Singh Kesar, a well-known critic, named it as 'new progressive poetry in Punjabi'(95). Due to its overt combative tone and explosive temper, this poetry marked a 'militant phase of Punjabi progressive poetry'; other labels such as 'naxalite Punjabi poetry' or just 'revolutionary Punjabi poetry' were also invoked inter-changeably for this kind of poetry. Satinder Singh Noor, another eminent critic, approached this poem regarding a composite reaction to both *prayogwad* and *pragatiwad* (18–20). Later detractors termed it as poetry of noise and 'militant bravado' (Gurbachan 1972: 89) or just 'murderous poetry.'[21] Some critics and contemporary poets while acknowledging its unflinching popularity, found this poetry too idealistic and loud-mouthed to sustain the test of time.

II

(a)

There was yet another very controversial streak of *jujharvadi* poetry which has often been underplayed, ignored or even deliberately erased to keep the canon straight and comfortable. It might sound ironical that a movement which was so pronouncedly that of the ultra-left, in moments of stalemate began to fall back on martial Sikh past for sustaining its guerrilla instincts. This kind of primordial pull towards religion was understandable on two counts – one, right from Singh Sabha to Babbar Akali movement, Sikhism always loomed large as a possibility of cultural stay throughout, and two there had been a glaring lack of a robust local intellectual tradition of Marxism in Punjab.[22],[23] The irony becomes all the more poignant when one learns that during the rise of militancy in Punjab during the 1980s the prime target of terrorist violence were the comrades of the Naxalite movement. Pash was killed by Khalistani militants on 23 March 1988 when he was all set to fly to the US. He was just 38 then. And his death coincided with the 57th death anniversary of Shahid Bhagat Singh.

Deep down Naxalite poetry in Punjabi struck a distinct religious note, and in hindsight, it tended to hark back to hard-core militant Sikhism. Though in the beginning, this element did not emerge with as much belligerence as it did in its latter phase, yet one could sense an uncanny symbiotic relationship between radical Sikhism and Punjabi Naxalite poetry throughout. Pash valourised the Naxalites as new obedient Sikhs of Guru Gobind Singh who would stand by him in the face of gravest threat:

> Gone wild with their fiestas
> They have owned your teaching
> And Machiwara's wild growth
> Has disfigured their faces,
> Their Jafarnamas being written

> By lice festering over there
> They exalt them as martyrs
> > ('The Disowning Letter,'
> > *Reckoning with Dark
> > Times*, trans. Tejwant, 23)

Writing back to his senior comrades, reminding them of their rather quasi-intellectual brand of socialism, Pash in his subtle ways invoked *dasham* Guru Gobind Singh, the saint-soldier, thus,

> You have never perceived words
> As eggs animated with chickens
> Or sun-light dissolved
> In the rain-soaked mid-day dark.
> I have suffered words with their sharp edges,
> In their bid to escape the severity of winter
> I have provided them shelter in my blood.
> With no claim to emulate the tenth Master
> I have bitterly lamented
> After putting them in poetic armour
> > ('Taking to a Comrade,' *Reckoning with
> > Dark Times*, trans. Tejwant, 108)

It can be argued that in the poetry of Pash and his contemporaries, the images of Sikh heroes or martyrs occur or operate more or less as quick references, or as extant cultural tropes shared by the semi-literate masses of rural Punjab. And, it can also be reasoned that to lend thick texture to a poetic argument, the poets, irrespective of their ideological intentions, often exploit religious metaphors. But there are ample instances where the progressive poets tend to go overboard in their invocation of the patently religious metaphors, bringing therein an avoidable communal fervour to their poetic output.

In the verse quoted next, Darshan Khatkar in his oft-quoted poem "Prun" ["Oath"] from his collection 'Sangi Sathi,' for instance, conflated *dharma-yuddha* (religious war) with *lok-yuddha* (people's war), thus,

> Today Guru's sons have taken a vow
> Whether we are of the age of sixteen or twelve
> Would leave Anandpur

And cross Sirsa
This is our dharam and this is our karam
Whether it is the wall of Sirhind
Or police post of Banga
Whether we are buried alive in brick wall or are beaten blue
the trumpet of dharam-yuddha, and the slogan of lok-yuddha would reverberate
today the khalsa of guru has taken a vow
("Prun," *Sangi Sathi*,19)

The *dharma-yuddha* and the *lok-yuddha* feed each other and in the process lend continuity to a history of militant protest that characterises Sikh past. When Darshan Khatkar was asked about the over-use of Sikh symbols and history in Naxalite poetry in general and in his poetry in particular, the poet claimed, 'During Naxali movement the re-writing of Sikh history was done on a large scale, something which even Shiromani Committee could not have done!' (quoted in Parwana, *Kala, Jindagi te Naxali Sarokar*,94) In other terms, it means that what Sikh clergy fails to do, the Naxal poets succeed to do with elan and passion. Variam Singh Sandhu, another Naxal writer, who sought to replace Marxist thinkers with Sikh gurus and heroes as source of inspiration for armed resistance was asked by an interviewer,

[T]his is often said that in the rise of Khalistani movement there is a role of that tendency in the Naxalites under which they while re-writing Sikh history, bring into foreground the militant aspect of it. Even in your writing, there is a glorification of this militant past. What do you say?
(Quoted in Parwana, *Kala, Jindagi te Naxali Sarokar*, 123)

Of course, the writer defended himself, but the very question itself points towards the ideological overlap of the left and the right.

In his later poetry, Sant Ram Udasi increasingly went back to Sikh martial past and wrote poems which were overtly religious. There are poems of Udasi that cater to both the communal and the communist ways of life, without causing any ideological dissonance: 'Even though the number may go from/ twenty five to twenty five thousand/ Or even from forty to forty thousand/ The Sikhs would not piss over reward/ for Khalsa can never be a traitor'('*Do*

Raah,'Udasi: Jeevan te Smuchi Rachna, 258). Or, in another verse, the target was Delhi, and the rhetoric continued to be that of the medieval past: 'We will raise the fort of Delhi to dust/ in front of the mud fortress of Chamkaur./Do not regret the fall of Anandpur fort;/ each shack, we will turn into a fort'('*Chamkaur de Gadi vich Singhan da Jera,'Udasi: Jeevan te Smuchi Rachna*, 172). In such poems, the references to Gobind Singh's encounter with Aurangzeb's army at Chamkaur Garhi repeatedly occur, almost as a given and ready trope of radical heritage:

> Therefore, I deem myself both the guru and his disciple/ so that the master-servant relation ends in the world./ Therefore, I waged a war from inside the fortress of Chamkaur/ so that the castles and towers may be humbled before the mud hut.
> ('Guru Gobind Singh Ji da Lokan de Naam Antim Suneha,'Udasi: Jeevan te Smuchi Rachna, 152)

Of course, the first two lines lean towards the ideology of the left, but after that it is all surcharged with religious imagery.

An editor of the collection of his poems, Rajinder Rahi very significantly suggested Sant Ram Udasi's leanings towards ultra-right towards the end of his life thus:

> Just two months prior to his death in Sept. 1986, one revolutionary literary organisation recorded an interview with him. This cassette was taken by Baru Satwarag with a promise that he would make printable script from the conversations. . . . He later told that had we published that interview, the established image of Udasi would have suffered and secondly it would have emboldened Khalistani wave.
> (XXXI–XXXII)

The editor added, 'In this interview, Udasi emphasised on two things. One, the Naxalite movement was not just a movement, it was an action plan. Second, Khalistani wave can be described as a peasant movement that came in the form of the reaction of Sikhs against oppression. He openly endorsed this wave. When asked that Khalistani killed his closed associate Baldev Singh Mann, he had to say that such mishap does occur in any movements. When we reminded him that his songs based on historical past provided moral support to Khalistanis, he said that whenever anyone takes on oppression, whether he is a Khalistani or a Naxalite, his songs would inspire him' (XXXII).

Sant Ram Udasi's elder brother Gurdas Singh Gharu in his autobiography '*Pagdandiyan ton Jeevan Marg tak*' (2000) chronicled the last phase of the revolutionary poet regarding his disillusionment with life. From a devout teetotaller Namdhari, Udasi ended up as a compulsive alcoholic:

> As after 1980, the revolutionary wave ebbed, Udasi was utterly disappointed. Within his household, quarrels started. Even his friends started criticising him. We in Jagmalere, received reports of Udasi's despair and drinking. Before this, I had never seen drinking so much of wine.
> (173)

Overall, as Amarjit Chandan in an interview in a reputed Punjabi little magazine, *Hun* also confessed, 'Naxalite were inherently Sikhs' ('*Anokha te Ekalla Amarjit Chandan,*'*Hun*, 6). Pritam Singh in an article on the sweep of Marxism in Punjab further explains the narrow social basis of the cadres of radical Marxists thus: 'Marxism as a social-political movement in Punjab was/is mainly confined to the Jat Sikh land-owning peasantry and this caste-religious-social group also provided the major chunk of the activists and political leaders of the communist movement in Punjab'(543). This regressive propensity attained rather dangerous proportions in the latter-day poetry of these poets, so much so that the ideological distinction between the left and the right became almost unsustainable.

(b)

The Naxalite phase of Punjabi poetry did not last very long and was soon busted or lost steam on its own in less than a decade. The imposition of Emergency followed by the rise of the ultra-right movement for Khalistan in a way usurped the space of protest which hitherto was with ultra-left Naxalites only. Thus we have seen that throughout Naxalite phase of Punjabi literature, the discourse of radical Sikhism remained integral to its revolutionary zeal. The ideological poetry couched in the language of militant religiosity did provide cultural legitimacy to those Naxalite who joined the ranks of Khalistani separatists.[24] Later observers, including those who once empathised with them, termed Naxalites as *Kalyugi* Gobinds who were only eager to showcase their heroics at a very personal level. Some of these poets even went on to prove their status at par with Guru Gobind Singh in terms of their audacity to take on the enemy.

III

In the third section, I intend to discuss the fate of those *jujharvadi* poets who survived not the only Naxalite phase but also the Khalistani movement. As both the extreme left and the extreme right suffered a reversal, the erstwhile *jujharvadi* poets underwent bouts of ideological confusion. Of course, some poets chose to remain in a state of denial and continued to write in radical terms without necessary intellectual self-reflexivity. Some decided to go abroad and began to re-discover themselves in extremely provincial terms. Some stayed back and toned down their radicalism and relapsed into lyricism of the popular kind; some while acknowledging the failure of their youthful radicalism, turned reflexive without ever giving up their progressive leanings. The argument is that the so-called *jujharvadi* poets ran a crisis of relevance and it distracted into different directions to carry forward their poetic urges. Its ideological scaffolding suddenly becomes untenable and even self-defeating.

(a)

The latter phase of Pash's poetic trajectory needs to be re-assessed regarding its ideological veracity. It is often maintained that had Pash not been killed by the Khalistani militants in 1985, he would have produced a formidable corpus of radical Punjabi poetry. These are purely conjectural positions, but the fact of the matter is that Pash himself admitted of facing a stalemate in his life. In a diary entry of 13 June 1982, he wrote,

> On 4th January 1974 I do not know under what spell or belief I had written in a diary that 'My poem would never become silent.' Now it is almost six years that no poem has come out of me, but still I have a blind faith of the religious kind that it can never be so. Only the nature of happenings in my life has changed and my sensibilities to accept them have also taken a different turn. My new nature and new sensibilities have yet to arrive at a point of coincidence. This is all a process of a new

poetic style. The span of the longings of the body is about to be over. After I fold their death-carpet, only then shall I be able to write something. In the last six years I really never felt the desire to write. This is a matter of consolation. I salute myself. I never forcibly hold my pen to do some kind of verbal jugglery. Does this not make sense? After all writing poetry is not like a bitch giving birth to puppies!

(qtd. in Pash, *Khilre Hoye Verke*, '*Pash de Kavita*,' Ed. Amarjit Chandan 16–17)

This is not just a case of what is sometimes described as the writer's block. Of course, he did write some poems later and never really abandoned his anti-establishment position, but more or less he withdrew from the volatile field. Significantly enough, the poet was no longer inspired to write. This lack of motivation to write poetry does speak about the dwindling ecology of revolutionary fervour.

In the diary entry quoted earlier, there is a suggested shift in the poetic make-up of Pash, as a poet. From youthful aggression to mature cogitation, from mere rhetoric to thoughtful confession and from mere sloganeering to the need of evolving an idiom of measured ethical sensibility, he seems to veer towards a post-ideological stance that is directed towards the emancipation of Punjabi culture on the whole.[25] Amarjit Chandan's observation sums up how the orthodox Marxist critics fail to locate Pash beyond the narrow limits of violent Naxalism:

Unabashed anger was the insolent aspect of militant poetry. This can be understood in the context of the so-called Cultural Revolution during the Charuite terrorist era. Then, Pash and other poets and activists thought the movement of murder and martyrdom and the book burning to be the best thing they would do. This was the reason Pash in his poetry written during the times, makes fun of the beards of Tagore and Ghalib and sees the great poet of Punjab, Waris Shah, as 'a corpse grown like a cactus on the body of society.' Later on, Pash stopped this name calling. In 1973, he wrote in an open letter to a self-styled critic that all the anger in militant poetry was, in fact, futile outburst against the oppression. He accused the critic to have 'developed bad habits.' He came to realise that the anger of an insolent child cannot be the right human behaviour. But even after so many years, some critics present his curses of the Charuite phase to be the poetics of Pash and say [like the iron] 'Red hot in the fire of anger, the poetic language of Pash is its best.' They seem to ignore Pash's remarkable poems like 'Raat Nu' (To the Night) and 'Barsaat' (Rain) in his collection *Loh Katha*.

(Ferrous Story)[26](*'Pash di Kavita,'*
Amarjit Chandan, 19)

Ideology, in its unconcerned pure form, became an encumbrance for Pash as a poet, and he was too eager to go beyond its constraints. Even as he struggled to re-invent himself, the orthodox left critics kept branding him as a Naxal poet.

(b)

The Naxal poets, on the whole, become far less productive; only those who change planks could re-invent themselves. Darshan Khatkar writes one more collection that too after a gap of about 35 years. In this group, we come across a sober Khatkar who turns self-reflexive and diffident:

> The unease is too much
> Don't know what to do and what not to do
> Ever since the market has usurped you in
> the open market
> neither there is any ransom,
> nor is there any freedom to you.
> ('Bazaar Vich Agwa,'Ulte Rukh
Parvaz 2010: 34)

Of course, while conceding to the might of "the global" (20), he refuses to accept the proposition of the end of history given by the champions of late capitalism. Of all the major *jujharvadi* poets, it is mainly Khatkar who continues to remain within the ideological fold with the only difference that from being a dreamer of revolution, he becomes sceptical about its possibility.

(c)

Amarjit Chandan, who once heralded 'handcuffs, chains, rifles/ utensils of prisoners' (*'Kise vi Saaz da Naam Lau,'Kaun Nahin Chahega,*

19) as instruments of music, now undergoes bouts of self-reflexivity to sustain his post-progressive poetic propensities. In a collection entitled *Kavitavaan* (1984), from being an activist-poet, he increasingly turns into a pensive poet who postpones the possibilities of plunge for his survival. Very significantly he uses two quotes – one from Kafka and another from Kabir as epigraphs revealing his preferences for the existential.[27] Having suffered long spells of incarceration and the perpetual threats of police encounters, he now prefers the value of stoic experience: 'This time we want to make our own another Hindustan/ we want to be released from this prison/ we want to live all over again/ the history's most condemned times to the hilt' (*'Naxali Shahidaan de Swa-Padchol,'Kavitavaan*, 50). In poems like *'Kudi te Nehri,'*the ideological impetus is lent artistic indirection through innovative correlatives. The "dust storm" does not stand for disruption, it rather stands for rejuvenation with 'a promise of rain' and 'a clear sky' (*'Kudi te Nehri,'Kavitavaan*, 51) after that.

In the collections that are published subsequently, we come across the mellowed Chandan, who yearns to hear melodious hymns from the distant lands of the First World where he had migrated in the early 1980s: 'We shall hear shabad of Guru Arjun from the mouth of Bade Gulam Ali/ we shall hear bani of Nanak from the mouth of Subba Lakshmi'(*'Punjab de Katilaan Noon,'Jarhaan*, 109). The existential no longer remains the fulcrum of his stay; it only withholds but does not nurture:

> I have become a prisoner of time
> How do I break these invisible walls?
> Which earth shall I dig to make a tunnel?
> Even if I escaped
> Is there any place to go to?
> Whose hand I'd hold?
> Whose embrace I'd fall into?
>   ('Dupahir,'Jarhaan, 51)

As the displaced poet clamours for a cultural anchor, he resurrects the familiar tropes of belongingness such as familial past, mother tongue and the native folklore for the necessary umbilical pull: 'Looking at these roots/ I come face to face with the image of our great ancestor Dhareja/ . . . whose roots flow into my veins'

(*'Jarhaan,'Jarhaan*, 13). Punjab and Punjabi – the native space and its language – overtake Chandan's youthful infatuation with ideology.

In *Bijak*, except for some poems like 'Lal Dandora'(14) or 'Dholak'(45) wherein Chandan's erstwhile Marxist leanings strike back, it is largely the legacy of Sufi and Bhakti metaphysics that seem to besiege him in fundamental ways. Some of the early poems bear titles such as 'Manglacharan'(1), 'Shukarana' (2), 'Aarti' (3), 'Deepdaan' (40 and 'Jot'(31). In such a poem, the gap between a prayer and a poem almost vanishes, and right at the outset, the reader is lifted beyond the realm of this-worldliness. In some of the other poems such as 'Garabhpaat' (27), 'Jeevan Marag' (39), 'Mout da Khooh'(40) and 'Photo Khichwan Lagga Baccha' (41), the poet does work out his metaphysical leap through an encounter with ordinary events of life. Cylcing, which in an earlier poem – 'Cylce Chalaundiyan' (Jarhaan, 64–66) – was a metaphor for collective progressive movement amongst the proletariat, now stands elevated as a metaphor of metaphysical surge: 'This is not cycle, nor even a flying saucer/ flying above the roofs of Begumpura/ as fast as wind, whistling/ I cycle with hands off the handle' (*'Jeevan Marag,'Bijak*, 39).[28]

In *Chhanna* (1998) and *Gurhati* (2000), Chandan tends to sound more abstract and absolute. From the flatness of ideological rhetoric, he leapfrogs into the roundness of mysticism, bypassing in the process, the severe pangs of becoming.[29] The poet who once surmised – 'if conversations are not bombs, at least they can surely turn into abuses' (*'Khabraan,* Bomb, *Gahlaan,'Kavitavaan*, 29), 'now pines for silence – a silence which is inside the grand-explosion of a seed/ . . . /inside the squall of the sleep/' (*'Chup,'Chhanna*, 39). In another poem, the poet attempts to define 'this': 'This is not day/ This is not night/ . . . / This is some entity/ without any name' (*'Eh,'Gurhati*, 45). Writing a note for his collection *Chhanna* (1998), Satyapal Gautam writes,

> Again someone asked a naughty question: first your poetry was clearly revolutionary and now it has become mystical. How does this miracle happen? Chandan with all humility, which was difficult to trace in his nature earlier, replied: what you term as miracle, I also accept that as a miracle
>
> ('Maan Boli Simardiyan,'Chhanna, 11)

In another interview when accused of being heretic and a renegade, Amarjit Chandan justifies his change of stance thus:

> They dare not look at me in the face and call me a renegade or a heretic. I haven't made any compromises to this day. But look at them: on the one hand, they are enjoying all the benefits offered by the government they call oppressive, authoritarian and corrupt; and on the other hand, they fancy themselves as revolutionaries. I am not afraid of questions. I even question myself in my poems. Even Marx said we must doubt everything. And these blind followers of his ideology don't doubt anything?
> (Interview with Dhiman, The Sunday Tribune)

Writing as a poet residing outside his country, Chandan thus changes planks; there is a movement from Naxalism to theological Sikhism. In the same interview, he goes on to admit that 'Naxalism was a suicidal movement; it was never a people's movement. It was a movement of murder and martyrdom' (Interview with Dhiman, The Sunday Tribune). Bhagwan Singh Josh tends to look upon this shift regarding Chandan's liberation from ideology: 'The element of spirituality is embedded in the poems included in his collection Jarhaan, which otherwise was absent in his early poetry. The poet by invoking tradition, appreciating its greatness has lent aesthetic ease to his modernity.'('Vichardhara ton Mukt Kavita,' http://amarjitchandan.tripod.com/Bhagwan1.pdf).

(d)

The latter-day Lal Singh Dil also emerges as a disillusioned Naxal:

> It turned to be just a dream/ that we will cover the heads of the evil gentry with caps/ they will be forced to trace lines on the floor with their noses/ and will give account to people of their deeds/ on the contrary the feet of revolution turned towards our own chests/ to be humiliated, it seems, is our only halt.
> ('Ult Inqlab de Pair,'Naglok, 150)

In another poem 'Comradaan da Geet'(*Naglok*, 130), the poet takes a dig at those loquacious 'noble comrades' who give extended lectures but are wary of sacrifice. He questions the very idea of socialism in which individualism remains intact; figuratively, he puts it, 'Fish is cooked/ and yet it seeks to remain alive'(*'Samajvad,'Naglok*, 132).

Later, partly to conceal his identity as a runaway Naxal, partly to camouflage his background of being a low-caste and partially to satisfy his inner spiritual urges, Dil converts to Islam. Amarjit Chandan observes,

> The conversion of Lal Singh Dil as Muhammad Bushra Jan Wali Muhammad was his answer to the lethal philosophy of terrorism and anarchism, and to the insecurities of a low-caste in a caste-ridden society, its aspects of gender-oppression included as well.
>
> (*'Sampadki,'Naglok*, 98)

In fact, Dil goes on to express his quandaries after his conversion into Islam thus:

> How could one be a Communist, with being a Muslim? I used to believe that Islam is quite akin to Communist culture. The only difference is that the former is theistic, and the latter is atheistic. I thought that till Communist culture is not achieved, I should convert to Islam but at the same, I should stick to my atheism. This was a strange idea that I should become a Muslim, and yet remain an atheist.
>
> (Dil, *Dastan*, 130)

In a passionate letter written to Amarjit Chandan in 1973, he writes,

> [Therefore] I am a sympathiser of the community of Mao and Ho Chi Minh because this is one halt in the politics of Allaha. The rising tides within a culture do please me, but I am one among the devouts of Allaha.
>
> (Quoted in Amarjit Chandan's *'Bahut Chup Kitiyan da Kavi,'Naglok*, 28)

Towards the end of his life, Lal is appropriated by the Punjabi Dalits as their poets, and he also goes on to accept, though reluctantly, the status of a caste-poet. In fact, he would, later on, grudge: 'There is caste in literature too. Everyone talks about Pash. Because he is a son of a jatt. Lal Singh Dil is not even read by people' (quoted by Gurbachan, '*Lal Singh Dil: Viralaan chon Jhakda Jahar,*'*Naglok*, 153). In his long descriptive poem 'Ajj Billa Pher Aya' (2009), the frustration of a being a Dalit is expressed thus: 'For us/ fruits do not come to trees/ . . . / for us/ revolutions do not happen' (72). In the poem, Dil plays to the hilt his identity as a Dalit, which otherwise remains understated in his earlier collections. Dil's poetic journey in a way becomes the tragic locus of jujharvadi disposition for it begins with a sense commitment to ideology, then it drifts towards religion and, finally, it culminates in his casteidentity.

(e)

Jagtar, who 'slid into the fashion with a quiet hope to lead the [*jujharvadi*] movement' (Gurbachan 1972: 90), after the mid-70s becomes more contemplative and thoughtful. In poems written around the pre- and post-Operation Blue Star and 1984 anti-Sikh Delhi riots, the poet, who was once scripting "lahoo de naqsh" (the imprints of blood) begins to sound helpless and turns sceptical about the credo of violence and terrorism:

> I have read the orders of my murder
> But wait
> There is none left in the basti,
> Let me write my will to the trees...
> My friends
> After me
> Come what may
> You have to become the pillar of a falling roof
> You have to become the lathi of a man in need
> But do not become the grip of a sword.
> ('Vasiyat,'*Chanukari Sham*, 57)

As Jagtar survives past the history of what is often called 'Punjab crisis,' he loses the ideological sting, and his ghazals tend to be more saturnine and gloomy; he emerges more as a 'poet of concern'(Sukhdev 2007: 70) than of activist intentions.[30] The existential or the philosophical take over the political: 'That I may not lose my identity by merging into the sea/ I remained all my life a flowing river' (Ghazal no. 193, *Mere Andar Ek Samundar* 2001: 292).[31]

(f)

Surjit Patar, in his collections published post-1990s, increasingly writes in a mixed vocabulary – of resistance and renunciation, of confrontation and confession and of loss and love. This is how he responds to the Naxal rage: 'From inside me many voices speak/ Nehru speaks, so does Mao. . ./ But if anyone whose voice is missing/ It is mine' (*'Gharar,'Hanarey Vich Sulgadi Varnamala*, 26). What prompted Patar to write this poem 'was a protracted debate . . . about the role of the poets of the [naxalite] movement, and also about the deep concerns of Punjab' (*'Kavita da Janam*,*'* 185). In his latter-day poetry, as the poet negotiates with disparate discourses of nativism, Sufism, theological Sikhism, progressivism, existentialism and romanticism, he seeks refuge at the altar of words. All through his poetic journey, the poet is smitten by virtue of words and their surcharged alphabets (*Hanarey vich Sulgadi Varnamala*) as they bristle in the darkness. He emerges as a poet of Arnoldian mindset who seeks redemption in poetry as both institutionalised religion and doctrinal ideology fail to enamour him[32]: 'O poetry, I return to you/ your high pedestal/ where music echoes eternally/ and every pain is sublimated'(*'Hey Kavita,'Lafazaan de Dargah*, 18). The epigraph to *Lafazaan de Dargah* reads: 'Transmuting sorrow into a song/ does offer me a way to redemption/ if there is no other door [I can knock at]/ there is at least this shrine of words' (7).

IV

Overall, the *jujharvadi* poets, major or minor, evidently enough undergo ideological entropy. The Punjabi imagination consequently splinters in many directions, with ideology no longer the cementing impulse. In fact, as the *jujharvadi* temper wanes, Punjab is left with hardly any composite alternative to providing a steady cultural stay to the restless and dynamic Punjabi imagination. The rise of multiple Dalit movements, the proliferation of deras and other competing discourses of identitarian claims within Punjab add to the ideological problem. The burgeoning diaspora, on the beats of pop-bhangra and kitschy music, is all set to overwhelm the contemporary youth towards popular entertainment and drug-induced escape. The species of revolutionary *lok-kavis* that used to sway the rural masses with their passionate lyrics is all set to be replaced by a horde of Punjabi pop-singers and standup comedians in the post-90s Punjab. The ideology which seemed to hold sway for a while stands sucked first by the black hole of religion and later on by the equally compelling discourses of identity politics based on caste, gender and location. If *jujharvadi* poetry is any measure, it can be surmised that ideology does have its spasmodic presence, but it does not constitute the blueprint of identity in the South Asian context.

Notes

1 The author of the chapter, unless mentioned otherwise, has translated quotes taken from Punjabi and Hindi poetry and prose, for illustration. The translations are of working nature only.
2 'Ideology' is a secular category for unlike the mythologised belief systems of organised religion, it stands for an intellectual approach to this-worldly human experience. Of course, religion can be used as a political resource to control and coordinate human experience, but it is distinct from ideology: 'A religion is a system of faith, worship and conduct. If it could be said, like an ideology, to contain an explanatory doctrine, its explanations are always regarding a divine order; they are never, as the doctrine of ideology, centred on this world alone. Religion certainly does not need to have a programme of political and social action, although it may have a vision of just and decent social order. The emphasis of religion is on inwardness, and the redemption of each human soul: while an ideology speaks to the mass man, to the class or group or nation or crowd. Religion recognises its debt to faith and revelation; whereas ideology believes that it lives by reason alone' (Cranston 1979: 59).
3 As an ideological category, the term 'Left' begins during the French Revolution, and those who supported values of republicanism, democracy and socialism (as against French monarchy) were called Leftists. Later on, the discourse of the left was appropriated by Marx and Engels with their radical ideas of communism, classless-society and revolution. Today 'left' is an umbrella term used for all shades of socialism – ranging from communism to Naxalism.
4 Eugene Lyons, an American journalist, in his book *The Red Decade: The Stalinist Penetration of America* (1941), underlined the overwhelming threat of penetration of communism in America and other countries of Europe during the Cold War. George Kennan in his article 'The Sources of Soviet Conduct,' (1947) published in Foreign Affairs suggested a policy of containment through which the expansion of the ideology of the left could be arrested in the US and elsewhere.
5 Besides other aspects related to the role of writers and literature in general, the Manifesto adopted at the AIPWA meet, clearly evinced a Marxist slant. It vowed 'to take our literature and other art forms from the monopolistic control of priests, pundits and other conservatives . . . bring [them] nearer the people' (Jalil 436). It further iterated that 'the

new literature in India must respect basic realities of our present-day life and these are the questions of our bread, plight, our social degradation and political slavery' (Jalil 436). For a nuanced and critical reading of different versions of the Manifesto read, Rakshanda Jalil's Linking Progress, Loving Change: A Literary History of the Progressive Writers Movement in Urdu (2014)

6 In their 'Introduction' to *Punjab Reconsidered* (2012), Anshu Malhotra and Farina Mir points towards the rather enigmatic phenomenon of syncretic Punjabis atavistically lapsing into communal or religious grids every now and then: 'We know why/how religious antagonisms became entrenched in society, but less about mental states, for example, that encouraged the shared veneration of saintly lives. We know how different religious communities came to see themselves as distinct from each other, and how soured relations between them sowed the seeds of an irrevocable political parting of ways. . . . And despite, over a half-century of interrogation into communalism – often, however, with a telos to Partition – much work is yet to be done' (xxxvii–xxxviii).

7 One may argue that Sikh is not a primordial identity and that its rise can be historically mapped during the colonial period and after that. Gopal Singh, an eminent scholar, describes the growth of national consciousness among the Sikhs: 'Therefore, I believe that the nationality formation of the Sikhs took place during last 120 years or so, i.e. from the beginning of the Namdhari or Kuka movement to the end of the 1980s and through the various struggles against and the persecutions by the ruling powers. Baba Ram Singh and his followers of the Kuka movement fought against British imperialism on the one hand and for reforms in Sikhism on the other. . . . Another massive upsurge which was in congruence with Sikh national aspiration was to be seen during the Gurdwara Reform Movement' (1920–25). During this movement, hundreds of unarmed non-violent Sikhs were done to death when they went to liberate the gurdwaras (particularly Nankana Sahib) from the corrupt "mahants" and thousands were put into jail. Also, the breakaway faction of the Sikh youth known as Babbars took to militancy. The point which I want to emphasise here is that the heroic sacrifices made by Kukas and Babbars did create a national consciousness among the ordinary Sikh masses, particularly those inclined to puritanism' ('Complexities of the Question of Sikh Nationality' 1882). In his critical intervention on the possible origins of Sikh identity Harjot S. Oberoi's goes back to what he terms as 'The Guru Phase' (1600–1707) thus: 'Some of the elements that provided significant axes of identity in the history of the embryonic community are well known: allegiance to the person of the founder of the Sikh faith, Guru Nanak, and his nine successors; identification with their teachings (bani); the foundation of congregations (sangats); the setting up of pilgrim centres at places like Govindwal and Amritsar; the convention of a communal meal (langar); and the compilation by Guru Arjan of an anthology that ultimately became the sacred scripture of the community, making Sikhs, like the Judeo-Christians, into a people of the Book' (Oberoi 31).

8 Dipankar Gupta also observes that towards the end of the 1970s, the communalisation of Punjab begins with the rise of what he terms as "new minority" (1185) of Sikhs within the nation-state. Both the leftists and the liberals pitch in this process of the communalisation of the space of Punjab. He observes, 'The entire gamut of left politics is quite rudderless. Several discordant voices pulling in different directions can be heard from the ranks of even the CPI (M). Many leftists, particularly in the CPI, even found words of praise for the Operation Blue Star which killed hundreds of innocent pilgrims to claim the lives of approximately fifty militants led by Bhindranwale. Many among them also considered the Anandpur Sahab resolution as one potent with mischief which only reveals that they have either not read the resolution or did not like the confident look of the Sikhs' (1186).

9 The ideology of Left has undergone a process of expansion as it moves away from a rather economically determined dialectical materialism of Marx to the everydayness of cultural materialism as theorised by Raymond Williams. Raymond Williams in his book Marxism and Literature (1977) overturns the orthodox way of approaching culture only as a part of the superstructure (75–82). He insists that culture determines material practices as much as material practices determine the culture. He goes on to include the category of the 'residual,' along with the categories of the dominant and the emergent to map the make-up of culture at any point in time (121–27).

10 Of course, right from Daniel Bell's apocalyptic pronouncement about the death of ideology in 1960s in his *The End of Ideology* (1960) to Francis Fukuyama's equally sensational thesis of the end of history in his book *The End of History and the Last Man* (1992), the role of ideology in the formation of cultural identity has been questioned and even summarily dismissed by a host culture critics, but in the Indian context, Sekhon was perhaps the first one to use the expression of 'post-progressive.'

11 The modernist and experimental poets like Haribhajan Singh, Ajaib Kamal and Meesha (one might add names of Sati Kumar, Jasbir Singh Ahluwalia, Surjit Haans, etc.), and romanticists like Shiv Kumar, and idealists like Sukhpal Veer Singh Hasrat, among others collectively steered modern Punjabi poetry towards a different direction of aestheticism, away from the clutches of ideology which their predecessors had imbibed to a large extent.

12 Gopal Singh, a well-known Punjab scholar, sums up the negative fallouts of the Green revolution thus: 'The green revolution has resulted in an uneven development not only in different regions of the State but also for the population within a region. This unevenness has resulted in a growing pauperisation of marginal and poor peasants, thus adding to the army of the landless, who have no employment avenues in urban areas because there is insufficient industrial development. . . . The fruits of the Green Revolution appear to have been grabbed by just 20 percent of Jat landlords who own more than 60 percent of the total land' ('Socio-Economic Bases of the Punjab Crisis,' 42).

13 Naxalbari is the name of a village in the Darjeeling district of North Bengal in eastern India . . . tea plantations abound. There Charu Majumdar organised the workers and peasants against the feudal forces. On 24 May 1967, a large police force tried to enter a village that was waging a new struggle. . . . The rebellion was crushed within a short time in the place of its birth. However, it raised waves of struggle' (Bhattacharyya 2016: 37).

14 Dalit Panthers was a radical anti-caste organisation, full of young neo-literate Dalits. It was founded by Namdeo Dhasal and J V Pawar on 29 May 1972 in Mumbai. It was modelled on the lines of Black Panthers (US).

15 This is how a commentator describes the turbulence of the late '60s in the US: 'The decade began with hopeful idealism – symbolized by the student sit-ins, the rhetoric of the Port Huron Statement (founding manifesto of the New Left) and John F. Kennedy's call to service. It reached its apogee in mid-decade with the Mississippi Freedom Summer, the Berkeley Free Speech Movement, and Lyndon Johnson's electoral landslide. Then, in the context of an escalating and bitterly divisive war in Vietnam and growing social dislocation at home, the idealism curdled into disillusionment and despair. The year 1968 – which witnessed the assassinations of Martin Luther King and Robert Kennedy, and the riot at the Democratic Party's national convention in Chicago – marks the symbolic end of "the sixties": with the New Left and civil rights movements in decline and mired in factionalism, the liberal consensus unravelling, and Richard Nixon triumphant. The strains of "We Shall Overcome" were displaced by cries of "Burn, Baby, Burn" (Hall 655).

16 The rhetoric of martyrdom begins to acquire a place of importance in Sikh texts after 1700, which Harjot S. Oberoi terms as "metacommentaries" of "the heroic age." He refers to some them such as 'Sainapati's Sri Gur Sobha (1711), Sukha Singh's Gurbilas Dasvin Patsahi (1797), Koer Singh's Gurbilas Patsahi, and Sohan's Gurbilas Chhevin Patsahi (the last two texts were written in the first half of the nineteenth century) – are devoid of any representation of Punjab in Sikh identity. Their dominant concern is to exhibit the lives, valour and battles fought by the sixth and tenth Sikh Gurus. Sikh identity in these metacommentaries begins to be defined through a powerful myth of origin, whose principal characteristics are bravery, suffering, persecution, blood, sacrifice, and martyrdom. The climax of the heroic age is reached by Rattan Singh Bhangu's influential metacommentary Prachin Panth Prakash finished in 1841. He further enlarged the corpus of the Sikh origin myth through an exegesis of the conventions noted above. The Khalsa community was born out of blood and martyrdom' (34). Later on, ideologues of Singh Sabha buttressed this sentiment of martyrdom as central to Sikh way of life.

17 Amarjit Chandan, during his days as an active Naxal, also edited a journal *Dastavej* in which he carried out poems, stories and articles of the underground revolutionaries. Though he was not in the vanguard

of the radical Punjabi progressives, yet he did a seminal job of collating and editing Naxalite literature produced during the 1960s and 1970s. It was in this journal that the poets like Pash and Dil were published for the first time. It had a short run of seven editions, and it did not deliberately carry the name of the press and the publisher to escape the backlash of the state. Chandan himself informs in an interview that neither he nor anyone else possesses any copy of any edition of Dastavej today (*Anokha te Ekalla Amarjit Chandan,Hun*, 5).

18 Irfan Habib and S. K. Mittal inform, 'The Naujawan Sabha openly held Gandhi responsible for the death of Bhagat Singh and his comrades. "If Mahatma Gandhi had made it a condition of peace, the execution might not have taken place"' (37).

19 Amrita Pritam describes the poetry of the '60s as the poetry of "hot blood": 'The new poetry here means only such creation that has come from one's hot pulsating blood. Whatever is written for cheap popularity is mere versification. . . . Strangely enough, the writers who have lent their voice to the times and have written about this life have been labelled difficult, immoral and unhealthy. . . . A good writing is not that attracts applause but one that causes thinking' (1971: 47).

20 During the early 1970s in Hindi poetry, for instance, a school of anti-poetry called akavita or *nishedh kavita* employed the same kind of language. Here is one example:

> . . . and from the debris
> I choose a half-burnt girl
> Who could be prepared for producing offspring
> Excuse me, my times
> I cannot be of any use to you right now
> Because I. . .
> Am undergoing treatment for my impotence.
> ("Mukhbir," *Nishedh*, Vinay, 64)

21 Tejwant Singh Gill sums up the murderous credo of jujharvadi poetry thus: '[It] was written through the barrel of a gun rather than through the point of a pen.' He buttresses his observation through a quote of Haribhajan Singh, a poet who was often pilloried for his rather too experimental reflective poetry thus:

> What sort of poetry is this o friends,
> That rather than the heart comes from the barrel of a gun
> Not meant for hearing, it is fired instead
> What sort of a couplet is it o friend, that upholds murder,
> Written not with one's own but other's blood.
> (Quoted by Tejwant Gill, 200–201)

22 'The Singh Sabha movement arose as a systematic attempt to purge these impure internal 'Others' from the Sikh 'Self' by redefining Sikh identity in the light of the institutional and conceptual innovations of colonial modernity. After 1849, Sikhs and other Punjabis were confronted by unprecedented cultural challenges. . . . These included the influence of both Christianity and the secular 'ideologies' of Liberalism

Ideology as identity 97

and colonial difference upon 'traditional' religious beliefs and practice. . . . Under siege, on the one hand, from Christian missionaries aligned with British administrators and, on the other, by the semitized neo-Hinduism of the Arya Samaj, Sikhs endeavoured to work out their [own] modernity' (Shani 2008: 32). And The Babbar Akalis were members of the Babbar Akali Jatha, a militant organisation which, unlike other Akali jathas, sanctioned the use of violence against mahants and their British protectors in the Gurdwara reform movement between 1922 and 1923.

23 Pritam Singh points towards the lack of intellectual tradition among local Punjabi Marxists thus: 'In fact, there has been a culture of anti-intellectualism in the Left parties. . . . A critical attitude is not only not encouraged. It is consciously curbed. . . . The official literature produced either by Moscow or Peking is considered as the only desirable reading material' ("Marxism in Punjab," 544). Another commentator on Punjab politics Bharat Dogra also corroborates: 'Thus those who came to the leftist movement initially attracted by vague notions of socialism did not get the sort of education or guidance which would have strengthened these vague notions into strong, clear concepts or programmes which could have secured their wholehearted commitment' (565).

24 Many former revolutionaries, later on, turn out not just sympathisers but supporters of Khalistani movement. Santokh Singh Dheer observes Sant Singh Sekhon: 'Intelligent men like Sekhon during the Khalistani movement turned into fascist writing in favour of the killers of the innocents as young, innocent, revolutionary children' (*Hun* 5, 23). Ajmer Singh who was a leading Naxalite, after 1984Operation Blue Star, becomes a passionate votary of Khalistan. Ajmer Singh introduced the cover of his book *Sikhaan di Sidhantak Gherabandi* (2015) as follows: 'For about one and a half decade, he gained from close quarters the experience of communist revolutionary movement in disguise. But in 1984 following the attack on Shri Darbar Sahib, he was thoroughly shaken, and he gradually drifted towards realising his own cultural roots and legacy, he emerged as an analyzer of the concerns of Sikh struggle' (Inside Cover).

25 In his brief write up on Pash, Rajesh Sharma also tends to trace post-ideological tendencies in the poetry of the poet thus: 'This suspicion of ideology is a grim warning against ideological complicity, including our own, in a so-called post-ideological world. Against ideological straitjacketing, Pash pits existential experience which the poetic language for him has, as it has for Heidegger, the strength to protect' (29).

26 Amarjit Chandan has translated his Punjabi quote into English.

27 Amarjit Chandan quotes Kabir from an unknown source thus: hum sabh maye, sabh hai hum maye, hum hai bahuri akela [we are in all, all are in us, we are very forlorn]. One of the entries from Kafka's Diaries is also quoted along with the earlier line from Kabir: 'Anyone who cannot cope with life while he is alive needs one hand to ward off a little his despair over his fate . . . but with his other hand he cannot jot down what he sees among the ruins for he sees different and more things than

others; after all, he is dead in his own lifetime and the real survivor' (Diaries, 19 October 1921).
28 Begumpura is Guru Ravidass's utopia – a land without sorrow and pain. Shabad 3 of his amritbani – Begampura sahar ko naoo!! /Dukh andohu nahi tihi thaao!!/ . . . (Ravidass, 72–73) – means that Ravidass is a citizen of the world known as "Begampura" that is devoid of any grief. There is no room for any pain and worry in that world.
29 Patrick Grant in his book *Literature of Mysticism in the Western Tradition* explains the poetics of roundness thus 'One characteristic of great writing on the subject of spiritual progress is, therefore, to take a certain position, and to proceed along a definite way, and yet to make of the commitment something infinitely suggestive of realities that lie outside of its path or trajectory. There is a certain 'roundness' to such writing which is partly the fruit of an ability not to identify wisdom literally with any method or sequence of steps or stages, while nonetheless holding that we are creature of contingency' (130).
30 'Many definitions serve to explain the Punjab crisis, each naturally implying different remedies. The definitions fall into three main groups, depending on the level of organisation one looks at. At the household level in Punjab, it is primarily economic; at the level of state-wide political discussions, it is legal and constitutional. Only at the national level is it primarily religious, and this construction is mainly the product of actions of the central government, more specifically the government of the late Indira Gandhi, and not the people or politicians of Punjab' (Leaf 1985: 475–76).
31 However, the possibility of atavistic returns to the credo of sword can still be seen in a ghazal written as late as 2006: 'Why should I fear the harshness of sun/ I am protected by the shadow of sword on my head/ The blood on its own has moved towards the battle-ground/ it is not under my control' (Ghazal no. 258, Jagtar, *Mere Andar Ek Samundar*, 358).
32 Matthew Arnold, a Victorian poet and culture critic, held that since creed and dogma had lost credibility, serious poetry would provide "an ever surer stay" (1973: 161) in the age of doubt. He wrote, 'More and more Mankind will discover that we will have to turn to poetry to interpret life for us, to console us, to sustain us' (161).

References

Ahmad, Aijaz. "The Progressive Movement in Its International Setting." *Social Scientist* 39 (11–12) (November–December 2011): 26–32.
Arnold, Matthew. 1973. "The Study of Poetry." In *Matthew Arnold: English Literature and Irish Politics*, edited by R.H. Super, 161–188. Michigan: University of Michigan Press.
Bell, Daniel. 1960. *The End of Ideology: On the Exhaustion of Political Ideas in the Fifties*. New York: The Free Press.
Bhattacharyya, Amit. 2016. *Storming the Gates of Heaven: The Maoist Movement in India*. Kolkata: Setu Prakashan.

Chandan, Amarjit. 1975. *Kaun Nahin Chahega*. Chandigarh: Rangshala Prakashan.
———. 1984. *Kavitavaan*. New Delhi: Navyug.
———. 1995. *Jarhaan*. Ludhiana: Aesthetic Publications.
———. 1996. *Bijak*. New Delhi: Navyug.
———. 1998. *Chhanna*. New Delhi: Navyug.
———. 2000. *Gurhati*. New Delhi: Navyug.
———. 2005. "Anokha te Ekalla Amarjit Chandan: Gallan" (An Interview given on 10 April 2005 at London). *Hun* (June–December): 1–18.
———."Bahut Chup Kitiyan da Kavi." Lal Singh Dil's, *Naglok*, 19–24.
———. 1989. "Pash di Kavita." In *Khilre Hoye Verke*, edited by Amarjit Chandan. New Delhi: Navyug.
Cranston, Maurice. "That Is an Ideology?" *Revue européenne des sciences sociales*, T. 17, No. 46, L'ubiquité de L'idéologie: Hommage à Raymond Polin,1979. 59–63. JSTOR.
Dhiman, Kuldeep. 1999. "Real Home of Man Is Where He Has Dignity." Interview with Amarjit Chandan, *The Sunday Tribune*, June 6.
Dil, Lal Singh. 2007. *Naglok: Kavitavaan*. Ludhiana: Chetna Prakashan.
———. 1998. *Dastaan*. Ludhiana: Chetna Prakashan.
Dogra, Bharat. 1986. "Communal Tensions and Left Forces." *Economic and Political Weekly* 21 (14) (April 5): 565–66.
Fatehjeet.1973. *Kachi Mitti de Baune*. Jallandar: Lokayit Prakashan.
Fukuyama, Francis. 1992. *The End of History and the Last Man*. New York: The Free Press.
Gautam, Satyapal. "Maan Boli Simardiyan Hoye." Amarjit Chandan's, *Chhanna*, 11–18.
Gharu, Gurdas Singh. 2000. *Pagdandiyan ton Jeevan Marg tak*. Sirsa: Sant Ram Udasi Yaadgari Parkashan.
Giil, Tejwant Singh, trans and ed. 1999. *Reckoning with Dark Times: 75 Poems of Pash*. New Delhi: Sahitya Akademi.
———. 2006. "Reading Modern Punjabi Poetry: From Bhai Veer Singh to Surjit Patar." *Journal of Punjab Studies* 13 (1–2): 185–214.
Grant, Patrick. 1983. *Literature of Mysticism in the Western Tradition*. London and Basingstoke: Palgrave Macmillan.
Gupta, Dipankar. 1985. "The Communalising of Punjab 1980–1985." *Economic and Political Weekly* 20 (28) (July 13): 1185–90.
Gurbachan. 1972. "Punjabi Literature in 1971 – A Critical Survey." *Indian Literature*15 (4): 89–98.
———."Lal Singh Dil: Viralaan chon Jhakda Jahar." Lal Singh Dil's, *Naglok*, 153–59.
Habib, Irfan, and S. K. Mittal. 1979. "Towards Independence and Socialist Republic: Naujawan Bharat Sabha, Part Two." *Social Scientist* 8 (87) (October): 31–40.
Hall, Simon. 2008. "Protest Movements in the 1970s: The Long 1960s." *Journal of Contemporary History*43 (4) (October): 655–72.

Hall, Stuart, and Paul du Gay, ed. 1996. *Questions of Cultural Identity*. London: Sage.
Halwaravi, Harbhajan. 1981. *Paun Udaas Hai*. Ludhiana: Lahore Book Shop.
Jagtar. 2001. *Mere Andar Ek Samundar*. Jalandhur: Deepak Publishers.
———. 2003. *Lahoo de Naksh*. Revised ed. Chandigarh: Lokgeet Prakashan.
———. 1990. *Chanukari Sham*. Jalandhur: Deepak Publishers.
Jalil, Rakshshanda. 2014. *Linking Progress, Loving Change: A Literary History of the Progressive Writers Movement in Urdu*. New Delhi: Oxford University Press.
Josh, Bhagwan Singh. "Vichadhara ton Mukt Kavita." http://amarjitchandan.tripod.com/Bhagwan1.pdf. Accessed on August 23, 2016.
Kennan, George.1947. (published under the anonymous name of "X"). "The Sources of Soviet Conduct." *Foreign Affairs* (July) Issue. ww.foreignaffairs.com/articles/russian-federation/1947-07-01/sources-soviet-conduct. Accessed on September 12, 2016.
Kesar Singh, Kesar. 2005. *Pragativadi Vichardhara te Punjabi Kavita*. Ludhiana: Chetna Prakashan.
Khatkar, Darshan. 1973. *Sangi Saathi*. Amritsar: Balraj Sahni Ghrelu Yadgar Pustakshala.
———. 2010. *Ulte Rukh Parvaz*. Ludhiana: Chetna Prakashan.
Leaf, Murray J. 1985. "The Punjab Crisis." *Asian Survey* 25 (5) (May): 475–98.
Lyons, Eugene. 1941. *The Red Decade: The Stalinist Penetration of America*. Indianapolis: Bobbs-Merrill.
Malhotra, Anshu, and Farina Mir, eds. 2012. *Punjab Reconsidered: History, Culture, and Practice*. Oxford and Delhi: Oxford University Press.
Noor, Satinder Singh. 1972. *Naveen Kavita: Seema te Sambhavna*. Ambala Cant: Vidvan Prakashan.
Oberoi, Harjot S. 1987. "From Punjab to 'Khalistan': Territoriality and Metacommentary." *Pacific Affairs* 60 (1) (Spring): 26–41.
Parwana, Balbir. 2004. *Kala, Jindagi te Naxali Sarokar*. Barnala: Tarakbharati Prakashan.
Pash. 2002. *Sampooran Pash-Kavi*. 4th ed. 2008. Ludhiana: Chetna Prakashan.
———. 1989. *Khilre Hoye Verke*. Edited by Amarjit Chandan. Nakodar: Lok Katha.
Patar, Surjit. 1979. *Hava Vich Likhe Haraf*. 6th edition. 1998. Ludhiana: Lahore Book Shop.
———. 1992. *Birkh Arz Kare*.10th ed. 2014. Amritsar: Lok Sahit Prakashan, Chandigarh: Lokgeet Prakashan.
———. 1992. *Haneri Vich Sulgadi Varnamala*. New ed. Ludhiana: Shabadlok, Chandigarh: Lokgeet Prakashan, 2014.

———.1999. *Lafzan di Dargah*.2nd ed. 2000. Ludhiana: Lahore Book Shop.

———. 1998. "Kavita da Janam." In *Surjt Patar de Kavita da Samvad*, edited by Satinder Singh Noor, and Vanita, 184–88. New Delhi: Punjabi Akademi.

Pritam, Amrita. 1971. "Punjabi: Hot Blood Poetry." *Indian Literature* 14 (1) (March): 46–51.

Rahi, Rajinder. 2011. "Dooji Vaar Sampadki." In *Sant Ram Udasi: Jeevan te Samuchi Rachana*. Ludhiana: Chetna Prakashan.

Ravidas. 2013. *Amritbani Satguru Shri Ravidass Maharaj Ji* (Steek). Trans. Shri Piare Lal. Jalandhar: Ravi Parkash Printing Press.

Sandhu, Sant. 1970. *Sis Tali Te*. Amritsar: Sudarash Press.

Sekhon. Sant Singh. 1955. *Kaav Doot*. Ludhiana: Lahore Book Shop.

———. 1963. "Uttar-Pragativad." *Alochana*, February, 4–9.

Shani, Giorgio. 2008. "From Panth To Qaum: The Construction of a Sikh 'national' Identity in Colonial India." In *Sikh Nationalism and Identity in a Global Age*, 17–39. London and New York: Routledge.

Sharma, Rajesh. 2014. "Pash – Killed, Not Finished." In *In/disciplines: Notes on Politics, Education and Culture*, 27–36. New Delhi: Three Essays Collective.

Singh, Ajmer. 2015. *Sikhaan di Sidhantak Gherabandi*. Amritsar: Sikh Brothers.

Singh, Gopal. 1984. "Socio-Economic Bases of the Punjab Crisis." *Economic and Political Weekly* 19 (1) (January 7): 42–47.

Singh, Gopal. 1994. "Complexities of the Question of Sikh Nationality." *Economic and Political Weekly* 29 (29) (July 16): 1877–82.

Singh, Mohan. 2012. *Prof. Mohan Singh Rachnavali*. Edited by Dr. Dhanwant Kaur.2nd ed. Patiala: Publication Bureau Punjabi University.

Singh, Pritam.1985. "Marxism in Punjab." *Economic and Political Weekly* 20 (13) (March 30): 543–44.

Singh, Takhat. 1956. *Vangaar*, 60. Jalandhur: Hind Publishers Ltd.

Sukhdev. 2007. "Jagtar-kavi de Vicharparak Sarokar." In *Kavi-Vihar*, 70–82. Chandigarh: Lokgeet Prakashan.

Williams, Raymond. 1977. *Marxism and Literature*. Oxford and New York: Oxford University Press.

Chapter 5

Flying high or lying low?
The moral economy of young women in higher education in Punjab, India

Navtej K. Purewal and Manpreet K. Gill

This study builds on evidence from secondary data sets which point to trends of changing participation patterns in higher education. While at a glance an increase in women's enrolment in higher education might be interpreted to reflect a rising value being placed on women's education, our qualitative assessment of this increase reveals a more complex picture in which women's education has become incorporated into broader aspirations around migration and marriage which are shaping the moral economy and its gendered value, with new and oftentimes more restricting cultural values being associated with women's educational pursuits.

* * * * *

Introduction

The college or university campus has provided a ready-made set for countless Indian films in showing storylines in which young men and young women intermingle and pursue academic and personal aspirations on the oasis-like campuses in these cinematic depictions. While the fantasy of film accentuates the liminality of college-going as a time of opportunities for freedom and youth romance as a precursor to familial obligation, marriage and working life, film fantasy is not so distantly removed from the experiences of young women and men who attend college and university. The dreams, fantasies and aspirations that college-going represents at this age are universal. It is their symbolism and links to social and economic lived realities which we are concerned with and will be exploring in this chapter.

In India, the picture of the expansion of higher education shows that the demand for places in higher education institutions is increasing but that enrolment trends are gendered. The total gross enrolment in higher education in India is 19.4%, while it is 20.8% for males and 17.9% for females. While state-wise data show evidence of higher ratios of female enrolment in states such as U.P., Meghalaya, Himachal Pradesh and Kerala, the focus of our study is on the northwest state of Punjab where the differential in gross enrolment ratio (GER) shows 23.6% male and 14.5% female GER, respectively, one of the highest gaps in India from the available statewise data. While higher education discursively presents emancipatory potentials for young women through professional training and career paths, this study finds that any examination of enrolment and attendance must be viewed regarding how education is socially embedded. The family, in particular, regulates and values women's education through strategic decision-making, thus presenting pressures for women to not necessarily 'fly high' for personal motivations, but to navigate broader collective family attitudes and goals. While the gender impacts of the Green Revolution's capitalist agriculture on Punjab in the 1970s were recognised by Sharma (1980) as withdrawing women of land-owning families in particular from the public sphere as a sign of status, our exploration of women's higher education in the contemporary context of Punjab shows that the regulation of women's mobility as a sign of status and respectability has continued through the subsequent decades.

The global context of higher education attainment highlights the new meanings being attached to women's education as a tool for social mobility through marriage alliances and global migration as this relates to their families' aspirational desires. The evidence of more women pursuing higher education shows how education as a principle is being promoted on the grounds of uplifting women in encouraging them to "fly high" according to aspirational and globalising discourses. Meanwhile, the perception of young women's education by parents continues to circulate as a threat to the social order in which young women are encouraged to "lie low." One might also assume that "flying high" refers to either or both the aspirations to achieve and the desire to migrate abroad. In examining this metaphor, the chapter draws on Bourdieu's logic in exploring how the gender context of the Punjabi household is engaging with the heightened participation of young women in higher education showing how the objective logic exists as an ideal is shaping women's educational experience, attainment and outcomes. The chapter will argue that higher education institutions are promoting education for women within this objective logic resulting in a mixed picture of raising young women's aspirations while simultaneously containing them.

The logic of practice: the moral economy of young women and higher education in Punjab

Punjab is associated with agriculture and, as such, has been popularly coined as the "breadbasket of India." Studies of the development of capitalist agriculture and its socio-economic impacts have charted the transformations to social and class relations resulting from the Green Revolution strategy for agricultural growth through mechanisation, chemical inputs and new forms of loans for financing investment for farmers (Byres 1981; Frankel 1971). However, as Bhalla (2004) states, 'Punjab today presents a paradox. . . . The state boasts of one of the highest per capita incomes in India . . . but the number of girls has shrunk alarmingly.' The moral panic of the sex ratio constitutes a significant and pervasive public discourse in Punjab. The campaigns have been carried out in the state to mete out the 'culprits' of sex-selective abortions and to 'discipline the sex ratio' through both criminalisation of sex selection and incentives to uplift the status of the girl child (Purewal 2014, 2018). The scarce women scenario in Punjab has seen its inclusion in India's '*kurhi maru*' list of states identified by the central government's tracking of sex ratios (see Table 5.1).

Table 5.1 highlights the profile of the state of Punjab in its high rank regarding per capita income since 1961 and its near bottom ranking in comparison to other Indian states in terms of the sex ratio. As can be seen in the table, there is an inverse relationship in Punjab between per capita income and sex ratio which has further been explored by some in terms of a 'parity effect' seeing an intensification of male bias despite decreasing rates of fertility (Das Gupta 1995; Das Gupta and Mari Bhat 1997) and by others in terms of how masculinist models of social organisation and economic growth have historically led to deepened gender inequalities (Oldenburg 2002; Purewal 2010; Kaur and Larsen 2013). Punjab thus provides a context in which to explore these multiple facets and outcomes of patriarchal and masculinist development resulting in 'scarce women' and 'surplus men,' the lens through which we now will analyse women's presence in higher education.

Table 5.1 Rank-wise per capita income and sex ratio across the states of India

STATE	Per capita income						Sex ratio					
	1961	1971	1981	1991	2001	2011	1961	1971	1981	1991	2001	2011
A.P.	9	16	18	13	10	13	9	7	5	5	4	3
ARUN. P	NA	20	22	14	18	12	23	28	27	28	24	17
ASSAM	6	7	8	10	21	24	26	20	21	15	14	14
BIHAR	16	21	23	23	28	28	6	9	11	21	20	23
JHARKHAND	NA	NA	NA	NA	26	23	10	12	14	16	13	16
GOA	NA	6	1	1	1	2	1	4	6	7	11	9
GUJARAT	4	9	10	9	9	5	13	16	13	13	19	22
HARYANA	5	1	3	3	3	3	27	25	25	27	28	28
H.P	NA	4	5	5	5	10	14	8	7	3	8	11
J&K	10	5	4	11	19	20	24	22	22	22	25	27
KARNATAKA	7	14	15	16	8	11	11	10	9	8	9	10
KERALA	11	3	7	7	7	9	2	1	1	1	1	1
M.P.	12	15	17	19	23	25	18	18	17	19	21	19
CHHATTISGHAR	NA	NA	NA	NA	24	21	5	2	2	2	2	5
MAHARASHTRA	1	8	6	4	4	4	16	17	15	14	18	20
MANIPUR	17	18	14	18	22	26	3	5	8	9	5	4
MEGHALAYA	NA	NA	11	12	17	15	15	13	10	10	6	6
MIZORAM	NA	NA	NA	NA	11	16	4	11	18	17	15	8
NAGALAND	NA	NA	9	6	13	14	19	24	26	23	22	18

(Continued)

Table 5.1 (Continued)

STATE	Per capita income						Sex ratio					
	1961	1971	1981	1991	2001	2011	1961	1971	1981	1991	2001	2011
ORISSA	15	12	16	22	25	22	7	3	3	6	7	7
PUNJAB	**3**	**2**	**2**	**2**	**2**	**8**	**28**	**26**	**24**	**24**	**26**	**25**
RAJASTHAN	8	11	11	15	20	19	20	19	19	20	17	21
SIKKIM	NA	NA	NA	NA	14	1	22	27	28	25	27	26
TAMIL NADU	NA	10	13	8	6	6	8	6	4	4	3	2
TRIPURA	14	19	19	20	15	18	17	14	12	11	12	13
U.P.	13	17	20	21	27	27	12	15	16	12	10	12
UTTARAKHAND	NA	NA	NA	NA	16	7	21	23	23	26	23	24
WEST BENGAL	2	13	12	17	12	17	25	21	20	18	16	15

Source: Census of India 1961, 1971, 1981, 1991, 2001, 2011

Flying high or lying low? 107

The gendered dimension to the agricultural base shapes how the education of boys and girls is viewed under gender norms and ideals. While landless and poorer families are unlikely to send their male or female children to colleges out of economic necessity for their labour contributions to the household, landed and more privileged families in the region have been known to withhold their daughters from further education beyond primary schooling due to heightened regulation of girls' mobility and codes of humility and honour which can be viewed as compromised by girls' mobility in the public sphere (Mandelbaum 1988). Sengupta and Guha (2002) argue that while parental education, income and occupation have the strongest impact on girls' schooling opportunities and attainments, daughters of agricultural families have the lowest participation at higher levels of education. However, land-owning families, because of land, are also known to invest in their daughters' education and not in their son's education, to keep them in agriculture (Heyer, this volume). While the material base of agricultural families posits girls at a distinctive disadvantage within this context of decision-making associated with education, the post-Green Revolution context of Punjab is seeing immense changes to rural sensibilities, requiring more qualitative assessment of this evolving picture.

The moral economy of peasant societies require customs and social 'norms' to survive, as systems which are governed by mutuality within social networks of economic actors and social units (Scott 1977). In this respect, the moral economy of the Punjab rural household operates as a system of surveillance of women's mobility and their access to public space due to women's necessary compliance with kinship custom and arrangements (Purewal and Hashmi 2014). It is here that we apply Bourdieu's (1992) thesis around the objective logic of the household within this moral economy of insecurity. We highlight that young women venturing into the public domain is often perceived as a risk-invoking act. Thus, the objective logic of the rural Punjabi household in the decision-making processes around young women's access to higher education is shaped by the symbolic function of female education within this moral economy of 'scarce women' in the forms of heightened moral policing of young women's movements as well as of women's higher education as an opportunity or hindrance for family-building strategies. Bourdieu's focus on the symbolic function of education is particularly useful for understanding how a discriminatory logic against young women's education exists alongside a strategising use of women's education for wider goals. Where education can serve these collective goals, young women are encouraged to "fly high," but where education presents threats to the patriarchal status quo by providing tools for women to challenge or question the status quo, they are encouraged to "lie low" in order to preserve cultural gender norms which constitute the practical logic informing the 'habitus.'

Our focus on the rural context of Punjab exhibits how the household unit acts as a site where decision-making, as well as discrimination, exist within its walls. The domestic mode of production, as highlighted by materialist feminists, points to the complex economic, social and cultural dynamics of the household stemming from the economic base of patrimony, gifts, inheritance, power and hierarchies of status and entitlements within the family (Delphy 1988). Diane Leonard's translated edition of Delphy's (1984) book Close to Home uses the rural context of France as a means of examining the significance of the family as a non-market sector of the economy in which agricultural families' identity and livelihood is centred on land and inheritance through male heirs, and this inheritance is not doled out equally. While sons are given land and property in their inheritance, daughters are given gifts or dowries which require them to marry and exist non-autonomously, thus entrenching them within the patriarchal structures of not only their natal family but also their marital family. Such an exploration of the sociology of children raises further questions about the position of children within family structures regarding sibling and generational relationships in which daughters' entitlements are undermined by their circumscribed position as non-inheriting members of the household unit. Feminist economists have probably contributed to the exploration of not only equality of opportunities but shifted the lens towards reproductive and productive labour and the equality of outcomes (Berik et al. 2009; Elson 1994; Chant 2011). Croll (2002) similarly highlights the structural position of girls vis-à-vis the family which is culturally embedded and has resulted in the sex ratio outcomes of discrimination against girl children. The material base of the household in deeming entitlements through patrimony across a range of contexts are significant in understanding the position of girls in the family where decisions around education are made.

The household unit is thus based on gendered differentiation which Delphy (1984) argues places the male patriarch at the centre through his discretionary powers to bestow inheritance according to his choice and preference, instilling hierarchies of authority and entitlements. She extends this notion of inheritance beyond property to include social and cultural capital which, for our purposes, would consist of the opportunities to access education. The negotiated hierarchies of gender through women's power must also be understood in terms of how the patriarchal family is not comprised of merely male authority but also of both women's complicity and active participation (Kandiyoti 1988). Applying this to the Indian context, Agarwal (1994), whose analysis of the structural dimensions of the household unit, utilises similar tools of understanding differential entitlements and gendered outcomes of systems of inheritance which create systemic barriers for women, explaining the resistance to women's access to property through the biased attitudes and practices against women's economic rights which argue that 'endowing a daughter with land is seen by the natal family as bringing little reciprocal benefit, and any land inherited by her as lost to the family'(2003: 204). Women's access to education and the understandings of the benefits (or risks) of investing in daughters' education must be situated within this a framework which considers not only the cultural attitudes towards gender but also the economic base which measures considerations around investments and benefits. This moral economy of higher education is gendered and informs our analysis here.

While the human capital discourse on girls' and women's literacy envisages a liberating effect of education on women's and families' lives (Colclough 1982), our analysis aligns with Kapadia's (2002) argument that the orientation of development processes is the cause for worsening status of women and declining sex ratios. The penetration of capitalism has resulted in what both Bhalla (2004) and Kapadia (2002) have characterised as a paradox of development. On the one hand, the household unit is becoming increasingly dependent on the domestic mode of production requiring women's continuing focus on the domestic, household sphere while, on the other hand, the marketisation of education presenting 'choices' to parents of girls as part of a broad schema of concerns laden with cultural values, rationalising assessments of returns, normative gender ideals and the domestic mode of production. These concerns constitute the gendered nature of the material relations of the family which are being challenged and reworked through the objective logic discussed earlier. It is these concerns regarding the domestic mode of production which is shaping girls' opportunities for being educated, and choices become narrower as they progress to secondary and then higher education. However, the picture is not as simple as this. While education is becoming commodified, the value of education within a society which places so much emphasis on kinship relations is also affecting women's access to education in evolving ways. Education can also present opportunities for families for whom social mobility and migration within the global circuits of settlement and 'arranged' marriages are taking place. In this light, the local market of education can be understood through the demand for skills in terms of how, for instance, English language and I.T. course offer new dimensions to how women can access education for ends tied to both individual aspirations as well as collective goals of the family. Higher education, thus, is expanding in subjects related to professional degrees such as medicine, engineering and law, but also other subjects which are deemed suitable, less ambitious and thus 'respectable' for young women to pursue and to still be rendered marriageable, or, as we have connoted, 'lying low.' As our qualitative material will highlight, the values which are comprised by kinship concerns and common family strategies are being routed through the educational system in which young women's aspirations are simultaneously raised through higher education while also systematically curbed through the educational experience.

The higher education data from the Punjab Statistical Abstract 2011–12 indicates that while there has been an increase in girls' share of enrolment since the 1990s in some courses (B.A, B.SC., M.A.) (Table 5.2), there are still more male students enrolled than girls in engineering, medicine and architecture (Table 5.3).

While Tables 5.2 and 5.3 show an increasing rate of women's participation in higher education by women, this is also subject-specific. Further to this, when we delved into these findings on a qualitative level, we found that women pursuing higher education negotiate a highly gendered terrain of parental and extended family discretion with regards to whether or not the opportunities to continue higher education should be awarded to them by their families. Thus, not only is the decision to go to college or university shaped by economic considerations (returns of the investment of education in light of conventions around women's imminent departure to their marital homes) but also culturally shaped gendered ones which deem girls' and young women's mobility in the public sphere a risk to her humility and the family's honour and respect.

Table 5.2 Percentage of students by gender enrolled at undergraduate level in Punjab

Year	B.A/B.A. (Hons.) Boys	Girls	B.Sc/B.Sc. (Hons.) Boys	Girls	B.Com/B.Com.(Hons.) Boys	Girls
1980	54.75	45.25	69.62	30.38	94.09	5.91
1990	43.98	56.02	53.73	46.27	68.69	31.31
2000	45.61	54.39	46.24	53.76	53.50	46.50
2008	42.92	57.075	31.58	68.42	50.08	49.92
2009	41.69	58.31	30.74	69.26	51.25	48.75
2010	42.30	57.70	30.60	69.40	50.25	49.75
2011	46.18	53.82	29.01	70.99	45.98	54.02

Source: *Punjab Statistical Abstract 2011–12*

Table 5.3 Percentage of students by gender enrolled in selected subjects in Punjab

Year	B.E./B.Sc.(Eng.) Boys	Girls	M.B.B.S Boys	Girls	B.Ed. Boys	Girls
1980	98.18	1.82	73.51	26.49	37.40	62.60
1990	92.04	7.96	55.08	41.56	30.98	69.02
2000	81.53	18.47	52.81	47.19	29.42	70.58
2008	78.22	21.78	49.96	49.38	26.48	73.52
2009	74.62	25.38	50.81	49.19	17.48	82.52
2010	74.98	25.02	45.86	37.17	17.48	82.52
2011	73.94	26.06	40.04	32.62	16.84	83.16

Source: *Punjab Statistical Abstract 2011–12*

Methods

This study draws on the trends of increased participation and subject-specific areas of representation of women in higher education as identified in the data sets of the University Grants Commission (UGC) and state government of Punjab Statistical Abstract (Tables 5.2 and 5.3). While the juxtaposition of the sex ratio with per capita income for the state highlights an inverse relationship or a paradox, women's education presents a slightly less straightforward picture. We intend to examine this increasing participation of women in higher education and to pursue questions around whether or not this represents a reversal of discrimination against girls and women and what these trends might be reflecting about more extensive socio-economic developments in terms of how women's status relates to education.

Our study is based on sites selected from two districts in Punjab: Moga and Jalandhar. The context of the sex ratio in Punjab and its districts can be seen in Table 5.4 where the sex ratio for Moga and Jalandhar is 893 and 915, respectively.

In focusing on the objective logic of the moral economy of rural households with development, we chose to focus on sites in Moga and Jalandhar, both districts showing some evidence of improvement in the sex ratio. Coupled with a heightening presence of women in higher education in these two districts, we intended to explore the dynamics at play behind the data in terms of decision-making, attitudes towards women's mobility and the value associated with women's education. We selected three colleges where six semi-structured interviews and nine focus groups were conducted between 2013 and 2014 (Table 5.5).

Table 5.4 Sex ratio in the districts of Punjab

Districts	1951	1961	1971	1981	1991	2001	2011
Gurdaspur	846	869	890	907	903	890	895
Amritsar	841	854	856	871	873	871	889
Tarn Taran	NA	NA	NA	NA	NA	887	900
Kapurthala	880	886	889	898	896	888	912
Jalandhar	**857**	**867**	**883**	**890**	**897**	**887**	**915**
Hoshiarpur	877	902	899	919	924	935	961
Rupnagar	812	812	854	862	870	889	915
Ludhiana	852	856	848	860	844	824	873
Ferozepur	835	840	876	884	895	885	893
Faridkot	856	849	866	879	883	883	890
Muktsar	862	846	863	885	880	891	896
Moga	**867**	**862**	**866**	**881**	**884**	**887**	**893**
Bathinda	839	834	851	861	884	870	868
Mansa	824	830	852	869	873	879	883
Sangrur	820	832	840	860	870	870	885
Barnala	NA	NA	NA	NA	NA	907	876
Patiala	809	831	850	870	881	875	891
Fatehgarh Sahib	773	815	831	841	871	854	871
PUNJAB	**844**	**854**	**865**	**879**	**882**	**876**	**895**
INDIA	**946**	**941**	**930**	**934**	**927**	**933**	**943**

Source: Director, Census operations Punjab

Table 5.5 Sampling of the qualitative study

	Interviews	Focus group discussions
Women's college Moga	1 teacher 1 principal	2 (women-only)
Co-ed college Jalandhar	1 teacher 1 principal	1 (mixed) 2 (men only) 1 (mixed, teachers)
Women's college Jalandhar	1 teacher 1 principal	2 (women-only)
Parents	–	1 (mixed)
Total	6	9

Source: Authors

The interviews included teachers, principals and young women and focus groups were conducted with female and male college students, teachers, principals and parents. All of the interviews and focus group discussions (FGDs) were recorded, transcribed and coded.

Our interest in employing qualitative methods in this study was to delve beneath the surface of the discourse around 'missing girls' and to develop an understanding of new meanings, changes and responses that are emerging with respect to the statistical evidence showing increasing women's participation in higher education in a state of consistently masculine sex ratios. Therefore, our sample reflects our interest in exploring the attitudes and reflections of teachers, parents, principals and, of course, students themselves. The remits drawn around young women's education in a context in which education is being promoted provided the central principle in directing our questions within the qualitative fieldwork in terms of how families, educational institutions, young men and, young women are responding. These remits are reflected on the qualitative data through the recurrent themes and concerns which emerged from the coded material.

Extending patriarchy: the threats of young women's education

The annual review for 2013 of one of the colleges focused on in this study was entitled 'chirhiyaan da Chamba' (transl. flock of birds), using the metaphor of the 'flock' to signify the home or college environment as the protective space for young women. The bird is popularly referred to highlight girls as temporary in their parental homes before 'flying off' to their marital homes explicitly rooting the metaphor in the social 'norms' of the moral economy. Thus, by evoking the flock of birds metaphor, the college projected itself as providing a 'safe' environment much like the home where young women are 'looked after' during the important years between the stages of unmarried youth and marriage. This must be understood both in terms of the depiction of the college space as a 'safe' place for young women as well as an extension of the household's moral policing role into the public educational and institutional spheres. In an interview with the principal of this women's college, she states that there is reluctance from parents to send their daughters to college and situates this reluctance within concerns around respect, a generational exertion of authority and a general lack of interest or commitment to women's education:

> Yes, there is an improvement from before, but only by a small percentage. Only a few parents really value the education of girls. . . . They don't see that a girl who studies won't just get married and move to their marital home but that her life will improve with the benefits that education brings to girls which they bring to themselves and their families.
>
> (Interview, August 2012)

To 'really value' the education of girls, as the principal here highlights, means to forego the risks associated with having a daughter who might have difficulty in eventually finding a suitable marriage match. The 'norm' of marriage appeared throughout the FGDs and interviews as a primary concern often in conflict with the education of young women at higher levels. This principal went on to say that the risks associated with daughters' education extend further:

A lot of parents say that by going to college, their respect will be ruined. They think that by going to college, they are risking tainting the respect and honour of their families by coming into contact with boys at college. From being a principal, I have the experience of seeing that the biggest responsibility to encourage girls to attend college is mothers. The grandmother (paternal) of the girls has the most say in this matter because often she is jealous because she did not have the opportunities and that she thinks 'why should these girls have the opportunities that we did not?' This is where the izzat factor comes in again and is used as an excuse for not sending girls to college. But more educated parents do not stop their girls in this way from attending college. They are more likely to support their girls in obtaining higher education.

It is within this understanding that the college utilises the flock of birds metaphor to highlight the college's commitment to showing its concerns for the safety of girls and of maintaining the respect of their families. Thus, the patriarchal ethos is extended from the home to the college as a continuum in which young women are looked after first by parents and then by the college as a form of extended patriarchy.

While most parents and teachers reflected overtly on the need to 'protect' girls as a duty of both family and college, the material base of gender relations is what informed how the value and threat of young women's education was being understood in terms of land, property and the gendered relations of the household unit, influencing relationships with siblings, especially brothers.

As a male I.T. teacher commented, 'Boys don't like the idea of their sisters having rights to half of their share of any family property' (age 43). In direct response, a female science teacher commented in defence of the patriarchal unit. She situated girls' attachment with their parents and siblings within the emotional ties and bonds which make daughters non-demanding entities within the economic realm of their natal household:

> Parents give their daughters so much love that why would girls want to take any land? Parents go out of their way to educate their daughters. Their prayers and blessings for their brothers and parents are their biggest role. I only wish for my brother's happiness. I would never take my share. Boys have the duty of serving and looking after their parents, so it is their right. . . . Girls also don't ask about their parents. It's not necessary that girls should look after their parents only because they have some rights over property. If a daughter is needy, then help should be given. Otherwise, nothing needs to be given. We, women, believe that we have to have good relations with our brothers, so what's the need for land and property?
>
> (Age 52)

The resistance from family members to permit girls to study backed by the moral policing of girls and young women framed most of the discussions around girls' experiences of education. The mother of a young woman who had recently completed her degree at the nearby college commented, 'My sons didn't want my daughter to continue studying, but we (my husband and I) ignored their complaints, and we made sure she completed her B.A. studies. Her Dad also supported me.'

One of the female colleges, also considered a 'safe' choice to send daughters to, was described by students:

> This college is near to our villages, and our parents don't want to send us to a co-ed college. When we are coming from home, boys tease and harass us so many parents don't send their daughters to study fearing this, especially in the villages.

The underlying patriarchal framework which frames the worth of investing in daughters' education or taking the risk to send daughters to college within a context of moral policing is necessarily an issue of women's autonomy which extends beyond the idea of having access to education into a comparative notion of rights relative to their male kin. Thus, the flock of birds metaphor which operates on an emotional as well as economic level is simultaneously bolstered by the *paraya dhan* (transl. 'others' property) depiction, in which women are married off and leave their natal homes to become a part of their in-laws' home, thus having no claims to parental property or inheritance. This presents the foundation for how the young women in our study are navigating the gendered and mediated access to education. A teacher in one of the colleges expressed this unequivocally by stating that not only are girls *paraya dhan* but sons, regardless of anything, are one's own. 'Girls become other people's property [*paraya dhan*] when they are married because sons are the ones who will be living with their parents. Whether they are alcoholics or taking drugs, a son belongs to his parents. Girls become a part of their in-laws' family.'

The young women in this study voiced some criticisms of this framing in an emerging determination to prove to family members that they can achieve, despite the characterisations of their weakness and vulnerability. One young woman vocalised this by stating: 'Girls can bring respect and pride to their parents by studying, and we should show them that girls can also do many things in spite of people continually stopping them.' In a focus group in one of the co-educational colleges, a young man highlighted an underlying tension around the question of the limits and threats of women's education when he commented on his preference regarding the ideal type of woman he would like to marry:

> She should be simple but educated, to educate the children. But she shouldn't have a job. Because if she works outside of the house, who will manage the household? Who will educate the children? Our parents have worked all their lives, so if she goes out, then who will look after my parents. I want to give them relief.

Thus, as this quote expresses, young women's education, while being necessary for the progress of the family, should be limited for the household to benefit in terms of her nurturing and caring functions, an embedded part of the moral economy, rather than as a professional or an income-generator. This notion is what lies at the crux of our title 'flying high, lying low.' While we are not using 'lying low' as a marker for women who do not pursue careers, what we are saying is that the curbing of women's aspirations and ambitions through higher education in order for them to not threaten the patriarchal order presents pertinent questions around how higher education is being inculcated into cultural and economic norms. Thus, to 'fly high' can often be viewed as a threat of women's education which can potentially destabilise the ideals of family, young women's respectability and the balance of the patriarchal order.

Arrangements of marriage and migration: evolving values of women's higher education

Migration abroad emerged as a significant theme in our exploration of higher education. Punjab is known as a for its steady flow of out-migration to places such as the USA, Canada, the UK, Australia and other parts of the world, particularly over the past six decades. Other studies which have focused on the impacts of global migration on Punjab either through labour migration and subsequent remittances or marriage and transnational kinship practices (Ballard 1990; Gardner 2006; Charnsley and Shaw 2006). We posit that education and higher education are rapidly becoming new arenas and institutions which are acting as conduits for migration, whether in terms of real strategies and realised plans or in terms of aspirations and imagined futures.

The educational system from primary to higher levels is rapidly expanded and shaped to fit with the demands that globalisation processes are presenting to Punjab. The cultural politics around migration and settlement abroad find a platform through education for the aspirations of young people and their families in strategising their futures (Qureshi and Osella 2013). However, we have found that the globalising influences, including aspirations around migration through education, do not entirely present a liberating picture for young women. Gender 'norms' of the moral economy is being reworked into the educational system rather than being challenged, as the flock of birds annual review poignantly illustrated. However, higher education's recent expansion and intensification in India has meant that it has not been part of this discussion to date. Our study of colleges in rural Punjab highlights how higher education has become a means by which the picture of the value and worth of women's credentials is extending the patriarchal ideology of the family while also intensifying it through institutions, creating certain contradictions around how to contain aspirations meanwhile capitalising on the education of women for family-building. As stated,

> A daughter is a big responsibility. If she is to go abroad, then she should get married and then go so that we will be relieved of our worries. If she goes abroad to study unmarried, then our worries will never end.

These concerns or 'worries' are encapsulated through the threat of a young woman migrating abroad to study without the protection of her male kin. Women's autonomy presents a threat to the social order, and thus education is commonly understood in this light. A young woman commented on her own experience of visiting relatives (not to migrate) and how local relatives reacted when she returned from her trip:

> Girls want to go abroad to have freedom. They want to escape from the pressures of brothers and parents. I went to Dubai, and I really liked it because no one interfered. . . . But after I returned I went to visit relatives in another village, and I found out that local people had begun to gossip saying that 'the girl must have run away.'

Thus, the 'safety' of girls is understood in regard to the threat of unwanted male attention, harassment or even the threat of daughters forming relationships. However, one of the biggest threats perceived was that of gossip. To avoid 'what people will say,' parents were known to make hasty decisions to marry daughters off to avoid such threats of dishonour via gossip. The classic mode through which gender relations and women's autonomy are commonly understood is through dowry (Sheel 1999). However, dowry as an institution is evolving and changing to the new functions of the family in the economy and therefore, it is not surprising that our study has found that dowry is being reworked through higher education as a means by which the family can negotiate the new terms and social contracts implicit in the establishment of social and kinship relations. The same female teacher who had earlier unquestioningly evoked the *paraya dhan* (others' property) depiction of girls also made the connection between dowry and education: 'Now, many parents are changing. If they don't have the money, they can't pay for dowries. And then, they value education in the hope of finding a good match for their daughters where they won't have to pay a hefty dowry.'

Her sense of a 'good match' is reliant on the assumption that educated people do not practice dowry. However, as a male teacher commented on how the expansion of education is not changing the attitudes towards gender and the role of dowry: 'Attitudes need to be changed. Education doesn't make a difference.' Perhaps more relevant are how young women themselves are viewing higher education as either a route to escape or challenge prescriptive roles for marriage or as a means by which to gain access to the diaspora through marriage abroad. In both of these scenarios, the notion of the daughter as a burden parents are intent on 'marrying off' lies at the centre of the decision-making process in terms of not wanting to bear the responsibility for the unmarried, 'unprotected' daughter:

> I am doing a dress-designing course, and then I will go abroad. But if I don't get admission onto a course abroad, then I'll get married and go. Parents prefer to get daughters married first so that their husbands will look after and take responsibility for them.

The emotional and moral responsibility is matched by the economic rationale for not taking a risk or investing finances into daughters' education, as is reflected on by another female student: 'Some parents think that if you're going to spend money on sending a daughter abroad, then it's better to just spend on the marriage to send her.' The blurring of priorities between educational investment and fulfilment of responsibilities for daughters' marital futures highlight the moral framework within which decisions are made which shape attitudes towards girls' and young women's education. The aspirations to study were not all met by the desire to migrate, though migration emerged as a theme in the context of possibilities and routes after graduation. The determination of the young women to prove to natal relatives that they could achieve despite the barriers and tacit negativity towards women's education was the overarching sense which we found from our focus groups and interviews. Young women in Punjab are also highlighting that there is a strong critique of the rhetoric to promote girls' and women's education while simultaneously discouraging and erecting barriers for them, especially in the face of heightening economic insecurity and the assertion of masculinity through the family and the public sphere. Agarwal (2003) notes,

> In the absence of an effective state social security system, brothers are seen as an important source of security, especially in case of a marital break-up. Cultural constructions of gender, including how a 'good sister' should behave, also discourage women from asserting their rights, as does the emphasis on female seclusion in many areas.

Our study points to this cultural construction in how moral policing is used to curb and regulate young women's access to not only education but also women's autonomy and access to public spaces. As one young woman commented: 'Girls can bring respect and pride to their parents by studying, and we should show them that girls can also do many things in spite of people continually stopping them.' Thus, it is clear from this young woman's statement that, despite structural obstacles and surveillance of their educational experiences, young women are conscious of the policing and the attitudes behind the decision-making around their education. This explains for why the college campuses and students covered in this study were replete with determination by so many young women to achieve in the face of tacit permission or even discrimination against them pursuing studies beyond secondary school.

Conclusion

As this chapter has highlighted, the moral economy within which young women's education is valued and permitted is constituted by an objective logic which positions women's educational access and opportunity within the collective concerns of gender norms and the patriarchal household's family-building strategies. Young women are popularly characterised in traditional sayings and songs and understood in their natal homes as *paraya dhan* (others' property) or *chirhiyaa da Chamba* (flock of birds). Meanwhile, the moral panic of 'scarce women' and masculine sex ratios or 'surplus men' points to a highly fraught scenario of women being simultaneously viewed as others' property while being in need of protection by one's own natal family. While we have argued that there is little scope for the expansion of higher education to provide liberating effects on women's aspirations due to the pervasiveness of this objective logic, our study highlights how young women and their parents and teachers are subversively answering back to these constructions of their structural vulnerability. In Punjab, a state where there is relatively high per capita income is also a place where grave concerns about young women's education are expressed as a challenge to the social order. However, despite negativity by parents which could deter many young women from pursuing their educational ambitions to 'fly high,' many continue to persevere and study under these conditions of tacit negativity about their desires to study further. So while there have been improvements in women gaining access to higher education in Punjab overall, the gendered terrain of attitudes towards women's autonomous ambitions still exists within the objective logic of the family, parental controls and how parents will be able to negotiate and even contain the impacts of higher education on their household and family aspirations in light of the potentially transformative impacts of young women's education.

As the colleges in our study have shown, the objective logic is being extended and expanded into educational institutions who appeal to the sentiments of parents, rather than challenging restrictions on young women to maintain the social order of the moral economy and the domestic mode of production. Thus, as we have highlighted, young college women often 'lie low' within the parameters of the patriarchal values while, as an act of persistent defiance or resistance, also project their aspirations and desires to 'fly high' beyond the gendered expectations placed on them. Young women are challenging this pigeonholing and patronisation in the *chirhiyaa da Chamba* depiction both regarding criticisms of their male kin as well as in terms of how they show they are aware of how they can utilise higher education as a means to navigate patriarchal restrictions. However, the limits of this are clear, and until women can challenge the material, economic base in asserting themselves beyond being non-inheritors or as *paraya dhan*, then we are looking at a future of scarce women becoming increasingly controlled, regulated and commodified in a moral economy in which higher education is providing new and evolving local and global circuits.

References

Agarwal, B. 1994. *A Field of One's Own: Gender and Land Rights in South Asia*. Cambridge: Cambridge University Press.

———. 2003. "Gender and Land Rights Revisited: Exploring New Prospects Via the State, Family and Market." *Journal of Agrarian Change* 3 (1–2): 184–224.

Ballard, R. 1990."Marriage and Kinship: The Differential Effect of Marriage Rules on the Processes of Punjabi Migration to Britain." In *South Asians Overseas: Contexts and Communities*, edited by C. Clarke, C. Peach, and S. Vertovek, 219–49. Cambridge: Cambridge University Press.

Berik, G., Y. Rodgers, and S. Seguino. 2009."Feminist Economics of Inequality, Development and Growth." *Feminist Economics* 15 (3): 1–33.

Bhalla, M. 2004. "The Land of Vanishing Girls: Sex Selective Abortion in Punjab." In *The Unheard Scream: Reproductive Health and Women's Lives in India*, edited by Mohan Rao, 259–78. Delhi: Zubaan.

Bourdieu, P. 1992. *The Logic of Practice*. Cambridge: Polity Press.

Byres, T. 1981. "The New Technology, Class Formation and Class Action in the Indian Countryside." *Journal of Peasant Studies* 8 (4): 405–54.

Chant, S. 2011. "Female Headship and the 'Feminisation of Poverty.'" In *Transnational Feminist Perspectives on Women*, edited by Women Worldwide, 334–36. New York: McGraw Hill Higher Education.

Charnsley, K. and A. Shaw. 2006. "South Asian Transnational Marriages in Comparative Perspective." *Global Networks* 6 (4): 331–44.

Colclough, C. 1982. "The Impact of Primary Schooling on Economic Development: A Review of the Evidence." *World Development* 10 (3): 167–85.

Croll, E. 2002. *Endangered Daughters: Discrimination and Development in Asia*. London: Taylor and Francis.

Das Gupta, M. 1995. "Fertility Decline in Punjab, India: Parallel with Historical Europe." *Population Studies* 49: 481–500.

Das Gupta, M., and P.N. Mari Bhat. 1997. "Fertility Decline and Increased Manifestation of Sex Bias in India." *Population Studies* 51 (3): 307–15.

Delphy, C. 1984. *Close to Home: A Materialist Analysis of Women's Oppression*. Translated and edited by D. Leonard. London: Hutchinson.

———. 1988. "Patriarchy, Domestic Mode of Production, Gender and Class." In *Marxism and the Interpretation of Culture*, edited by Cary Nelson and Lawrence Grossberg, translated by D. Leonard, 259–67. Urbana: University of Illinois Press.

Elson, D. 1994. "Micro, Meso, Macro: Gender and Economic Analysis in the Context of Policy Reform." In *The Strategic Silence: Gender and Economic Policy*, edited by I. Baker. London: Zed.

Frankel, F. 1971. *India's Green Revolution: Economic Gains and Political Costs*. Princeton, NJ: Princeton University Press.

Gardner, Katy. 2006. "The Transnational Work of Kinship and Caring: Bengali-British Marriages in Historical Perspective." *Global Networks* 6 (4): 373–87.

Kandiyoti, D. 1988. "Bargaining with Patriarchy." *Gender and Society* 2 (3), 274–90.

Kapadia, K. 2003. "Introduction: The Politics of Identity, Social Inequalities and Economic Growth." In *The Violence of Development: The Politics of Violence, Gender and Social Inequality in India*, edited by K. Kapadia, University of Chicago Press, 1–40.

Kaur, R., and M. Larsen. 2013. "Signs of Change? Sex Ratio Imbalance and Shifting Social Practices in Northern India." *Economic and Political Weekly* xlviII (35) (August 31).

Mandelbaum, D. 1988. "Women's Seclusion and Men's Honor: Sex Roles in North India." In *Bangladesh and Pakistan*. Tucson: University of Arizona Press.

Oldenburg, V.T. 2002. *Dowry Murder: Imperial Origin of a Cultural Crime*. Oxford: OUP.

Purewal, N. 2010. *Son Preference: Sex Selection, Gender and Culture in South Asia*. Oxford: Berg.

———. 2014. "Disciplining the Sex Ratio: Exploring the Governmentality of Female Feticide in India." *Identities: Global Studies in Culture and Power* 21 (5): 466–80.

———. 2018. "Sex Selection, Neoliberal Patriarchy and Structural Violence in India." *Feminist Review* 119 (1): 20–38.

Purewal, N., and N. Hashmi. 2014. "Between Returns and Respectability: Parental Attitudes Towards Girls' Education in Rural Punjab." *British Journal of Sociology of Education* 36 (7): 977–95. DOI:10.1080/01425692.2014.883274.

Qureshi, Kaveri, and Filippo Osella. 2013. "Transnational Schooling in Punjab India: Designer Migrants and Cultural Politics." In *Refugees, Immigrants and Education in the Global South: Lives in Motion*, edited by L. Bartlett, and A. Ghaffar-Kucher, 99–115. London: Routledge.

Scott, J.C. 1977. *The Moral Economy of the Peasant: Rebellion and Subsistence in Southeast Asia.* New Haven: Yale University Press.

Sengupta, P., and J. Guha. 2002. "Enrolment, Dropout and Grade Completion of Girl Children in West Bengal." *Economic and Political Weekly* 37 (17): 1621–37.

Sharma, U. 1980. *Women, Work and Property in North-West India.* London: Tavistock.

Sheel, R. 1999. *The Political Economy of Dowry.* New Delhi: Manohar.

Chapter 6

Dalit assertion and different shades of movements defining Dalits
From accorded nomenclature to asserted one

Vivek Kumar

Introduction

Dalits were referred with different nomenclatures like *Asprishyas* (untouchables), *Antyajas* (last born), *Antvasin* (last to reside), *Panchamas* (fifth class), Chandalas, etc., at different points in history. However, they were internally differentiated in some endogamous groups called caste with different names like Chamars, Mahars, Mangs, Malas, Modigas, Holiyars, Chakkiliyars, Pulayas, etc., to name just a few. One can easily argue that these were the accorded nomenclatures to this 17% population by the so-called upper castes of the Hindu social order. Dr Ambedkar, their emancipator, addressed them as depressed classes. With the coming of India act of 1935, a schedule of the castes noted earlier was drawn. Since then they were referred to as Scheduled Castes which continue even today. Hence, Scheduled Castes is a constitutional reference for the erstwhile untouchables of Indian society. In the 1970s, a group of young ex-untouchables formed the political party called Dalit Panthers (Murugkar 1991). They argued that 'are they so enfeeble that they cannot have their own name and have to depend on others for their nomenclature.' Hence they propounded a name 'Dalits' for themselves. Here Dalit literary means 'crushed to pieces.' Hence the Dalits moved from accorded nomenclature to self-asserted nomenclature. However, they created confusion because they included along with ex-untouchables, the tribals, women and poor people of every caste. In the same vein in the late 1970s, to be exact in 1978, 'Bahujan' was another nomenclature mooted by the ex-untouchables for themselves by the organisation BAMCEF. Like Dalit Panthers, they also argued that 'Bahujans' include Scheduled Castes,

Scheduled Tribes, Other Backward Castes and converted minorities-Muslims, Sikhs, Christians and Buddhists (Oommen 1990). However, when we analyse sociologically at an epistemic level, the sources of exclusion of ex-untouchables differ from that of tribals, women, poor people, converted minorities and other backward castes. Hence in this chapter, the term Dalit has been used exclusively for ex-untouchables of the Hindu social order (see Kumar 2014).

Dalits or ex-untouchables constitute approximately 17% of the Indian population. As victims of a rigid social structure, they were cumulatively excluded, notably, from social, economic, political, religious and educational rights (Kumar 2014). The assertion for their existence and their right to be treated as human beings led them to launch different shades of movements. However, these movements have manifested some hierarchical order and sequence. In other words, the Dalit movements, in temporal history, first manifested against socio-cultural oppression, followed by economic, political, educational and assertion in other spheres. The rationale for this hierarchy of movements is, in the words of Oommen, 'a collectivity subjected to multiple deprivations will protest first against those disabilities, which it perceives to be the most inhuman and unbearable' (1992:47). Therefore, he opines that 'it is no accident that Dalit protest in India first crystallised against socio-cultural oppression' (ibid.). In the light of the aforementioned hierarchy of movements, it will be pertinent to map the different shades of Dalit movements.

Evolving a typology Dalit movements

Different shades of Dalit movements have emerged due to specific assertions of Dalits and the socio-political and economic changes ushering in Indian society. These movements can be broadly classified into the following categories: 1. Socio-religious reform movements, 2. Political movements, 3. Dalit literary movements and Dalit intellectual movement, 4. Movements of Dalit employees, 5. Movements by Dalit voluntary associations, 6. Dalit women's movement, 7. Dalit Media Movement and 8. Dalit diaspora movements.

The various types of Dalit movements mentioned earlier are, however, not an exhaustive list. There are also other sub-types of Dalit movements that do exist. For instance, socio-religious movements can be further divided into several sub-types (at least five types). Some of these sub-types shall also be considered in the course of the discussion.

Socio-religious reform movements

Dalits use a multi-pronged approach to liberate themselves from extreme forms of exclusion, oppression, exploitation and for gaining social mobility and dignity. It is considered that, since time immemorial, Dalits have been organising socio-religious reform movements. Dalit leaders would ask their caste members to leave carrion-eating, observe teetotalism, give up hereditary occupations, etc., which were stigmatised by the so-called upper castes (Kumar 2002).

The socio-religious reform movements are discussed under the following heads:

(a) socio-religious reform movements to remain within the pale of Hindu social order;
(b) to convert to other religions of Indian and foreign origin; and
(c) to claim the identity of the original inhabitants.

The socio-religious reform movements for remaining within the pale of Hindu social order are associated with sanskritisation (Lynch 1974; Rudolph and Rudolph 1987; Cohn 1990; Mathew 1986) and Bhakti Movements like Raidasi, Kabirpanthi and Satnam Panth (Gooptu 1993; Dube 2001), etc. Through the Bhakti movement, Dalits established their own *panths* (sects) during fifteenth and seventeenth centuries where they worship a formless God to emancipate themselves (Lorenzen 1996). While the Bhakti movement of the thirteenth to seventeenth centuries sprang up because of extreme caste oppression of Dalits, the nineteenth-century Bhakti movement amongst Dalits emerged due to the paradoxical social milieu. Gooptu (1993) argues that the British needed menial labour to serve soldiers. Hence, they imported the Dalits from villages. Once the Dalits came to the Army Cantonment, they felt free from their caste shackles. However, in civil society, they still faced discrimination as they had no access to religious places. Hence, they started their sects in the Raidas, Kabir and Sivnarayni Sant Sampradaya, which was started in Allahabad later on (Gooptu 1993). Similarly, Dube (2001) highlighted Satnami sect movement amongst the Chamars of Madhya Pradesh (1780–1950).

Conversion to Islam, Sikhism, Christianity (Webster 2002) and to Buddhism (1892, led by Ayothee Dass and then by Ambedkar in 1956) are examples of religious movements to sever relations with the Hindu religion. It is difficult to give exact figures of conversion of Dalits to Islam for the paucity of data. However, the vast numbers of Dalit Muslims prove the point that they converted to Islam. According to Webster, Dalits have also converted to Sikhism. I quote,'Chuhra Sikh were called Mazhabi Sikhs and were kept at a distance by other Sikhs . . . despite giving up polluting work and habits (of eating carrion)'(Webster 2002:16). The 1891 Census explained that '[i]t is impossible to tell from them whether the Balasahis and Valmiks are the same, whether the Balmikis are a section of the Lalbegis or vice-versa, or whether they are two independent sects' (Webster 2002:17). Vicziamy and Mendelsohn (1998:78–79) argue that

> [i]n the first period many untouchables, particularly in South India were converted to Christianity. Conversion . . . began to affect untouchables late in the century. The mass conversion movement began in the 1870s and was largely spent by the early years of the present 20th century.

On the impact of Christianity on Dalits, they opined that 'the churches represented a store of instruction as to how Untouchables might better themselves, and . . . by then, as opposed to their earlier stance, the churches were beginning to take up issues of social justice in India' (ibid.).

Conversion to Buddhism was prevalent in Tamil Nadu during the latter part of the nineteenth century (Aloysius 1999). Then, Ambedkar converted to Buddhism on 14 October 1956 in Nagpur with hundreds of thousands of his followers. After that, thousands of his followers converted to Buddhism all over the country turning it into a movement. Ambedkar was criticised for his conversion. Some opponents alleged that Ambedkar had converted to gain political favours for his people. However, Zelliot (2001:195) argues that

> [w]hat possible political advantage does conversion offer? Conversion to Buddhism immediately cuts off deserving governmental benefits to Untouchable castes. Ambedkar's delayed conversion came long after the period of combining the conversion idea with political expediency, and by then, a reference to

conversion as a political threat had lost its significance. Instead, it had reference to the great Asian Buddhist world, the reputation of Buddhism as an important religion both in India and the West and the possibility of Buddhism as a moral force.

The third stream of socio-religious reform movement launched by Dalits highlights the fact that Dalits are the original inhabitants of this land. Through these movements, Dalits asserted that they have their own identity separate from the Hindus, such as Adi Hindu, Adi Dravid, Adi Andhra, Adi Karnataka, and Adi Dharma. By these identities, the Dalits tried to moot a racial theory in which Aryans were depicted as outsiders who have subjugated the indigenous. Four Adi Hindu conferences were organised in Hyderabad between 1912 and 1924 (Omvedt 1994:122). The Adi Dravida identity emerged amongst Tamil speaking Dalits who claimed to possess separate history, philosophy, civilisation and culture, etc., from Hindus. Dalit leader M.C. Raja gave legitimacy to the nomenclatures like Adi Karnataka and Adi Dravidian conferences during 1923 and 1925 under his President-ship (ibid.). Led by Bhagya Reddy Verma and Arige Ramaswamy, Adi Hindu movement emerged amongst the Malas of Hyderabad (Omvedt 1994). Reddy established an organisation named Manya Sangam in 1912 and later transformed it into Adi Hindu Social Service League. Adi Dharam movement of Dalits came into existence in Punjab with Mangoo Ram as President (Juergensmeyer 1982:145).

Causes of failure of Bhakti and socio-religious reform movement

The socio-religious movement failed to bring about desired changes in the socio-economic status of Dalits. According to Gupta (1985), Neera Desai gives reasons for the failure of the Bhakti movement to bring about change amongst the Dalits. He quoted her thus:

> The socio-religious Dalit leaders of the Bhakti movement argued against the caste system, ideology, social evils and corrupted form of Hinduism. They could not be successful in transforming the society, mainly because the movement fostered equality only in the religious sphere and not in secular. The movement offered no new alternative programme of social and economic organisation. . . (and) never built up the organization, which

could carry out any positive social programme; at best they produced individual (and) not collective opposition to the status quo.

(Gupta 1985:148)

Similarly, Ambedkar also provides reasons for the failure of saints to bring about social change in society. He argues,

> They [saints] have been ineffective. . . . Firstly; none of the saints ever attacked the Caste System. On the contrary, they were staunch believers in the System of Castes. Most of them lived and died as members of the castes they respectively belonged. . . . They were not concerned with the struggle between men. They were concerned with the relation between man and God. They did not preach that all man were equal. They preached that all man were equal in the eyes of God.
>
> (Ambedkar 1979:87; parenthesis is mine)

Dalit political movements

The Dalit political movement emerged during the late nineteenth century after the British introduced changes in India. Ambedkar's effort further strengthened independent Dalit political movements. Since the Dalit movement is actualised through its leadership, it will be necessary to evaluate the nature of Dalit political leadership. The Dalit political leadership can be divided into two broad categories – 1. Dependent Dalit Political Leadership and 2. Independent Dalit Political Leadership (Kumar 2003: 49–50). The first type of leadership functions in political parties led and dominated by the so-called upper castes like the Indian National Congress (hereafter Congress) and the Bharatiya Janata Party (hereafter BJP). The Dalit leaders in these political parties are often made to look after specific party-level units like the SC/ST cells (*Anusuchit Jati Avam Anusuchit Jan Jati Prakoshta*) of their respective political parties. Therefore, the Dalit leaders are often deprived of the opportunities to raise their voice in the parliaments or state assemblies but are conditioned to speak only the language of their party to the public.

The Independent Dalit Political Leadership is found in the movements and parties led and dominated by the Dalit themselves. They have their independent ideology, agenda, parlance, symbols and style of mobilisation. The Independent Dalit Political Leadership and its movement began in 1936 with the establishment of Independent Labour Party (ILP) under the leadership of B. R. Ambedkar. Since then (after nearly 79 years), the independent Dalit political consciousness has grown by leaps and bounds. The development in the political consciousness was visible in the launching of Dalit-based organisations and political parties, such as Scheduled Caste Federation (established in 1942), Republican Party of India (formed in 1957), Dalit Panther's Party (launched in 1972) and Bahujan Samaj Party (floated in 1984).

Impact of independent Dalit political leadership

Independent Dalit Political Leadership has not only contributed to the development of Dalit movement but has also paved the way for 'Dependent Dalit Political Leadership.' It has indirectly forced the Congress and the BJP to provide them with a dignified position in the government and the party organisations. In fact, with the emergence of Bahujan Samaj Party in Uttar Pradesh in the 1990s, some Dalit leaders were elevated to respectable positions. There are many instances that substantiate this phenomenon. For instance, K.R. Narayan was elevated to the post of Vice President and the President of India by the Congress. G.M.C. Balyogi, a Dalit from Andhra Pradesh, was elected as the speaker of the Lok Sabha. Another significant development was the appointment of Meera Kumar as the speaker of the Lok Sabha by the Congress in 2009 and elevation of Bangaru Laxman, a Dalit from Andhra Pradesh, as the national president of the BJP. Along with this, both the Congress and the BJP elevated some Dalits as governors of different states and nominated them to the Planning Commission and the Rajya Sabha.

The political Dalit leadership has also given separate identity to Dalits and has certainly helped to carve out a distinct community with a vast vote bank. It has given self-confidence to the Dalits and helped them play significant roles in the contemporary polity. In fact, they are no more mute spectators and passive recipients in today's political realm. This phenomenon has also influenced Indian democracy to come closer to the masses. It has transformed Indian democracy from representative to participatory and thereby strengthened it. This movement has been successful in keeping the Dalits in the fold of democratic politics and kept them away from being lured by the violent politics of Naxalite groups. It has not only challenged the political hegemony of the so-called upper castes but has also started mobilization to bring them within its fold – a process, which is quite evident in Uttar Pradesh (Kumar 2006). Along with its success, the independent Dalit political movement is marked by three crises. It has failed to unite different shades of independent Dalit political movements, it has failed to provide a unified identity to Dalits, and it has failed to provide a genuine political ally of Dalits in Indian polity (Kumar 2002).

Dalit literature movement and Dalit intellectuals

A clear upsurge of Dalit intellectuals is visible. They are trying to redefine the contours of Indian academia by questioning existing knowledge systems in the Indian society (Kumar 2014). Starting from the Dalit literature movement to the publication of various types of magazines and newspapers, Dalits are involved in expressing their views at every level, which has taken the shape of a movement. A few examples may be worth mentioning. During 1997–1999 three Dalit history Congresses were organised in Delhi in which Dalits tried to highlight the fact that 'Indian history' has blacked out the Dalits. In recent years, Dalit sociologists at Jawaharlal Nehru University, New Delhi have also been attempting to develop an alternative perspective, i.e., 'Perspective from Below.' They argue that the Indian social reality elucidated by Indian Sociologists is 'Brahmanical' in its content and worldview (Kumar 2014).

Dalits trace the history of Dalit literary movement with couplets of fourteenth- to fifteenth-century saint poets, such as Raidas or Ravidas. They have begun to critically look at the nature of existing literature. Wankhade highlights the situation of a Marathi writer that 'understanding of life is restricted by his birth and upbringing in a particular caste and class. . . . He has never seen . . . suffering, distress, struggling, howling world, burning with anger from within like a prairie fire'(Wankhade 1992:316).

To counter the total exclusion of the Dalits, their movements, icons, experiences, worldview, etc., the Dalits were forced to write their own experiences. The process assumed such a proportion that it took the shape of a movement, and thus the Dalit literature movement was born in 1960 in Maharashtra. Specifically, the literary writings in contemporary Dalit literature emerged in Maharashtra in modern India in the 1960s (Wankhade 1992:316) under the influence of Ambedkar's social and political philosophy. This movement is carried forward by the written and codified languages in small weekly, fortnightly, monthly or annual journals, magazines and newspapers published in different languages. Devy argues that 'when Dalit literature started emerging in the 1960s, Marathi literary taste dominated by a narcissistic tendency that fore-grounded, namely, formalistic, non-confrontationist, and titillating works' (Devy 2003: xx).

Kuhn's (1970) view on the revolution of scientific knowledge appears to be rather relevant in the intellectual discourse of the Dalits. He argued that revolution in the scientific knowledge comes about not through the accumulation of data alone but a change in the paradigm when the framework of explanation or the hypothesis is altered, or a new set of questions is posed. In this context, one can locate Dalit writers as changing the paradigm and raising new hypotheses about their existential and experiential realities in their writings. The Dalit writers have been attempting to reject the explanations given by the mainstream Indian writers about the permanent structures of the Indian society like caste, village, religion, etc. While every other mainstream writer tries to highlight these institutions as functional for every section of Indian society, the Dalit writers would provide the rationale and substantiate as to how these institutions are dysfunctional for the Dalits and other marginalised sections (cf. Ambedkar 1979; Ambedkar 1989:19–26; Valmiki 2003). Therefore, it is no accident that the Dalit writers have been criticising Hindu religion. They are sceptical about the powers of Gods and Goddesses and have even questioned the very sanctity of the Hindu religious texts. Dalit writers have also attempted to de-construct the negative and stigmatised image of Dalit society by writing extensively on the contributions of Dalit saint poets and social reformers. In this way, Dalit literature has carved out a new iconography parallel to the so-called upper-caste iconography. Of late, the Dalit writers have also been urging for the quantification and measurement of their labour, which contributes significantly to running the economy and society.

Movement of Dalit employees

Dalits employees' movement goes back to the British colonial days when Gopal Baba Walankarand (later known as Ambedkar) had submitted a petition on behalf of Dalits for their recruitment in British Army. Ambedkar had also demanded inclusion of Dalits in the civil services. After independence, Dalits were granted reservation in government services and public sector undertakings under Article 335 of the Indian Constitution. But the Dalit employees were discriminated within the structures of bureaucracy. Therefore, they launched their employees' movement. However, a more organised effort was made by the Dalit employees of Pune, when in 1971, Kanshi Ram and his colleagues established the Scheduled Castes, Scheduled Tribes, Other Backward Classes and Minorities Employees' Welfare Association. This was duly registered under the Poona Charity Commissioner (Viczany and Mendelsohn 1998:220). The primary objective of this organisation was, 'to . . . find out quick and equitable solutions to the problems of injustice and harassment of . . . employees in general and the educated employees in particular'(ibid.: 220).

In another important development, Kanshi Ram and other leaders established 'All India Backward and Minority Employees Federation' (BAMCEF) in 1976 which was re-launched with greater fanfare on 6 December 1978, with claims of 2,000 delegates in New Delhi (ibid.: 221). Through BAMCEF, Kanshi Ram constructed an 'Other' for Dalits against whom a battle could be pitched. He divided the whole society between 85% Bahujans which included a majority of Dalits, tribals, other backward and converted minorities and 15% Manuwadis, which included the Brahmins, Kshatryas and Vaishyas, the beneficiaries of the system. With a dedicated cadre, propaganda materials like 'Ambedkar Mela (fair) on Wheels.' In between April and June 1980, the BAMCEF highlighted the discrimination of Dalits in thirty-four destinations of nine states of North India. Mobilisation was done with the aim to ask the Dalit employees to 'pay back' the community as they have benefited from the reservation. The BAMCEF gave birth first to a semi-political organisation of Dalits – DS-4 (Dalit Shoshit Samaj Sanghrush Samiti) on 6 December 1981whose primary objective was to agitate for the issues of the whole Bahujan society. This organisation, in fact, laid down the foundation of Bahujan Samaj Party (BSP) on 14 April 1984, the only national political party of the Dalits, minorities and the Other Backward Classes (OBC). However, after contributing to the formation of BSP, Kanshi Ram made BAMCEF a shadow organisation. This led to its first division in BAMCEF in 1986. Today, the biggest Dalit employees' group BAMCEF is led by B.D. Borkar. It is still a non-political, non-religious and non-agitational organisation with 25,000 members having units in 18 states. The organisation brings out six fortnightlies in six languages. It has a 28-acre campus for developing leadership. They produce audio and video cassettes on issues related to Dalits and maintain a website. Since 1993, this group has also propagated "Moolnivasi" identity – that is original inhabitants' identity.

Dalit women's movement

The assertion amongst the Dalit women has been invisible, though Dalit women have been participating in the Dalit movement since time immemorial. Yasudasan (1999) argues,

> The historical invisibility of Dalit women is because we look for them exactly where they were denied entry. We look for women's history in the activities of the savanna women where we cannot find Dalit women. We cannot find them in the struggle against polygamy or enforced widowhood. But we do find them in the struggle against slavery. And we still find them in the struggle for human dignity.
> (p. 334)

He further opines,

> They (Dalit women) have actively participated in thousands way in which Dalit communities tried to liquidate slavery and caste oppression. Dodging masters and overseers, they escaped into jungles along with their men and set up maroon settlements. Conversion to Protestant Christianity was an important form of anti-slavery struggle where we find the initiative and drive of Dalit women. . . . Conversion was a manifestation of Dalit freedom struggle in Kerala. . . . The moral and spiritual contribution Dalit women made to this freedom struggle was significant. They worked hard with their menfolk to set up schools and attended them in spite of unfavourable weather and threats of persecution. . . . These literate women were writing history, writing some most stirring of the struggle for freedom from the genocidal epoch of slavery that for centuries treated them as non-humans.
> (Yasudasan 1999: 334–35; parentheses mine)

Yasusasan also cites examples of the active roles of Dalit women in the Dalit movements. According to him, Dalit women actively participated in Ayyankali's movement for Dalits' rights and in 1909 helped him to sustain a year-long strike at Venganur for educational rights. Further, in 1915, Dalit women resolve to throw many ornaments imposed on them as caste-marks and to cover their breasts defying savarna writs, which triggered off violent conflicts of Perinadu (ibid.: 335–36). Besides, Dalit women of Maharashtra actively participated in the movement led by Shivram Janaba Kamble. Devadasis of the area responded to the call of Kamble, and one of them wrote a long letter explaining the miserable condition of Devadasis. His propaganda against the Devadasi system was so effective that in the year 1909, not a single girl was offered to Khandoba as Devadasi and few male members married Devdasis (Moon and Pawar 2003: 48).

Dalit women also participated in Babasaheb's Mahad Satyagrihat Chowdar Tank on 20 March 1927. They also participated in the deliberation of the subject committee meeting in passing a resolution about the claim for equal human rights. Hundreds of Dalit women are said to have participated in Kalaram Temple (situated in Nasik) on 2 March 1930 and Pune Satyagraha against denunciation of 'Poona Pact.' They conducted sit-in protests in front of the temple and courted arrest. This movement lasted for five years until 1935. During this period Dalit women conducted meetings to support separate electorates for the untouchables. In May 1936, Dalit women held an independent conference in Bombay to support Ambedkar's declaration to convert to non-Hindu religions. At a later stage, at the time of formation of 'Scheduled Caste Federation' in July 1942, out of 70,000 members who participated in the event, 26,000 or one-third were Dalit women (Omvedt 1994:216). Shantabai Dani, who joined Scheduled Caste Federation in 1945 was responsible for organising the Women's Conference of the party. She also took part in the Bhoomeeheen (Landless) Satyagraha of the 1950s. Shantabai is also credited for her utmost effort in the mobilisation and organisation of people during the leadership of Gaikwad in rural Maharashtra. Dalit women in Bombay also organised the Dalit Stri Samwadini (Dalit Women's Dialogue) in 1986, probably the first women's literary conference in Maharashtra (Zelliot 2001:322).

In the 1990s, Dalit women's movement further gained independence. On 11 August 1994, National Federation of Dalit Women

(NFDW) was established at Delhi. By May 2001, NFDW organised seven conferences. Further, they independently participated in the international conference of NGOs on Racial Discrimination, Xenophobia and Related Intolerance organised by the United Nations Human Rights Commission (UNHRC) from 28 August to 7 September 2001 at Durban. Thus, it is observed that the movement activity and organisational network of Dalit women are wide ranging including regional, state and national levels. The increasing visibility of Dalit women in the power structure as sarpanch and as members of the Panchayat has, however, led to an increased backlash against Dalit women. The backlash is expressed through a range of humiliating practices and often culminates in rape or killing of their kin, etc. In this context, women from Dalit Action Research Centre, Chittoor are of the view that 'Dalit women's struggles find their place more naturally within the Dalit movement. . . . From an identifiable, strong position within the Dalit movement, the Dalit women should extend a hand and cooperate with the women's movement' (Bandhu 2003:112).

Movement of Dalit non-governmental organisations

Dalits have a long history of forming and establishing voluntary organisations which can be traced back to the mid-nineteenth century. During the 1850s, the Dalits in Kanpur, Allahabad, Varanasi and Lucknow had started their congregations to have social interaction amongst themselves (Gooptu 1993). At the beginning of the twentieth century many Dalits in south, Western and Eastern India formed caste and social organisations to assert and ameliorate their wretched condition. For instance, in 1903, Shivram Janab Kamble and Kisan Fogoj Bansode founded an organisation called 'Sanmarg Bodhok Nirashrit Samaj' (Depressed Class Society showing right path) (cf. Jogdand 1991; Omvedt 1994:121). The Chandal Movement (1872–73) established caste organisations in search of their rights. N. K. Bose states that a caste organisation exited under the name of 'Namasudra Hitashini Samiti' which was related to the Chandal Movement (Usuda 1997:229). Ambedkar, on his part, established his own voluntary association 'Bahishkrit Hitakarini Sabha' in 1924. Then, in September 1927, he started 'Samaj Samta Sangh,' and the same year he formed 'Samata Sainik Dal' (Rodrigues 2002:557). Ambedkar also founded 'Depressed Classes Education Society' on 14 June 1928 in Bombay and the 'People's Education Society Bombay' on 8 July 1945.

A renewed beginning of Dalit NGOs was made after the passage of 'Anti Atrocities (Against Dalits) Act 1989.' The Government of India, in its Five Year Plan, agreed to work with the NGOs which was, perhaps, due to the necessity for the involvement of the NGOs as this law had special and specific provisions which were to be disseminated to the Dalits. Subsequently, the Dalit Vikas Samiti, a voluntary organisation, was set up in Patna (in Bihar) in 1982 to take up this task. By 1990, the membership of the Samiti reached to 40,000, and the Samiti opened its centres in many other districts of Bihar (Sachchidanand 2001:193–95). The Dalit Vikas Samiti's main thrust was legal aid and education.

The era of globalisation since the 1990s introduced a new phase in the sphere of NGOs because the national and international institutions started playing a dominant role in overseeing the implementation of human rights of citizens. Moreover, more and more international voluntary organisations started funding and collaborating with Dalit NGOs. In this background, the National Campaign for Dalit Human Rights, a committee comprising some Dalit organisations had been born in 1995. The initiative developed into a campaign in 1998 and hence "National Campaign on Dalit Human Rights" (NCDHR) was launched (Kumar 2002:218). It ran a national campaign on Dalits' human rights from 10 December 1998 to 15 August 1999. It appealed the UNHRC to take note of violation of Dalit human rights in India because the Indian state has been playing a partisan role. The campaign, amongst others, stated,

> We, therefore, demand that in the 50th year of the Declaration of the Universal Declaration of Human Rights all the international human rights organizations give assurance to all the Dalits of Asia that the violations of their rights will be considered as violations of Human Rights and that the UN, in particular, will respond seriously to such violations through the appointment of a Special Rapporteur or Working Group on the practice of Untouchability in Asia and include caste discrimination in Article 1 of the 'Convention on the Elimination of Racial Discrimination.'
>
> (National Campaign Manifesto:34)

The NCDHR participated in the 'World Conference against Racism' held at Durban in South Africa in the year 2001 (Kumar 2004) with a contingent of 200 delegates from India. It formed a 'caucus' with the Dalits of other countries, such as Nepal, Sri Lanka, Pakistan, Japan, Nigeria amongst other things. Gradually, it has taken the shape of an NGO with its different wings, like advocacy, media, etc. This campaign also has an international network by being part of "International Dalit Solidarity Network" (IDSN) comprising members from more than 24 countries. Similarly, National Dalit Forum (NDF), National Conference of Dalit Organization (NACDOR), etc., and few other Dalit NGOs are running the movements for restoration of Dalit human rights.

On the whole, there are two views about the Dalit NGOs. One view about the Dalit NGOs argues that they are not grassroots organisations. They are merely funding bodies with grassroots façade. They are not people-based and spontaneous movements. Further, training in an NGO is based more on rights like – the right to health, right to education, right to access to land, water and other resources. Hence, it has blunted the Dalit political movement. On the other hand, there is a view amongst Dalits which sees that Dalit NGOs and other shades of Dalit movement work in tandem, especially the political movement, which can take advantage of an NGO. For instance, NGOs can provide much-needed information about socio-economic and educational status, etc., of Dalits. Secondly, NGOs can be provided with a much-needed platform to bring different shades of the Dalit movement, one platform to have a dialogue with each other and decide a unified direction (Gorringe 2005:75–77).

Dalit media movement

Apart from these, Dalits launched daily newspapers, TV channels (Lord Buddha TV is also available on cable. Also, Thiruma TV and Aawaj TV are available on satellite), E-magazines and hundreds of monthly and fortnightly magazines and newspapers as part of their movement. For example, Dalit Dastak (Dalit knock) is a monthly magazine published from Delhi. It now brings out some 10,000 copies and has a website with the name 'dalitdastak.com.' While going through the 60 issues, I was struck by the covers of the magazine. When asked why no one else than a Dalit or Bahujan has appeared on the cover of the magazine, the editor said that it is the policy of the magazine that this space belongs to Dalits and OBCs only. It is the fact that Dalits rarely get space on the front page of a magazine. The Dalit Dastak ensures that they get to be on the cover regularly. Soon the magazine is planning to launch a web channel. On the other hand, 'Moolnivasi Times' is the weekly newspaper published by BAMCEF as their mouthpiece. BAMCEF has also launched a monthly magazine in English. Above all, an analysis of 'Facebook' accounts of Dalit youths will give us an understanding that the use of Media by Dalits is ideological. They use it for questioning the social and bureaucratic system. Now on every auspicious occasion related to birth anniversaries of Dalit icons Dalits use SMS and Whatsup groups to convey greetings. This has increased connectivity within the erstwhile penury stricken and illiterate masses. It is interesting to note that Dalits have launched their songs on YouTube because no one was ready to air them. By launching their videos there, a number of singers have now become famous singers not only in India but also within the Dalit diaspora abroad. Dalit diaspora regularly calls them for performances. This a very new way of the assertion of their entity. Last but not least, in my fieldwork on political mobilisation in Uttar Pradesh, Dalits have started using mobile phones for communicating political messages. The Dalit Politicians argued that it has made their lives very simple because they did not have any means of communication in the past till the mobile phones came. In this way, Dalits have used different types of modes of communication as part of their movement to raise the level of consciousness amongst the masses and thereby augment the intensity of their assertion.

Movement of Dalit diaspora

The Dalit assertion has extended its contours from local to global especially with the help of Dalit diaspora. The Dalits settled abroad have by now turned into a close-knit community. Although they emigrated from different parts of India and belonged to different sub-castes and linguistic groups, they created their organisations to develop social solidarity. In this context, especially, members of 'new' Dalit diaspora took the lead. For instance, Dalits in the UK established Buddha Vihars (Buddhist praying centres), Gurudwaras (Sikh praying places) in the late 1960s. A Buddhist Council was also established in the UK in the year 1985. This council is a federation of seven Ambedkarite Organisations working for Dalit Indians which is called Federation of Ambedkarite and Buddhist Organization (FABO). Voice of Dalit International (VODI) is another organisation working in the UK. A more organised effort came in the United States from literate non-resident Indian (NRI) Dalits when they formed "Volunteers in Service to India's Oppressed and Neglected" (VISION) in 1975. The VODI report-2000 also mentions the establishment of Ambedkar Centre for Justice and Peace in Canada (cf. Kumar 2004). In the year 1999, the Backward and Minorities Employees' Federation (BAMCEF) was launched its international networking. Since 2003, the Ambedkar International Mission started working in the US.

It is observed that three countries, namely, the UK, Canada and the USA have been the hub of Dalit diaspora activities in recent years. In these countries, the Dalits would celebrate and commemorate the birth and death anniversaries of Ambedkar, Buddha and Ravidas, respectively. In the UK, the Dalits also organised the Ambedkar memorial lecture in collaboration with Manchester Metropolitan University for a decade. Dalit diaspora in the UK on 23 April 2003 established the Ambedkar Museum at Wolverhampton. They installed Babasaheb's Bust in the London School of Economics and the Indian High Commission office. The Indian High Commission office in London celebrates Babasaheb Ambedkar's anniversary on 14 April every year. In my fieldwork in Canada, three important centres of Dalit activities were found in Toronto, Vancouver and Calgary. In Vancouver, the Dalits have been living since 1906. They have installed Babasaheb's bust in San Frazer University library and have put up Babasaheb's portrait in the Mayor's office in Burnaby. They also own a huge Ravidasi temple. The Dalits in Calgary have instituted an annual Ambedkar memorial symposium in collaboration with the University of Calgary. In Toronto, the Dalits own two Ravidasi temples and one Valmiki temple. Dalit diaspora in the USA played a dominant role in getting Babasaheb's bust installed in the Columbia University and have established Ravidasi Gurudwaras in New Jersey, California and Houston. The organisation has also associated itself with the Indian Consulate office in New York and Columbia University. Lately, sometime in June 2013, they organised the 100th year of Babasaheb Ambedkar's journey to Columbia University. The movement has given self-esteem to emigrant Dalits and highlighted the fact that Indian diaspora is not a monolithic whole but is divided into caste lines. Last but not least, this movement has helped to unite the community by using the products of information technology (Kumar 2013:227–62).

Conclusion

Dalit movements have become a pan-Indian phenomenon cutting across geographical, linguistic and caste boundaries. They have gone beyond the national boundaries and have spread to different parts of the world, wherever Dalit diaspora live. The movement has acquired different shades in the process of struggle. The Dalits have suffered discrimination and exclusion in different institutions of the Indian society which were developed, especially after India got independence, in stark contrast to the universalistic principles which a democratic state like India is supposed to follow. Although the Indian Constitution has given the Dalits legitimate right to get access to institutions, the fact remains that they have been denied access to these institutions and spaces. Such discrimination, in fact, compelled the Dalits to organise themselves to demand their legitimate rights. Despite the difference in the frame of reference, the Dalit diaspora demand for solidarity and self-esteem identifies well with the demands of Dalits back home. Nevertheless, on the whole, different shades of Dalit movements have also led to the strengthening of Indian democracy.

References

Aloysius, G. 1999. *Religion as Emancipatory Identity: A Buddhist Movement among the Tamils under Colonialism*. New Delhi: New Age International Publishers.

Ambedkar, B. R. 1979. "Dr Babasaheb Ambedkar Writings and Speeches." *BAWS*, 1. Mumbai: Education Department, Government of Maharashtra, Mumbai (EDGMM).

———. 1982. BAWS, Vol. 2, EDGMM.

———. 1989. "The Indian Ghetto – The Centre of Untouchability-Outside the Fold." *BAWS* 5, EDGMM.

Bandhu, Pranjali. 2003. "Dalit Women's Cry for Liberation." In *Gender and Caste*, edited by Anupama Rao. New Delhi: Kali for Women.

Cohn, Bernard S. 1990. *An Anthropologist Among the Historians and Other Essays*. New Delhi: OUP.

Devy, G.N. 2003. *The Outcaste: Akkarmashi-Shravan Kumar Limbale*. New Delhi: Oxford University Press.

Dube, Saurabh. 2001. *Untouchable Pasts: Religion, Identity and Power among a Central Indian Community, 1780–1950*. New Delhi: Vistar Publications.

Gooptu, Nandini. 1993. "Caste and Labour: Untouchable Social Movements in Urban Uttar Pradesh in the Early Twentieth Century." In *Dalit Movements and the Meanings of Labour in India*, edited by Peter Robb. New Delhi: Oxford University Press.

Gorringe, Hugo. 2005. *Untouchable Citizens: Dalit Movements and Democratization in Tamil Nadu*. New Delhi: Sage Publications.

Gupta, S. K. 1985. *The Scheduled Castes in Modern Indian politics: Their Emergence as a Political Power*. New Delhi: MushiramManoharlal Publishers Pvt. Ltd.

Jogdand, P.G. 1991. *Dalit Movement in Maharashtra*. New Delhi: Kanak Publication.

Juergensmeyer, Mark.1982. *Religion as Social Vision: The Movement against Untouchability 20th Century Punjab*. Berkeley: University of California Press.

Kuhn, T. 1970. *The Structure of Scientific Revolutions*. Chicago and London: The University of Chicago Press, Ltd.

Kumar, Vivek. 2002. *Dalit Leadership in India*. New Delhi: Kalpaz Publications.

———. 2003. "Dalit Movement and Dalit International Conferences." *Economic and Political Weekly* (July 5). Mumbai: Sameeksha Trust Publications.

———. 2004. "Understanding Dalit Diaspora." *Economic and Political Weekly* XXXIX (1) (January 3–9). Mumbai: Sameeksha Trust Publications.

———. 2005. "Situating Dalits in Indian Sociology." *Sociological Bulletin* 54 (3) (September–December). New Delhi: Indian Sociological Association.

———. 2006. *India's Roaring Revolution: Dalit Assertion and New Horizons*. New Delhi: Gagan Deep Publications.

———. 2013. "The New Dalit Diaspora." In *Dual Identity, Indian Diaspora and Other Essays*, edited by K. L. Sharma and Renuka Singh. New Delhi: Orient BlackSwan.

———. 2014. "Dalits Studies: Continuities and Change." In *Indian Sociology (Volume 3): Identity Communication and Culture (ICSSR Research Surveys and Explorations)*, edited by Yogendra Singh. New Delhi: Oxford University Press.

Lorenzen, David N. 1996. *Bhakti Religion in North India: Community Identity & Political Action*. New Delhi: Manohar.

Lynch, Owen M. 1974. *The Politics of Untouchability*. Delhi: National Publishing House.

Mathew, Joseph. 1986. *Ideology, Protest and Social Mobility: Case Study of Mahars and Pulayas*. New Delhi: Inter-India Publications.

Moon, Meenakshi, and Urmila Pawar. 2003. "Dalit Women, Difference & Dalit Women's Movements." In *Caste & Gender*, edited by Anupama Rao. New Delhi: Kali for Women.

Murugkar, Lata. 1991. *Dalit Panthers Movement in Maharashtra: A Sociological Appraisal.* Bombay: Popular Prakashan.

Omvedt, Gail. 1994. *Dalits and the Democratic Revolution: Dr Ambedkar and the Dalit Movement in Colonial India.* New Delhi: Sage Publications.

Oommen, T. K. 1990. *Protest and Change: Studies in Social Movements.* New Delhi: Sage Publications.

Rodrigues, Valerian. 2002. *The Essential Writings of B.R. Ambedkar.* New Delhi: Oxford University Press.

Rudolph, Lloyd and Rudolph Susanne. 1987. *The Modernity of Tradition: Political Development in India.* New Delhi: Orient Longman.

Sachchidananda. 2001. "Voluntary Action for Social Development and Empowering the Marginalised in Bihar." In *Social Development and the Empowerment of Marginalised Groups: Perspectives and Strategies*, edited by Debal K. Singharoy. New Delhi: Sage Publications.

Usuda, Masayuki. 1997. "Pushes Towards the Partition: Jogendranath Mandal and the Constrained Namashudra Movement." In *Caste System, Untouchability and the Depressed*, edited by H. Kotani. New Delhi: Manohar.

Valmiki, Omprakash. 2003. *Joothan: A Dalit's Life* (Translated from Hindi-Joothan). Kolkata: Samay.

Viczany, Marika, and Oliver Mendelsohn. 1998. *The Untouchables: Subordination, Poverty and the State in modern India.* Cambridge: Cambridge University Press.

Wankhade, M.N. 1992. "Friends, the Day of Irresponsible Writers Is Over." In *Poisoned Bread*, edited by Arjun Dangle, translated from the Modern Marathi Dalit Literature. New Delhi: Orient Longman.

Webster, John C.B. 2002. *Religion and Dalit Liberation: An Examination of Perspective.* New Delhi: Manohar Publishers and Distributors.

Yasudasan, T.M. 1999. "Caste, Gender and Knowledge: Towards a Dalit Feminist Perspective." In *Dalits and Peasants: The Emerging Caste-Class Dynamics*, edited by Ashish Ghosh. New Delhi: Gyan Sagar Publication.

Zelliot, Eleanor. 2001. *From Untouchables to Dalits and Other Essays.* New Delhi: Manohar.

Chapter 7

The question of loyalty
Minorities and South Asian nationalisms

Tanweer Fazal

Loyalty as a problematic

Across the world today, and more so in South Asia, the problematic of loyalty has come to determine the course of national identity and citizenship. This question acquired colossal proportions for the first time in South Asia when formerly British India was partitioned into India and Pakistan. The enormity of violence that partition-induced transfer of populations triggered could not reconcile the problem of blood and belonging that majoritarian nationalisms on both sides had posed. Like the partition of 1947, the crafting of new state boundaries in 1971 that resulted in the formation of Bangladesh was preceded and followed by massive bloodletting, and a full-fledged war between Indian and Pakistan. However, the redrawing of South Asia's political geography miserably failed in settling the question once and for all. Suspicions regarding disaffection of their minority populations have not only kept the intelligence agencies and security establishments of South Asian states busy, but it also facilitated the rise of chauvinistic politics and anti-minority jingoism across the region. The question of loyalty poses varied political responses ranging from complaints of deep-seated prejudice, intolerance and discrimination to execution of extreme violence bordering on genocide.

Examples are simply far many. In India, for instance, a sort of religious profiling in the counter-terror operations has come to the fore wherein security agencies have had to bear allegations of selective targeting Muslim youth. Renewed demands being made on Muslims to make a visible demonstration of their allegiance to India is disturbingly frequent – more than ever before. Earlier, the Sikhs faced a similar situation when they came to be minoritised during the course of the Khalistan movement and in the aftermath of the assassination of former Prime Minister, Indira Gandhi. Muslims in India (and occasionally, the Sikhs and the Christians), Hindus in Bangladesh, Christians, Ahmediyas and Shias in Pakistan and the Rohingyas in Myanmar continue to suffer targeted violence. In Sri Lanka, the militarist solution to the existing nationality upsurge led to the killing of tens of thousands of Tamils. In neighbouring Bangladesh, the predicament of a Bengali or Bangladeshi nationalism has failed to address the citizenship quest of its religious and ethnic minorities. Most striking is the case of its Urdu speaking population, who after having survived the repugnance and immeasurable violence, have been left stateless and bereft of constitutional entitlements. The Nepalese speaking population in apparently peaceful Bhutan has been forced to leave the country and end up as refugees in Nepal.

The oddity of state formation in South Asia makes the problem far more vexed. Since the boundaries of partition were haphazardly drawn, therefore, a Europe-like situation, where cultural boundaries of 'nation' were somewhat in consonance with the political boundaries of the 'state,' could not be replicated. Most often, cultures in South Asia traverse and cross countries and state frontiers. The conundrum of dual identity – that of the cultural community and the other of the acquired one of a citizen of a given state thus comes under immense strain. Consequently, minority politics in South Asia seldom remains confined to the territories of a given state. Thus, the Tamil liberation groups in Sri Lanka could look towards the Indian Tamils for moral and material support. Kashmiris on both sides of the line of control (LOC), Indian and Pakistan-administered, are caught in a similar situation. The influx of Bengali refugees from erstwhile East Pakistan into West Bengal pushed Indian government into the war with Pakistan, while many north-eastern tribes find their ethnic homelands divided between India and Myanmar. This holds true of the followers of various religions of South Asia too. For instance, the demolition of the Babri Mosque had its reverberations felt in Pakistan and Bangladesh too. Conceivably, it was this intricacy of situation that prompted the early leaders of India and Pakistan to agree promising mutual comfort to their respective minority populations. The Nehru-Liaquat Pact (1950) between the prime ministers of the two countries assured protection of life, liberty and equal rights to religious minorities and paved the way for the setting up of minority commissions in the two states.

Nation-state framework in South Asia

Notwithstanding the poly-ethnic constitution of most South Asian states the desire to fashion a state anchored in a homogenous people or a nation has proved irresistible to state functionaries and sections of the national elite. Officially promulgated nationalism – state-led for Charles Tilly (1994) – is the vehicle to realise this convergence of culture and polity: the 'nation-state.' This presumed coterminality between state and nation led Rupert Emerson to term the 'nation-state' as a 'terminal community' – drawing the ultimate loyalty of the people to the 'nation-state': 'The largest community that, when the chips are down, effectively commands men's loyalty, overriding the claims both of the lesser communities within it and those that cut across it or potentially enfold it within a still greater society' (Emerson 1970: 95–6). In the given discourse, nationalism, defined as the finality of one's affiliations and loyalties, comes to be fiercely contested by minority groups resolute on preserving the pristine purity of their cultural inheritance.

The institution of the 'nation-state model,' it is assumed, would pledge legitimacy to the state, check estrangement of social groups and thus instil loyalty. It is noteworthy, however, that cultural nationalisms that South Asian states have nourished are only a euphemism for majoritarian inclinations. The rise of Hindu nationalism in India is thus not an aberration but only a fulfilment of a long-cherished dream of a section of the nationalist elite. It had its initial success by instituting Hindi as the *rajbhasha*. Resistance against Hindi from its southern states prompted this section of the cultural elite to push for Sanskrit as the national language. Following this, the Sanskrit Commission (1956–7) instituted by the Government of India to look into the language question made a strong plea for its adoption as the national language on the plea that 'Sanskrit' was 'the Great Unifying Force of India.' It credited Sanskrit for ensuring that 'India with its nearly 400 millions of people was one country, and not half a dozen 30 or more countries' (Ramaswamy 1999: 341). Similar anxiety to prevent further vivisection of Pakistan post-Bangladesh impelled Pakistan to move more decisively towards adopting Islam as the foundation of its nationality. Sri Lankan official nationalism today is more aggressively Sinhala-Buddhist than ever before while Bangladesh is caught in the puzzle of secular linguistic nationalism as against an aggressive Islamic identity.

Of the seven states (eight if Afghanistan is to be included) that comprise South Asia, at least five have adopted the faith of the majority as state religion. Besides, official language policies, carefully crafted by the elite, have been deployed in almost all states of the region to define national culture. Nonetheless, the states of South Asia, caught between the contradictory pulls of tradition and modernity, have desisted from becoming theocracies. It is also to concede that in most such states minority groups do enjoy recognition and constitutional protection to varying degrees. This chapter examines the perspective of minority identities as they negotiate their terms of co-existence, accommodation and adaptation with several other competing identities within the framework of the 'nation-state.'

Minorities: a typology

Sociologically speaking, the term minority refers to three different strains of cultural communities each specific regarding its composition and the politics that follow. One, cultural enclaves with real or fictitious association with a homeland. Oommen terms them as nations akin to those of the European type (Oommen 2004: 125). Two, communities that are culturally distinct but have no exclusive claim over territories they populate – the dispersed minorities. Usually, they share most cultural artefacts with the co-inhabitants of the region and differ from them on one or two counts such as religion that they follow. Three, the indigenous communities or tribes. They have all prerequisites of a nation – territory, language, religion – yet are dubbed in the South Asian literature as 'ethnic groups' referring thereby to their primordiality.

a. Minority nations

Nationalist expressions of minority nations look for congruity between power and culture by seeking either autonomy or secession. Cultural genocide coupled with state practices bordering on internal colonialism has impelled many minority nations in South Asia to seek the Westphalian solution, i.e., national self-determination. The Kashmiris, in both Indian and Pakistani Kashmir, the Nagas, the Mizos and many other groups in India's north-east, the Tamils in Sri Lanka or the Baluchs in Pakistan, took to armed rebellion against the might of the state to realise their objective. The claim to sovereignty of the people in all such cases rested on a supposed convergence of antiquity, homogeneity and territorial contiguity. Phizo, the author of Naga nationalism, in a speech delivered in 1951, thus made a case for plebiscite to achieve a separate Nagalim (Phizo 2018).

> Whether we call a national state or a country, both concerns the same thing: it concerns the territory of a people. Nagaland is the land of the Nagas; it is Naga country and nobody else. We are not refugees or immigrants in this beautiful land. Our own language tells exactly what a country is. We call country "Ura" which literally means 'we are first' (u, we; ra, ria, first). The root meaning of territory also developed from the same word; namely, "theria" meaning 'self first.' And our Naga language is certainly as old as human tradition and history cannot contradict us. No man can argue with fact and existence of Nagaland (Nagara) is a natural fact.

However, except in the case of Bengalis of East Pakistan, such insurgencies to realise separate ethnic homelands have only ended up in the further enslavement of the 'minority nation.' Claiming monopoly over violence, the states of South Asia have unleashed counter-terror to prevent the dismemberment of the 'national territory.' On this, the states of South Asia display a remarkable identity of approach. The promulgation of Armed Forces Special Power Act in the 'disturbed areas' of India, the brutality unleashed by the state on the tribal uprising in Frontier Pakistan, or more recently, the Sri Lankan army's annihilation of the Liberation Tigers of Tamil Eelam (LTTE) and the Tamils of the north-east region; the inviolability of the states' territorial sovereignty has been ruthlessly established. In hindsight, the insurgency in all such instances has only proved counterproductive. In the final analysis, the violence by the rebel groups has been dubbed as 'terror seeking' while that of the state as 'law enforcing' and legitimate.

Apart from the strategic naivety, calls to self-determination also suffer from epistemological double-speak insofar as political morality is to be taken into account. In all such upsurges for separation and autonomy, the fundamental issue at stake is the construction of the 'self' itself. The normative argument that every 'people' have the right to exercise territorial sovereignty as and when they demand, leaves minority cultures residing in such territories extremely vulnerable. The question to be asked is, whose 'self' and what about other 'selves' residing in the vicinity (Samaddar 2002: 20–34)? Since a perfect isomorphism between culture and geography is rare, contesting claims over territories regarded as ancestral and sacred obscure the issue further. For example, following a long spell of violence, the Indian state agreed to an ethnic homeland model to finding a Mizo majority province, Mizoram, but in the process left the concerns of the Reangs, an ethnic minority in the region, unattended. The Reangs have therefore organised themselves under a militant outfit to demand a separate district council. Bangladesh represents a similar case. The 'Bangalee nationalism' espoused by the state of Bangladesh required Bengali to be the primary identity of the citizenry. In effect, it pre-supposed either the extermination of non-Bengalis or their submergence in the larger collectivity. This implicit coterminality between citizenship and nationhood is resisted by minority nationalists. Chakma leader Manabendra Narayan Larma refused to be identified with the Bengali nation 'I am a Chakma, not a Bengalee. I am a citizen of Bangladesh, a Bangladeshi. You are also a Bangladeshi, but your national identity is Bengalee. . . . They (Chakmas) can never be Bengalee' (cited in Huq 1984: 51).

For most minority nations of South Asia, the 'principle of nationality' that nations are destined to realise themselves as a sovereign state is not a viable option. For firstly, the failure of movements for self-determination does not project an encouraging scenario. The cost/benefit ratio seems to be unfavourable. Secondly, by and large, the states of South Asia, particularly India, the largest one, have been successful in co-opting the counter-elites from minority groups. Apart from co-option, this has also required structural re-arrangement such as the distribution of linguistic provinces and adoption of three-language policy – measures that guarantee a limited federation in contrast to the unitary state structures in most countries of the region. The absence of a pluralist and accommodative structure has had unmistakable fallouts. After all, whereas the Pakistani state failed to contain resurgent Bengali nationalism leading to its vivisection in India, the Bengali cultural elite, the Bhadralok, came to be co-opted in the grand nationalist project to construct an 'Indian nation.' Similarly, if not for the centralising tendency of the Pakistani state, Baluch secessionist nationalism, in one opinion, could have been contained by facilitating and accommodating provincial nationalism centred around Baluchi history and culture.[1]

South Asia, in this sense, offers yet another advance in the study of nationalism, and this pertains to the flawed assumption regarding conjugality between state and nation. The partisan nationalist and the distant theorist speak in unison insofar as a nation and its association with the state is judged. A nation realises itself in a state or to the least, retains an ambition to do so. 'Nations dream of being free,' says Anderson, and 'a sovereign state' is the 'gage and emblem' (Anderson 1991: 7) of its freedom. Nationalism is then the ideology that aspires to state power. Breuilly is emphatic: 'Nationalism is, above and beyond else, about politics and politics is about power. The central task is to relate nationalism to the objectives of obtaining and using state power' (Breuilly 1993: 1). As cited earlier, Tilly's historical survey of the nationalist upsurges in Europe identified two divergent processes, state-led and state-seeking nationalisms. Apparently, at odds with each other, both reflected the nationalist resolve in bringing political and cultural sovereignty to coincide (Tilly 1994: 131–46). There are a sufficient number of instances mentioned earlier wherein such convergence was sought in the subcontinent too albeit with disastrous consequences. The survival of multinational states in the region, on the other, perforce draws our attention towards a parallel but largely overlooked occurrence, what has been termed as 'state-renouncing' nationalism, a phenomenon whereby minority nations 'insist on maintaining their cultural identity within a federal polity' (Oommen 2004: 126).

Thus, national self-determination as the avowed formula for the liberation of the people is abandoned in favour of certain forms of cultural autonomy and public recognition of these peripheral cultures. In many such cases of renunciation, nationalities forsook their separatist aspirations yet pitched hard for political and cultural autonomy. Tamils of India are one such example who, led by the legendary Periyar, denounced Indian nationalism as essentially Hindi imperialism and set out to chart a separate Dravidasthan for the Dravidian people. But save for the linguistic re-organisation of Indian states, Tamil nationalism felt content to co-exist in conjunction with all-encompassing Indian nationalism. Despite the accommodation, the claim of Tamils being a nation-in-themselves was never discarded. For C. N. Annadurai, DAMK leader and one of the main architects of this, the problem pertained to adjusting the national aspirations of the Tamil people within the framework of Indian Constitution (cited in Hardgrave 1964–65: 397):

> We say we demand unqualified enforcement of the theory of self-government or the State's sovereignty and autonomy. Our opponents have labelled this demand as aiming at secession. Our own comrades too have broadly understood this demand as meaning secession. The problem before us is: How are we to accommodate the theory of self-government within the framework of the anti-secession Constitutional amendment?

Following this, the DMK purged its Constitution of all references to the goal of independent 'Dravidasthan.' In the course of time, the issue of separate statehood receded as a feasible option even amongst the most nationalistic Tamils. The radical faction that deserted the DMK on its betrayal of the 'Tamil cause' failed to attract any mass support. In the DMK politics, Tamil nationalism is preserved in a new vocabulary – through the symbols of common Tamil culture, glorification of the Dravidian past and agitations against the imposition of Hindi (Hardgrave op. cit.: 401). The Mizos provide another such instance. In the early years of the post-British period, the Mizo middle classes, while conscious of their distinct identity, advocated an integrationist approach unlike the other ethnic groups such as the Nagas and the Meitees. However, in the early 1960s, led by the old aristocracy, Mizos, a conglomeration of various tribes started demonstrating secessionist inclination. The Mizo National Front initiated an armed revolution to seek independence from the Indian Union inviting brutal repression including the use of air power. However, a constitutional solution that paved the way for the unification of Mizo inhabited areas and the emergence of the state of Mizoram settled the issue. The Mizo Accord signed in 1986 between the Government of India and the Mizo National Front promised sufficient political and cultural autonomy (GOI 1986: 2).

> Notwithstanding anything contained in the Constitution, no act of Parliament in respect of (a) Religion or Social practices of the Mizos, (b) Mizo customary Law or procedure, (c) Administration of Civil and Criminal Justice involving decisions

according to Mizo customary Law, (d) Ownership and transfer of land, shall apply to the State of Mizoram unless the Legislative Assembly of Mizoram by a resolution so decides

In renouncing aspiration for separate statehood, are we to conclude that the minority nations of South Asia are analogous to the stateless nations of Western Europe? For both, the new nationalist aspiration in Europe and the South Asian nations, the scope of the action is not confined to the state alone. For ethnic nationalists, civil society provides a parallel space for cultures to thrive in. In India, Tamil film industry has been effectively used by the DMK and other Dravidian parties to keep the anti-Hindi linguistic nationalism of the Tamil people alive. Similarly, the proliferating Bhojpuri cinema, television channels, music and literary works have given a new thrust to a speech community that feared extinction following the assimilation of Bhojpuri as a dialect of *rashtrabhasha* Hindi.

The parallel with the European case, though, ends here for the new stateless nationalism of the Western type seeks to abjure state power or a desire for it in the context of the emergence of new suprastate institutions such as the European Union, Council of Europe etc. This surge for the non-state loci of power is also impacted by the erosion in capacity faced by the states in the era of globalisation. In the emerging scenario, the sub-state nationalism is seen to be operating at three different planes: a. at the regional plane where civil society is penetrated; b. at the level of 'nation-state' for want of recognition and representation and; c. at the European plane through institutional mechanisms such as the European Union's Committee of Regions or Council of Europe. Michael Keating sees such developments leading to 're-territorialisation of politics' that does not 'necessarily correspond to the nation-state' (Keating 1999: 74). Can the European solution be replicated in South Asia? This requires an enormous political will that allows for the abdication of centralising tendency on the part of the state and in reciprocation, the relinquishing of separatist dreams by minority cultures. Eventually, this might require new multilateral institutions at the regional plane where membership is not restricted to the states, rather is extended to the nations, nationalities and ethnicities of South Asia. Stateless minority nations, having found representation and reciprocal assurance by such institutions, could then rest content.

b. Dispersed minorities

In its scope and content, the subject minority nationalism for this chapter is not restricted to comprehending the aspirations of the territorially concentrated cultures or nations. The presence of dispersed minority groups, generally defined by the property of religion, adds to the complexity of the minority question in the region. Be it the Ahmediyas of Pakistan, Muslims and Christians of India or Hindus in Bangladesh; such communities, distributed as they are across the 'national' landscape, do not pose any territorial threat to the 'nation-states' as such. At the same time, their discreteness makes them most vulnerable and often places them at the receiving end of the violence perpetrated by a triumphalist majority. Fearing obliteration of their cultural practices and countenancing a gradual waning of political influence, such groups insist on recognition of their way of life in the public domain. The skewed constitution of the category 'public', where minority cultures are left unrepresented, comes to be interrogated. More often than not, this is followed by demands for an adequate share in recruitments and public life. Culture and power, as per this argument, invariably go hand in hand. This instrumentality of cultural rights discourse is distinctly South Asian, a significant departure from the Western debate on the subject. In India, the Sachar Committee instituted to study the status of its Muslim citizens, after having quantified their material deprivation, also took note of the power differentials that existed between Muslims and the rest (Government of India 2006).[2] In Pakistan, a separate electorate system was introduced at the insistence of the minority elites to ensure their representation. This separateness, however, has only served to further their remoteness.

How do such minority groups respond to the nationalism of the state? Living within the national territory, being daily consumers of national education policy, nationalist reconstruction of history and memory and an intrusive mass media, do the minority group members internalise officially fed nationalism similarly as do the majority? How is identity consciousness of such minority groups reflected in politics? In this context, statistics have a bearing on political consciousness although minority per se is more a state of material deprivation than of enumeration. In multi-party democracies, territorially dispersed, yet numerically substantial minority groups become strategically significant for electoral politics. This perceived indispensability in politics also enhances the identity-tempered minority politics producing what can be termed as 'minorityism.' Minorityism privileges culturalisms of various kinds and seeks succour in the reification of communities and groups through demands for 'cultural autonomy' and privileges for the elites. Statecraft informed by minorityism, instead of deepening citizenship amongst minority groups, negotiates and speaks through deliberately created and pampered 'cultural spokesmen' who thrive on perpetuating cultural boundaries and claiming to be the sole and authentic interlocutors of community consciousness. Inherent in minorityism is the tendency to even out internal differentiation and persisting hierarchies within minority cultures thus abdicating the moral obligation to address the concerns of 'minorities within a minority.' What is termed Muslim politics in India has been by and large plagued with such culturalisms. In Bangladesh, the Hindus constituting nearly 9% of the population are widely perceived as the vote bank of Awami League. This is to such an extent that political violence against League cadres usually ends up with violence against the Bengali Hindus.

The politicisation of dispersed minority groups takes a completely different route when they are numerically minuscule. The propensity towards collaboration and retreat from politics is observable in so far as the South Asian situation is concerned. Both, in Pakistan and India, Parsees or Zoroastrians are a small and diminishing minority and self-consciously stay away from politics. They have been second to none in expressing their adherence to the state.[3] Conversely, the loyalty of the Parsees is never called into question, neither by the votaries of Indian patriotism nor Pakistani. Similar proclivity is demonstrated by the Burghers in Sri Lanka, a microscopic minority that draws its lineage from the Dutch settlers. The enactment of 'Sinhala Only' Act, restrictions on Christian missionaries and an imminent economic downfall failed to politicise the community. The route adopted was that of defeatism and retreat (Peacock 2002: 170–6).

Given the common colonial past, the minority question in South Asia is rarely an internal subject. In the states of India and Pakistan, the partition of the subcontinent, the subsequent violence between communities and an unrelenting spell of hostility between the two countries impairs the minority situation to a significant extent. Indeed, at the time of partition, the issues concerning the identity and security of religious minorities appeared as important elements in the drafting of the foreign policy of the two states. The minority question was felt to be irresolvable without a pact between the two hostile states on the issue. The demolition of the Babri mosque by the shenanigans of Hindutva organisations spelt doom for the Hindu minorities in Bangladesh. The Tamil assertion in Sri Lanka frequently spills over across the Indian Ocean too, to the extent that it ended up with the assassination of a former Prime Minister of India. Sovereignty issues are frequently raised to deny cross-border interventions. However, in conditions of cultural boundaries transgressing international borders, such expressions of outrage have had little impact.

This follows that the 'other' in the nationalist discourse is both internal as much as external. In fact, external is only an extension of the internal and vice-versa. In such a situation, the loyalty of minority groups is forever suspected. Hindus of Pakistan and Bangladesh are perpetually suspected of retaining allegiance towards neighbouring 'Hindu' India. Similarly, the extra-territorial identity of the Indian Muslims connects them with the Pakistani state and people, it is believed. This amounts to erosion in the citizenship of minority groups leading to the birth of the term, 'second-class citizen.' In Pakistan, the chorus for declaring Ahmediyas as second-class citizen refuses to die. In Bangladesh, the 'Biharis' assumed to be collaborators of the Pakistani army during the war of liberation, are denied full citizenship. And in the slums of the cosmopolitan cities of India, Bengali-speaking Muslims hide their religious identity to gain employment and ward off the threat of being declared an 'infiltrator' from Bangladesh. The universality of citizenship comes to be tempered by the particularities of culture and religion. Very often such nationalist constructions attempt a hierarchy of loyalties and thereby, citizenship.

c. The question of indigenous people

The third dimension in the conceptualisation of minority identities is the question of indigenous people or tribes. As practitioners of a various form of animism, speakers of distinct languages with a spiritual association with the land and its ecology, the tribes display all symbolisms of a nation. However, over the years, the distinctiveness of their way of life has come under threat from a variety of sources. Epistemologically, colonial categorisation into scheduled tribe rendered them as primitive or 'people without history' and therefore lacking the wherewithal of being a nationality.

Their cultural expressions such as the specificities of religion and language are gradually lost owing to the onslaught of missionaries from organised religions such as Christianity, Hinduism and Islam as well as the state-induced homogenisation bid. Consequently, tribes as a religious community do not enjoy the status and recognition abrogated to the religious minorities in South Asia. Capitalist development alongside population influx from the mainland has further ravaged traditions, ecology and livelihoods of the indigenous people. The typicality of their situation necessitates nuanced handling. In India, the tribal question for long is caught between two divergent approaches: that between the integrationist or assimilationists and the isolationist or the protectionists. Quite obviously, policy orientation, wedded to the ideology of 'official nationalism,' has been distinctly skewed towards the latter. Tribal participation in national life has been sought through the instruments of protective discrimination, various schemes of tribal upliftment and retention of laws against land alienation. At the same time, capitalist exploitation of the forests for timber, minerals and other resources has pushed the tribals into an alien economic order (Sundar 1997).

As a final point, it is argued that the framework, minority and majority, are offshoots of colonial obsession with quantifying social categories. Once produced and mobilised, such consciousness played havoc in the lives of communities of the region of South Asia. Given the scale of hybridity amongst communities inhabiting the cultural landscape of South Asia, such imageries connoting neat compartmentalisation appear mythical. Boundaries are transgressed at will and majorities and minorities, almost habitually, exchange roles. Minoritisation is a process that produces context-specific minority groups out of communities without any history of possessing an awareness of kind. In Muslim majority Pakistan, there are still Pashtun, Baluch, Sindhi, Saraiki speaking Muslims who would not desire to be clubbed together as the majority in Pakistan. Hindus are a majority in India, but when analytically examined, assigning such a status to all the Hindus is ridden with self-doubt. Thus, the question, do Hindus in their entirety – Dalits and backward, speakers of Dravidian languages, the 'Hinduised' tribes of Central India, or the Meitees of Manipur – have similar access to power and privileges to constitute a majority that suits the definition? The minoritisation of Sikhs does not have a long history, and more recently Jains too have shown restlessness about their inclusion in the Hindu fold. Referring to the 'vertical and horizontal divisions of the Indian social structure,' Moin Shakir affirmed that the terms, 'majority' and 'minority' were 'imprecise.' 'There is no homogeneous oppressor "majority" which exploits other "minorities,"' he argued (Shakir 1982: 36–45). Stretching the argument a little too far, the single judge bench of an Indian Court declared the Hindus as the true minority if caste and sectarian divisions were to be taken into account (Allahabad High Court 2007). However, for scholarship on the subject, an acknowledgement of the ephemeral nature of such categorisation is to realise its dynamism, its historicity and its contingent flexibility, and yet not negate its persistence.

Conclusion

Very frequently, the relationship between official nationalisms and minority identities is presented as one under constant stress. The state-led nationalism is wary of the loyalty and allegiance of the members of the minority communities. As states tend to seek legitimacy within majoritarian constructs of nationalism, minority groups – whether religious or linguistic – develop deep-seated distrust in project homogenisation. The chapter argues that the question of loyalty may not necessarily pose an intractable problem for the states in South Asia. While aggressive nationalism and xenophobic patriotism tend to produce minorities as the alter ego of the national self, South Asia also provides examples of how deviation from the nation-state principle very often conditioned routes of integration. The question of loyalty, therefore, elicits variegated response depending on the structural constitution of the minority group, the legitimate entitlements that it aspires for and the prevailing ideological orientation of the state.

Notes

1 Hewitt, 'Ethnic Construction, Provincial Identity and Nationalism in Pakistan.' Hewitt argues that the Pakistani state's strategy of dealing with Baluch separatism remained short of success owing to its failure in patronising the emergence of a reformist Baluch ethnic identity that could be contained within the provincial framework.
2 Sachar committee is the popular name of the Prime Minister's High-Level Committee instituted of India to look into the Economic, Educational and Social Status of Muslims of India. The Committee submitted its report in 2006.

3 In Pakistan for example, the Parsee representative in the first Constituent Assembly of Pakistan vociferously supported the Islamic elements in the proposed Constitution of Pakistan. See Ghufran, 'Parsis: A Minority Community in Pakistan.' Similarly, the Parsee representative in the Indian Constituent Assembly declined the offer to have one permanent representative in the Parliament on the plea that the community would rather like to be part of the national mainstream.

References

Allahabad High Court. 5 April 2007. Committee of Management, Anjuman Madarsa Noorul Islam Vs the State of Uttar Pradesh.
Anderson, Benedict. 1991. *Imagined Communities: Reflections on the Origin and Spread of Nationalism*. London: Verso.
Bertram, Bastiapillai. 2002. "Minority, Nation and Identity Question: The Muslims of Sri Lanka." In *Religious Minorities in South Asia: Selected Essays on Pos-Colonial Situations*, edited by Monirul Hasan and Lipi Ghosh, 193–209. New Delhi: Manak.
Breuilly, John. 1993. *Nationalism and the State*. Chicago: University of Chicago Press.
Emerson, Rupert. 1970. *From Empire to Nation: The Rise to Self – Assertion of Asian and African Peoples*, 95–6. Kolkata: Scientific Book Agency, Indian reprint.
Ghufran, Nasreen. "Parsis: A Minority Community in Pakistan." In Monirul Hasan and Lipi Ghosheds, op. cit., 167–83.
Government of India (GOI). 1986. "Memorandum of Settlement (Mizo Accord)." https://peacemaker.un.org/sites/peacemaker.un.org/files/IN_860630_Mizoram%20Accord.pdf. September 5, 2018.
Government of India (GOI). 2006. *Report on the Social, Educational and Economic Status of the Muslim Community of India* (Sachar Committee Report).
Hardgrave, Robert L. Jr. Winter 1964–65. "The DMK and the Politics of Tamil Nationalism." *The Pacific Affairs* 37 (4): 396–411.
Hewitt, Vernon. 1998. "Ethnic Construction, Provincial Identity and Nationalism in Pakistan: The Case of Baluchistan." In *Subnational Movements in South Asia*, edited by S. K. Mitra, and R. A. Lewis, 43–67. New Delhi: Segment Books.
Huq, Abul Fazal. April 24, 1984. "The Problem of National Identity in Bangladesh." *Journal of Social Studies*: 45–58.
Keating, Michael. Winter 1999. "Asymmetrical Government: The Multinational States in an Integrating Europe." *Publius: The Journal of Federalism* 29 (1).
Oommen, T. K. 2004. "New Nationalisms and Collective Rights: The Case of South Asia." In *Ethnicity, Nationalism and Minority Rights*, edited by Stephen May et al., 122–43. Cambridge: Cambridge University Press.

Peacock, Olive. 2002. "Ethnic Conflict in Sri Lanka: A Case of the Burgher." In *Ethnicity and Polity in South Asia*, edited by GirinPhukan, 170–6. New Delhi: South Asian Pub.

Phizo, A. Z. September 5, 2018. "Plebiscite Speech." www.neuenhofer.de/guenter/nagaland/phizo.html.

Ramaswamy, Sumathi. 1999. "Sanskrit for the Nation." *Modern Asian Studies* 33 (2): 341.

Samaddar, Ranabir. 2002. "South Asia: Self Determination, Forms of Autonomy and Democratic Argument." In *Ethnicity and Polity in South Asia*, edited by GirinPhukan, 20–34. New Delhi: South Asian Pub.

Shakir, Moin. April 1982. "On National Integration." *Social Scientist* 10 (4): 36–45.

Sundar, Nandini. 1997. *Subalterns and Sovereigns: An Anthropological History of Bastar 1854–1996*. New Delhi: Oxford University Press.

Tilly, Charles. February 1994. "States and Nationalism in Europe." *Theory and Society* 23 (1): 131–46.

Chapter 8

Adivasi struggles in Chhattisgarh

'Jal, Jungle, Zameen'

Sudha Bharadwaj

Chhattisgarh, a state in Central-Eastern India, has a population of about 20 million with significant proportions of *Adivasi* (32%) as also of Dalit (12%) communities, in an area of 135,000 sq. Km, 45% of which is forest land.[1] Geographically, the "elongated pear" shaped region consists of a forested and hilly, mineral-rich outer ring populated largely by tribals, surrounding the plains area – once called a "rice bowl" for its thousands of indigenous varieties of rice – and presently home to large industrial areas stretching all the way down its length. Fifty years ago these industrial areas consisted of the state-owned steel, coal, aluminium and power companies and now increasingly house hundreds of sponge iron factories and private cement, steel and power plants. Chhattisgarh has significant reserves of high-quality iron ore, coal, dolomite, tin ore and even diamond which, respectively, make-up about 19%, 16%, 11%, 38% and 28% of the total Indian reserves. The state also has 5% each of India's limestone and bauxite.[2]

Whither self-rule? A betrayal of the constitutional scheme and protection for the tribal people

The prolonged and fierce resistance of the tribal people in large tracts of British India had forced the British administration to accept the areas dominated by tribal population as "excluded" or "partially excluded" areas (that is areas excluded from the general laws) and to bring in special laws – the Chota Nagpur Tenancy Act, the Godavari Agencies or Ganjam and Vishakhapatnam Act, the Santhal Parganas Tenancy Act or special provisions in existing acts such as in the Bombay Land Revenue Code. In these areas, by such provisions, the tribals were to be protected from exploitation of money lenders, their rights and title to enjoy the lands in their occupation were to be assured, and their autonomy and culture to be preserved. The infiltration of non-tribals, and the purchase of lands by them, except with the prior sanction of an officer appointed by the government in this behalf, was to be prohibited.

The Sarguja division of North Chhattisgarh (today the districts of Jashpur, Koriya, Sarguja, Surajpur and Balrampur) is inhabited largely by the Gond, Oraon, Kanwar, Nagesia, Kodaku, Cherwa, Khairwar, Agariya, etc. Tribes and primitive tribes such as the Pando, Pahadi Korva, Birhor, etc., are contiguous with the Chotanagpur region, now largely in Jharkhand. The Bastar division of South Chhattisgarh (now the districts of Bastar, Kanker, Sukma, Dantewada, Bijapur, Narayanpur and Kondagaon) is part of the Dandakaranya region stretching from Vidarbha in Maharashtra to Southern Odisha and is, apart from its urban areas, almost totally tribal in demography consisting of various branches of the Madia and Muria tribes speaking Gondi, Halbi and Bhatri languages. The western borders of the state (districts Kawardha, Mungeli and parts of Bilaspur) along with the adjoining districts of Madhya Pradesh are the area where the fast dying out a primitive tribal group of Baiga (now designated 'particularly vulnerable') reside. Though many of these areas have been the arena of tribal revolts of the past, their stories are more tucked away in local folklore than being alive in public memory, with the exceptions of the revolt led by Veer Narayan Singh in 1875 in the Kasdol block of the present district of Baloda Bazar; the Halba, Koi, Muria and Bhoomkal rebellions of Bastar in the British era; and post-independence – Praveer Chand Bhanj Deo's revolt in Bastar which was suppressed violently after killing him on the steps of his palace in Jagdalpur on 25 March 1966.

Post-independence, the 'partially excluded' and 'excluded' areas were more or less incorporated into the Fifth and Sixth Schedules of the Constitution. While the tribal areas of the north-east were covered by the Sixth Schedule which provided for autonomous district councils, the Fifth Schedule was conceived of as an area governed directly by the Union through the Governor who, in consultation with the Tribes Advisory Council, had powers of a legislative nature to repeal or modify, in the interest of peace and governance of the Scheduled area, any legislation of the State Assembly or the Parliament. Most of the tribes recognised by the British administration were listed as the Scheduled Tribes in various states. (Of course, there were tribes left out of the schedule and areas left out of the scheduled areas and those communities are struggling to assert their identity and autonomy even today.)

A very large proportion of Chhattisgarh's geographical area – 60.57% – is covered under the Fifth Schedule. Districts which are fully under the Schedule are – Surajpur, Balrampur, Sarguja, Koriya, Jashpur, Gariyaband, Kanker, Bastar, Kondagaon, Sukma, Dantewada, Narayanpurand Beejapur. Other districts like – Bilaspur, Raigarh, Dhamtari, Balod, Rajnandgaon, Baloda Bazar, Mungeli, Korba and Janjgir-Champa contain blocks which fall under the Schedule. With the passage of the Panchayat (Extension to Scheduled Areas) Act 1996, the constitutional principle recognising the special way of life, customary governance and autonomy of tribal people was implemented in statutory law. The terse act establishes the centrality and powers of the Gram Sabha. It empowers the Gram Sabha to safeguard community resources, approve development plans and projects, enforce prohibition or regulation of the sale of intoxicants and restore the unlawfully alienated land. Consultation with the Gram Sabha is required before acquisition or resettling of project affected persons, and its consent is mandatory for minor mining minerals. Most importantly the Gram Sabha can exercise powers over institutions and functionaries in the social sector, and the Panchayati Raj institutions at higher levels are forbidden from usurping its powers. Acts inconsistent with the Provisions of the Panchayats (Extension to Scheduled Areas) Act 1996 (PESA) were to have been appropriately amended or repealed within a year – by 24 December 1997. In other words, the PESA Act provided a template to exercise a substantial measure of grassroot democracy and autonomy and could have been the mechanism by which the tribal people could have engaged on their terms with the juggernaut of 'development' – the mining and corporate land acquisitions that were to follow.

Tragically that was not to be. As laid out, powerfully and simply, by Dr B. D. Sharma in his work 'Unbroken History of Broken Promises,' the laws for the scheduled areas were never effectively implemented. Governors failed to exercise their legislative powers. Even though they were not bound to act on the aid and advice of the Council of Ministers, they continued to act as if they were. The Tribes Advisory Council was rendered a formality. In Chhattisgarh, it is headed by the (non-tribal) chief minister. Many Governors did not submit their annual reports regularly, and those who did hardly conveyed the growing crisis in these areas. In Madhya Pradesh (and therefore in Chhattisgarh) despite a specific notification dated 31 January 2000 laying out in detail the manner in which the Gram Sabha is to be consulted prior to land acquisition, the interpretation that "consultation" is not "consent" have rendered the Gram Sabha powerless in even modifying let alone nullifying developmental projects. (It is quite another matter that while interpreting "consultation" in the appointment of judges, the Supreme Court has been quite clear that consultation is indeed consent!).

Again the historic 'Samatha' judgement[3] that held that private companies being "non-tribal" could not be permitted to mine, rather only government companies or co-operatives of the *Adivasi* people could do so, had provided an opportunity to organise Adivasi co-operatives and again engage with the developmental process on a level playing field. However, the "Samatha Committee" formed in Chhattisgarh does not appear to have interfered anywhere in the grant of mining leases to private companies to assert tribal rights. While the Samatha judgement has not been modified/ overturned by a larger bench of the Supreme Court, disparaging remarks have been made by coordinate benches not dealing specifically with the issues raised therein, thus eroding its credibility without an upfront challenge.

The Preamble to the Forest Rights Act 2006 admits correcting historic injustice and seeks to provide rights – both individual and communal – to tribal people and other traditional forest dwellers to live in, cultivate in, gather forest produce in and maintain *nistari* rights in forests – which since the British era had in the legal framework become 'state property' and in which framework the Adivasis, who had lived in and co-existed with the forests for centuries, had become 'encroachers.' While the critics of the Act rightly point out that the Act tries to limit and to privatise/ individualise ownership of forest lands, yet no doubt precious rights have been sought to be recognised by this Act. Chhattisgarh claims to be the 'No. 1' state in the Forest Rights Act (FRA) implementation. However, the ground reality reveals something else altogether, in fact yet more injustice – namely,[4]

1   More than 50% of all claims filed have been rejected, and the total land for which *pattas* have been granted is less than estimates made of forest encroachments in the erstwhile State of

Madhya Pradesh 20 years ago. The *pattas* granted have been very small parcels of land sometimes, as for the Baiga tribe, just homestead land.

2. Very few applications for community rights over forests have been accepted or processed, and, if granted, often contain unacceptable provisions making such rights subject to plans of the Forest Department. In fact, even the special application forms for rights on communal resources were not made available in most blocks in Chhattisgarh, and deadlines were repeatedly quoted for not accepting forms, despite clarifications from the Tribal Welfare Ministry.

3. The centrality of the Gram Sabha in the process of granting of forest rights; and the fact that, in the Act, the Gram Sabha is the investigating and certifying authority with regard to whether a forest dweller has been settled on a certain parcel of land, the acceptability of evidence necessary for establishing this and the period and extent of such settlement has been completely disregarded. As a result, it is the Forest Department that has de facto been the verifying or certifying authority, leaving the *Adivasi* at its mercy yet once more.

4. The provisions in the Forest Rights Act that explicitly lay down that the determination of the rights must be carried out before any displacement even when a forest is declared a Reserve Forest/ Eco-sensitive Area, is also being violated with impunity. Even otherwise, the explicit provisions prohibiting eviction of forest-dwelling communities during the process of determination of forest rights have been ignored in a large number of cases, where *dabang* (powerful) communities have evicted primitive tribal groups and Dalits with the tacit support of the authorities.

Intensification of the struggles over 'Jal, Jungle and Zameen'

With the intensifying global financial crisis, world capitalism has had only two difficult options – to reduce living standards in the developed world or to intensify the loot of natural resources in the developing world. In India we see corporates zeroing in on the mineral-resource-rich forested belt stretching all the way from North Bengal – Jharkhand, Odisha, Chhattisgarh, Bastar and upto Vidarbha, and a whole variety of tribal resistances ranging from peaceful to armed, springing up in reaction as a consequence.

On account of a large number of MOUs (121 as on 30 March 2011 as per the Chhattisgarh government website) to set up power plants, steel plants and cement plants, as well as the grant of a large number of Prospecting and Mining Leases (already more than 2 lakh acres have been covered under 354 MLs as on 30 March 2011),[5] a large-scale transfer of agricultural lands, commons and other livelihood resources – particularly forest lands and water (both surface and groundwater) – is occurring from the peasants and *Adivasis* (who enjoyed these earlier both privately and collectively) to private corporate entities. While this phenomenon is visible all across this mineral-rich state, it is particularly acute in the districts of Raigarh, Sarguja, Janjgir-Champa and Korba. This is causing a crisis of livelihood amongst a vast rural population, intensifying earlier trends of migration to brick kilns, human trafficking and other forms of bondedness.

In carrying out acquisitions of land the state government is misusing its powers of eminent domain in the name of 'Public Purpose,' whereas the reports of the Comptroller and Auditor General of India (CAG) of the state clearly indicate that in granting such largesse, corruption is occurring on a large scale, and private companies are gaining at a considerable loss to the state exchequer. (The case of allotment of coal blocks was an example in point where the spirit of the Directive Principles of State Policy was violated. Unfortunately, the legal challenge ended by equating auctions with transparency.) Similarly, the provisions for making objections under Section 5A of the Land Acquisition Act 1894 have been circumvented by misuse of the provisions for urgent acquisition under Section 17 of the Act. Despite the law being clear that the consent of both owner and occupier are mandatory for entry into private land for mining by a company (other than a government company under the Coal Bearing Areas Acquisition Act), the state acts on behalf of the private company to present the farmers with a fait accompli of having to accept compensation as if in the case of acquisition. Now, with the amendments in the Mines and Mineral Development Regulation Act, by which iron ore, limestone and bauxite have been designated notified minerals, and the possibilities of new mining regulations in the notified areas containing them, even these protective provisions may not survive.

Almost in all project affected villages there have been protests, some sporadic and short-lived, others more prolonged and determined, but all of them have faced state repression. The leaders of the protests and often large numbers of villagers have been victims of malicious prosecution by powerful corporates in which the local police and administration have been hand-in-glove. An extreme example of this is the case of the murderous attempt on the life of environmental activist Ramesh Agrawal at Raigarh by persons associated with the Jindal Steel and Power Limited.

Today in the Sarguja division of North Chhattisgarh, the Hansdeo Arand Sangharsh Samiti, Bharat Jan Andolan and Gondwana Gantantra Party battle against mining corporates destroying pristine and inviolate forests by demanding community forest rights and consultation with Gram Sabhas; the Gram Sabha Parishad struggles against the forced and unconstitutional urbanisation of village Premnagar, done only to bypass a robust Gram Sabha, which refused to permit establishment of a mega power plant. In Tamnar and Kosampalli villages, villagers surrounded by mines of the Jindal and Monnet companies fight never-ending legal battles against the fraudulent acquisition, receding groundwater levels and unacknowledged pollution.

In the still pristine district of Jashpur, villagers, particularly of the Christian Oraon community, march in tens of thousands to oppose plans to mine and deforest, and to protest the increasing elephant-human conflict that has become a serious threat not just to crops and granaries but human lives. Elephants driven out of adjoining parts of Odisha and Jharkhand by mining and fragmentation of their natural habitat have clashed more than 400 times with humans in the past three months in the Tapkara forest range alone.[6] Meanwhile, attacks on missions, demands de-reservation for Christian *Adivasis* and *Ghar Vapsi* campaigns by the Hindutva forces are the dangerous diversionary tactics which the corporate state is employing to ignore this groundswell. Korba town in Chhattisgarh – with its enormous ash dykes of power plants, regularly emptied by 'accidental' breaches inundating hundreds of acres of agricultural lands was declared the fifth-most critically polluted industrial cluster in India a few years ago. It is not a coincidence that the proposed elephant reserve of Lemru, lying in what was designated "no-go" forest in district Korba, was notified on the request of the Chhattisgarh government only to facilitate three new coal blocks.

The Chhattisgarh Bachao Andolan – a platform of anti-displacement movements is trying to forge unity and solidarity between anti-displacement movements and bring the burning issue of displacement onto the political agenda of the state. What needs to be appreciated is that the life and death struggle of *Adivasis* all over India for '*Jal, Jungle, Zameen*' is also the struggle for an ecologically sustainable path of development and the preservation of precious natural resources for the generations to come – indeed the rest of us need to thank these communities for refusing to allow a brutal and myopic paradigm of corporate loot to lead us to destruction.

Civil war and increasing militarisation in South Chhattisgarh – criminalising a people

The districts of Bastar division in Southern Chhattisgarh are the epicentre of the 3–4 decades long Maoist (Naxalite) insurgency, which has affected not only these tribal-populated and densely forested districts but also other neighbouring states and refuses to lie down and die despite increasingly heavy militarisation of these areas. A report of the BBC put the number of security forces per lakh population in Bastar presently as 1770, as compared to about 800 in Kashmir and 139 in India. Already, resistance to the military technique of 'strategic hamletting' – of emptying out the villages to bring the people to roadside camps – employed during the 'Salwa Judum' period and popularly perceived to be connected with a ground-clearing operation for mining the rich mineral resources of the region, has transformed the 30-year-old radical left movement into a wider tribal rebellion. The "collateral damage" of thousands of tribal villagers fleeing their villages and a large proportion of them retreating deeper into the forests, of large-scale arrests, killings and burning out of villages has been the subject of nationwide debate and important cases in the Supreme Court. The recommendations of the National Human Rights Commission of India (NHRC) in the Enquiry conducted on the directions of the Supreme Court in Nandini Sundar's case, namely that the displaced villagers be rehabilitated back in their villages and First Information Reports (FIRs) be lodged against all extrajudicial killings, has not been acted on at all by the state.[7] On the contrary, those NGOs which were trying to assist such rehabilitation and reparation were severely victimised. In the year 2011, the People's Union for Civil Liberties received a letter from a journalist in Bastar enclosing a list of 135 villagers alleged to have been killed during Operation Green Hunt between January 2009 and April 2010 alone, and this list has been filed with the NHRC.[8] Many of the incidents narrated could be correlated with newspaper reports and some news of protests by villagers. However, it has not been possible for independent civil liberties groups to carry out investigations to verify these serious allegations, mainly because there has been a denial of physical access. There has been an abject failure of constitutional remedies for such extrajudicial killings. A case filed in the Chhattisgarh High Court regarding the Singavaram fake encounter and demanding a Central Bureau of Investigation (CBI) Enquiry remains pending even after about eight years, while another case filed in the Supreme Court about the killings in Village Gompad also remains pending for the past five years. The exceptional case is of the Sarkeguda encounter of 2012 – in which 17 *Adivasis* including seven minors were killed.[9] This incident is being enquired into by a Judicial Enquiry Commission before whom the villagers have appeared and deposed. This has been possible largely because of the courage of a young health worker of the village – Kamla Kaka – who helped them to come forth and the support of the Jagdalpur Legal Aid Group (JagLAG) – a group of women lawyers doing pro bono work for *Adivasi* undertrials. Both Kamla and the JagLAG are facing serious harassment and threats as a consequence.

Now, an Army Headquarters is in the process of being set up in the Bilaspur district of Chhattisgarh and the Indian government, which leads the world in arms purchases this year, has bought drones, not only for surveillance but also from Israel, for the attack. Taken together with the statement of Prakash Mishra, DG CRPF, that 'drone attacks may be necessary' for 'clearing out Maoists deep within the forests of Chhattisgarh,' the possibility of aerial attacks in the future cannot be ruled out. The implications this would have for non-combatant civilians need only be seen from the example of Afghanistan.

In the name of dealing with Naxalism and Naxal supporters, the Chhattisgarh government has enacted draconian laws to suppress the freedoms of association and expression guaranteed in the Indian Constitution. According to journalists in Bastar there are tens of thousands of permanent warrants out for named and unnamed *Adivasis*, waiting to be executed. At least ten police stations in Bastar division have more than a thousand warrants each. While one can appreciate the complex conditions under which courts and jails function in this area, it is quite apparent that a large number of *Adivasis*, routinely picked up in searching operations, are being implicated in serious cases without the concerned magistrate exercising his/her judicial discretion independently. Once, being implicated in a serious "Naxal Offence," the undertrials are often not produced before courts for long periods of time, on account of there not being 'sufficient police guard.' They are refused bail so mechanically that lawyers have stopped moving bail applications altogether in these areas. A study by the JagLAG[10] based on 5 years of undertrial data shows that while a person is, on an average, 16 times more likely to get bail than acquittal in India as a whole and 8 times more likely to get bail than acquittal in Chhattisgarh, the ratio is 0.8 in Bastar division.[11] In other words, it is more likely that an undertrial is acquitted (though of course, that would take two to four years) than granted bail. Trials are held up for a single witness of the Naga Battalion or an investigating officer for years together but not closed because of the 'gravity of the offence.' Out of economic difficulty and for fear of harassment, family members of the undertrials are unable to visit them in jail, particularly in circumstances of physical and mental ailment. This makes the undertrials even more vulnerable. Since 'Naxal undertrials' are only kept in Central Jails, and since jails in Bastar are overcrowded four to six times their capacity, many of these undertrials are transferred to Durg or Raipur Central Jails, where they are even more inaccessible and too far away to be taken to court regularly. Seventy-nine undertrials facing trials in Kondagaon, who were sent to Durg Jail (more than 300 km away), had petitioned the Chief Justice of Chhattisgarh High Court in 2011 regarding their long incarceration of more than three years without trial.[12] Most lawyers never go to meet their client in jail in 'Naxal' matters for they would have to give a 'mugshot' and sign a separate register. This makes them amenable to pressures from the police. The vast majority of *Adivasi* undertrials speak only *Adivasi* languages, i.e., Gondi, Halbi, etc. However, it is shocking that even now courts in the Bastar region do not have official interpreters/translators and the *Adivasis* are unable to communicate with the Officers of the Court or otherwise effectively intervene in the judicial process. During the recent Vidhan Sabha elections, thousands of family members of *Adivasi* undertrials in Dantewada Jail had gathered to protest that these undertrials had been held falsely, that their trials were being unduly delayed and that they are released on bail. It is unfortunate that the Nirmala Buch

Committee, created in the wake of the abduction of Collector Alex Paul Menon, has neither been able to carry out a judicial review of the cases of *Adivasi* undertrials nor conduct a fact-finding mission to find out the actual circumstances of the arrest. Even in those cases where the Buch Committee has recommended that bails not be opposed, the courts have failed to grant bail. Another disturbing aspect of the functioning of the criminal justice system in Bastar is that political opponents or other "inconvenient" persons can easily be implicated in "Naxal offences" thus ensuring that they would be put away behind bars for several years. For instance, prior to the last Vidhan Sabha elections, many activists and *Sarpanches* of the Communist Party of India, a registered national political party contesting elections, were incarcerated, including Kartam Joga, a petitioner of the SalwaJudum case in the Supreme Court. Kartam Joga was finally acquitted but only after being in jail for three years. Today Soni Sori, Lingaram Kodopi, Arvind Gupta, etc., of the Aam Aadmi Party are being similarly victimised. Indeed as aptly put by Advocate Vrinda Grover in her study of undertrials in Bastar, the *Adivasi* undertrial has become a "Prisoner of War."

Which way – indigenous rights or genocide?

In the Bastar division, a proposed ultra-mega steel plant in Dilmili is facing mass protests, even as Tata waves goodbye to the land at Lohandiguda acquired at gunpoint. Recently, the people of 25 villages blockaded the roads to the National Mineral Development Corporation (NMDC) Bailadila Iron Ore Complex (district Dantewada) to protest its proposed expansion.[13] They were angered by the fact that so few local *Adivasi* youth had been employed, even though the Shankini and Dankini rivers have been running red with iron ore fines for the past few decades. The Polavaram dam which threatens to inundate scores of villages of Chhattisgarh-Odisha-Andhra is being constructed without Gram Sabha consultation, proper survey or rehabilitation of the project affected, as the *padayatra* of the *Adivasi* Mahasabha (affiliated with the CPI) has exposed. Approximately 7,443 hectares of land in Kanker, Narayanpur and Dantewada alone have been given out in prospecting leases to various private companies as per the government website,[14] yet in the case of villages falling within the proposed Rowghat iron ore mines in Kanker district, villagers and community workers marking their community forest boundaries with GPS machines were illegally detained by the Border Security Force. The government, which is forever exhorting the tribals of Bastar to shun extremism and join the mainstream, refuses to engage with these peaceful mass movements and only responds by treating all dissent as Naxalism.

The Government of Chhattisgarh admits that after Salwa Judum in the year 2005, 644 villages of the then Dantewada district, whose overwhelmingly *Adivasi* population was about 350,000, had been emptied out.[15] While a lakh of people might have fled to Andhra Pradesh/ Telangana, a large proportion of this population has gone deeper into the forests. With the withdrawal of educational and health services of the state as well as ration shops from these so-called 'Naxal' stronghold areas, a situation has arisen in which several lakh *Adivasis* have been automatically 'outlawed.' This population is being deprived of basic needs. Anti-Naxal operations in such an area could result in a virtual genocide and killings of unarmed civilians and non-combatants on a large scale. Additionally, the state programme of bringing *Adivasi* children to study in roadside porta-cabins and ashrams (where incidentally cases of food poisoning, medical negligence and sexual violence are regularly reported) and separating them from their families is repeating the "historical mistakes" committed by the Australian government on its indigenous peoples, for which the Australian prime minister recently rendered a public apology.

The Indian state claims that Naxalism is the 'internal security threat' and is justifying levels of militarisation akin to occupation and war. On the other hand, it refuses to accept the situation internationally as one of 'internal armed conflict' since that would mean permitting international observers such as the UN Special Rapporteurs, the International Red Cross, Amnesty International or Medicines Sans Frontiers to visit and ensure that all parties to the conflict abide by the Geneva Protocol. It would also mean ensuring the safety and welfare of non-combatant civilians caught in the conflict.

Historically, capitalism has come in riding on the back of indigenous genocides. But the recent meeting in Bolivia, where indigenous people from all over Latin America gathered and where they resolved to save Mother Earth, is perhaps the new direction the world needs to move in to survive.

Of late, an interesting phenomenon is occurring in Bastar. Thousands of villagers are gathering at police stations to protest against illegal arrests, detentions and tortures – at Kookanar, Kuakonda,

Tongpal. In many of these peaceful mass demonstrations, Soni Sori, who herself suffered custodial sexual violence and long incarceration on false charges and today dons an Aam Aadmi Party (AAP) topi is the organiser. In the past few months, she has exposed the fake encounter of Nuppo Bhima at Revali, of Podia Hemla at Nahadi and Bhima Mandaviat Nilvaya. An irate Inspector General (IG) (Naxal Operations) S R P Kalluri held a press conference urging people to socially boycott her. Recently, he had also been embarrassed by her press conference which revealed that out of 300 Naxal surrenders boasted by the police, 80% turned out to be unarmed villagers.[16]

The democratic voices in Chhattisgarh have been repeatedly demanding that the way to de-escalate violence in the Bastar region would be to rehabilitate people in their villages, allow them to rebuild their ravaged agrarian and forest-based economies, restore the civil administration and wholeheartedly comply with the Forest Rights Act and the PESA Act to give the *Adivasis* of the area substantial rights – rights to land, to livelihood and to life. Decisions to carry out large-scale mining and set up industries in that area can only be effective if carried out after genuine consultation with the people. It is only this, that can reduce the polarisation between security forces on the one hand and the *Adivasi* people at large on the other, and can prevent imminent genocide in the name of counterinsurgency.

Notes

1 Sudha Bharadwaj, "Some Experiences of Organising Workers in Chhattisgarh," *Aspects of India's Economy* (72–73) (May 2018), India's Working Class and Its Prospects, www.rupe-India.org/72/organising.html.
2 *Ibid.*
3 Sudha Bharadwaj, "Has India Betrayed Its Indigenous Peoples, the *Adivasis*?" www.sabrangindia.in.
4 *Ibid.*
5 "Chhattisgarh PUCL's Memorandum to the NHRC," https://kractivist.wordpress.com/2013/04/21/.
6 *Ibid.*
7 *Ibid.*
8 *Ibid.*
9 *Ibid.*
10 Bharadwaj, "Some Experiences of Organising Workers in Chhattisgarh."

11 *Ibid.*
12 "Chhattisgarh PUCL's Memorandum to the NHRC," https://kractivist.wordpress.com/2013/04/21/.
13 www.sabrangindia.in/article/has-india-betrayed-its-indigenous-peoples-adivasis.
14 *Ibid.*
15 *Ibid.*
16 *Ibid.*

Chapter 9

Was Bhagat Singh an internationalist?

Resistance and identity in global age

Aparna Vaidik

Introduction

Is there nationalism that doesn't nestle spatial imagery? The imagery of a bounded, finite and a closed space – a demarcated terrain – physical and imagined. Specific to anti-colonial variants of political nationalism is the imagery of space that the nation physically inhabits but may not be a sovereign of, space illegitimately usurped by internal and external 'others.' Nationalism, in this case, attempts to fuse the two, the physical space and the nation's sovereignty by wresting the latter back and investing it in the rightful inhabitants[1] (Ramnath 2011: 20). The idea of state, or statism, thus is the fundamental telos of political nationalism, as an opponent and as an aspiration. Internationalism, on the other hand, carries the spatial association of expansiveness and transcendence – a connectedness that goes beyond the more narrowly drawn physical and imaginative confines of political space. The very idea of internationalism, in its socialist avatar, necessarily posits an oppositional binary between itself and nationalism.[2] Not state but mythos – solidarity against oppression – is internationalism's professed telos. To be an internationalist is to appeal to a universalism that surpasses the purported insularity and inwardness of nationalism. This chapter interrogates these spatial imaginings associated with nationalism and internationalism to see whether the binary political identities that they generate (nationalist and internationalist) hold up to historical inquiry.

The category of 'internationalist' is often invoked to explain, categorise and classify Bhagat Singh on the Indian political spectrum. Why is Bhagat Singh despite never leaving India or working towards creating international ties known as an internationalist?

This tag lacking in definitional clarity leaves several questions unanswered: Is being an internationalist a claim to cosmopolitanism and universalism or a claim to representing higher consciousness than nationalism? What was the historical import of this category about the Indian nationalism? How does it help us understand the thoughts and actions of a historical person? Was Bhagat Singh an internationalist because he was reading and quoting from European and Russian texts, or he dreamt of a society where the proletariat was sovereign; or that his sources of inspiration were not just local and provincial? In interrogating the category 'internationalist,' the more significant historiographical question this chapter explores is whether and how far did individuals such as Bhagat Singh see themselves as warnings of a global phenomenon? Did he see himself as an internationalist? Is their location within a larger universal frame a historiographical or a historical one – did the global constitute his consciousness or is it the historian who locates them in a worldwide frame in order to understand their actions and persuasions?

Intertextuality of life and literature

The Indian revolutionary struggle arose in the 1890s. It thrived on diasporic and transnational links since its early days. The revolutionaries were not confined to the geographical boundaries of British India but were spread far and wide in United States, Mexico, Japan, Thailand, China, Singapore, Philippines and Malaya. The revolutionary centres included major cities across the world such as London, San Francisco, New York, Vancouver, Stockholm, Berlin, Tashkent and Singapore (Fraser 1977; Raucher 1974; Dmitriev 2002; Fischer 2007; Silvestri 2007; O'Malley 2010).[3] The early decades of the twentieth century also saw the birth of several revolutionary organisations in different parts of British India such as the Anushilan Samiti (1902) and Jugantar (1906) in Bengal, Abhinava Bharat (1904) in Maharashtra, Hindustan Republican Association (1924) in United Provinces, Naujawan Bharat Sabha (NBS) (1926) and the Hindustan Socialist Republican Association or the HSRA (1928) in Punjab under the leadership of Bhagat Singh (1907–1931) and Chandra Shekhar Azad[4] (1906–1931). The HSRA included revolutionaries active in British India since the early 1920s who regrouped under its banner in 1928. They espoused armed revolution and socialism as twin ideologies. Indian revolutionaries were mostly young college and university students who came from different cities and towns and belonged to families of the provincial middle class, including petty traders, well-off farmers or school or college teachers. Common to all shades of revolutionaries was their strident anticolonialism, a willingness to resort to political violence and broad-reaching political networks and diasporic connections. They carried out various acts – targeted political assassinations; raiding and looting for money or ammunition; illegally making bombs and acquiring arms; recruiting and training militias; and importing, writing, printing, translating and circulating 'seditious' literature. The HSRA revolutionaries became famous for having assassinated J. P. Saunders, the Assistant Superintendent of Police in Lahore on 17 December 1928 and for bombing Delhi's Legislative Assembly on 8 April 1929. The colonial police rounded up these young revolutionaries in June–July 1928 and put them on trial that came to be known as the Lahore Conspiracy Case Trial. It was unprecedented in the scale of public and media attention it attracted. While undertrial, the members of the HSRA disrupted the court proceedings in various ways before going on intermittent hunger strikes. They demanded better treatment and living facilities for the incarcerated political prisoners. The Government of India initially refused to indulge their demands let alone accord them the status of 'political' prisoners. The hunger strike and the attempts of the jail officials to force-feed the prisoners physically incapacitated the revolutionaries. The tempo of events acquired a painful crescendo when Jatindranath Das, a revolutionary from Bengal, succumbed to pneumonia and gangrene. These hunger strikes, the penal uproar and the revolutionaries' travails received extensive press coverage and galvanised the nationalist sentiments transforming the trial into a much-watched public and media spectacle.

For an analysis of the revolutionary ideology, historians have turned to Bhagat Singh's political writings and the HSRA's propaganda literature (i.e. its Constitution, public statements, court statements, polemical exchanges with Gandhi and the articles and essays written for public). These writings and materials are a significant exposition of HSRA's ideology and provide an insight into the full spatial and intellectual span of the radical imagination. It was evident that Marx, Lenin and Trotsky, Russian Narodniks, the Irish Sinn Fein, Italian leaders – Garibaldi and Mazzini, and the European anarchists ignited their minds and furnished them with strategies for framing their struggle. These influences have been an essential factor in Bhagat Singh's characterisation as an internationalist. This, in turn, has generated a misleading presumption that Bhagat entered the fray with a pre-fabricated identity of an internationalist. Despite being born in a political family and inspired by his Uncle Ajit Singh and Sardar Kartar Singh Sarabha with their links to the Gadar Party, a transnational revolutionary organisation with its base in California, Bhagat couldn't be classified as an internationalist when he left home in his teens to join the revolutionary struggle. His consciousness grew during the time he spent in the revolutionary movement observing, participating, learning, reading and studying about other revolutions and revolutionaries before rising as the leader and ideologue of HSRA.

A crucial aspect of Bhagat Singh's new consciousness was the books and pamphlets that he was consuming. Reading materials that nourished and nurtured his imagination; books that informed, shaped, moulded and radicalised his impressionable self; and books in which he found answers to his existential doubts and the problem of his country's enslavement. Bhagat Singh plainly acknowledged that the turning point in his revolutionary career from a 'romantic idealist revolutionary' to a more informed one came with the study of revolutionary literature: ' "Study" was the cry that reverberated in the corridors of my mind. Study to enable yourself to face the arguments advanced by the opposition. Study to arm yourself with arguments in favour of your cult. I began to study' (Singh 2006: 25). The dialectics between Bhagat Singh's political writings and actions and the books that he read were crucial to his becoming. That is, the intertextuality of life and literature made possible the intermeshing of the revolutionaries' present selves with the lives of the historical heroes is how Bhagat Singh came to imagine the revolution and himself as a revolutionary.

Some of these writers and books were Bakunin's *God and State*, Peter Kropotkin's *The Place of Anarchism in Socialistic Evolution and An Appeal to the Young*, George Woodcock's *The Anarchist Prince*, Bolton King's *The Life of Mazzini* and A. J. Sack's *The Birth of Russian Democracy*, Vera Figner's *Memoirs of a Revolutionist*, Dan Breen's *My Fight for Irish Freedom*, Upton Sinclair's *Cry for Justice*, Ivan Turgenev's *Fathers and Sons*, Savarkar's *The First War of Independence*, Bankim's *Anandamath*, Sachindranath Sanyal's *Bandi Jivan*, Soham Swami's *Commonsense*, Radha Mohun Gokul's *Communism Kya Hai* and Sakharam Ganesh Deuskar's *Desher Katha* to name a few. We know that Bhagat Singh was reading these books because he references them in his political writings and his jail diary. His associates Shiv Varma and Jaidev Kapur also mention these books and pamphlets in their reminiscences when they talk about the literature they were reading and distributing as part of HSRA's propaganda work.

Early influences of the literature that he read are visible in the naming of the organisations that Bhagat Singh founded and led. In 1924, Bhagat Singh came into the sphere of the United Provinces-based revolutionary group, the Hindustan Republican Association or the Hindustan Republican Association (HRA) named after Irish Republican Army and influenced by Mazzini's Republicanism (Gupta 297–98). Bhagat Singh founded the complimentary youth wing of HRA in the same year and called it NBS the Hindustani equivalent of Young Italy, Young Turkey and Young Ireland, all the revolutionary groups that he and his friends had read about while studying at the National College (Das 2007:14–15).

In 1928, the HRA morphed into the HSRA (the Hindustan Socialist Republican Association) when core cadre of HRA was wiped out in 1927 at the end of the Kakori Conspiracy Case Trial. It was at Bhagat Singh's behest that the word socialist was inserted into the name of the organisation when they regrouped in December 1928 on the grounds of Ferozshah Kotla in Delhi. The insertion of the word socialism reflected a transforming consciousness. Unlike the earlier cohort of HRA revolutionaries, the ones belonging to HSRA had different kinds of socialist literature that impacted their perception of themselves and the world around them. Since the early 1920s, there was a rapid upturn in the circulation of the socialist literature in British India. In 1923, S.A. Dange started publishing *The Socialist* series from Bombay that carried all kinds of books written by German radical socialists, social democrats, anarchists and Marxists (Varma OHT: 43).[5] Shapurji Saklatvala, a Parsee MP in London used to regularly send leaflets and pamphlets such as 'Tasks of the Youth' and 'What the Indian Youths are to do' to NBS (Varma OHT: 42).[6] Radhmohun Gokul, a socialist from Kanpur, undertook translation and publication of several socialist pamphlets in Hindi (Karmendu 2009). His writings were responsible for converting a high number of youngsters in Kanpur and elsewhere to the cause of socialism. Ganesh Shankar Vidyarthi, a Gandhian and the owner of Pratap Press in Kanpur actively participated in the publication of socialist literature and covertly aided the young revolutionaries.[7]

By the end of 1925, one could discern a decisive impact of the October revolution in popularising the idea of socialism amongst the Indian youth and the working classes. There were efforts to establish the Communist Party of India at Kanpur in 1925, the working-class struggles in the period of 1926–28,[8] the formation of Workers' and Peasants' Party and the Kanpur and Peshawar Communist Conspiracy Cases. Further, the formation of League Against Imperialism in 1926–27 in Belgium; Jawaharlal Nehru's visit to Brussels as the delegate of the Congress to the League and then to the Soviet Union in 1927, and the burgeoning Chinese Communist Movement fed the increasing fascination with socialism in India and nudged the HSRA group in that direction (Varma OHT: 39).[9]

Another clear testament to the intertextuality of life and literature were the political actions that Bhagat carried out. In December 1928, Bhagat Singh ideated and planned the murder of the Superintendent of Police in Lahore to avenge the death of Lala Lajpat Rai (1865–1928), the nationalist stalwart of Punjab. Earlier in the year, Superintendent James Scott had lathi-charged an anti-Simon Commission procession led by Punjab's most famous nationalist leader Lala Lajpat Rai. Lalaji suffered injuries in the scuffle that eventually led to his death (Chand OHT: 24–25).[10] The revolutionaries had planned to kill James Scott but ended up shooting his junior John Saunders because of misidentification by a member of the group charged with tracking Scott. The political assassination of Saunders seems inspired by a similar action carried out by Vera Zasulich (1849–1919), a Russian revolutionary 1878. Zasulich had fired point blank at the Chief of Petrograd Police, General Fedor Trepov, who was known for his brutality and for inflicting corporal punishment on political prisoners (Sack 1918: 51–52). After that, Vera was put on trial for murder and got an acquittal. The Europeans and the Americans besides Russian gentry, revolutionaries, litterateurs and the masses eagerly followed what became the most sensational 'trial of the century.' Vera Zasulich inaugurated an era of political assassinations in Russia and inspired an entire generation of revolutionaries across the globe to embrace violence and martyrdom (Siljack 2008). Bhagat Singh knew about Vera Zasulich. He mentions her in his essay 'Russian Nihilists' published in *Kirti* in August 1928 and the same essay he states reading Oscar Wilde's play *Vera; or, the Nihilist* (1882) based on the life of Vera Zasulich.[11] The HSRA revolutionaries were also reading Jaakoff Prelooker's *Heroes and Heroines of Russia: Builders of a New Commonwealth* (1908) and A. J. Sack's[12] *The Birth of the Russian*

Democracy (1918) that carry details of Zasulich's life (Prelooker 1908; Sack 1918). Jaidev Kapur mentions these books (in the oral history transcripts of the Nehru Memorial and Museum Library) being a popular read in the revolutionary circle.[13] The Ghadar press had also published a profile of Vera Zasulich in a collection of profiles of 'early anti-czarists and Russian socialists' presumably positioning Zasulich on the Indian revolutionaries' radar.[14] It's quite likely that Bhagat Singh was familiar with this publication as well.

The second decisive action carried out by Bhagat Singh was on 8 April 1929 where he and Batukeshwar Dutt threw two crude smoke bombs in the Delhi Assembly. They threw them behind the treasury benches so as not to hurt the Indian delegates of the Assembly who sat on the other side. The bombs burst with a loud crack filling the chamber with smoke. Pandemonium ensued. Bhagat Singh and Dutt tossed revolutionary leaflets into the assembly chamber and shouted slogans as they waited to surrender to the police. While on trial for bombing the Assembly, they stated in their defence that they did not intend to hurt or murder anyone but had used the bombs as a 'protest and warning' against the impending passing of the Trades' Disputes Bill and the Public Safety Bill.[15] The bomb was directed at the 'institution,' i.e. the Assembly, because it was a sign of 'India's humiliation and helplessness' and stood for 'overriding domination of an irresponsible and autocratic rule.'[16]

The inspiration for the Delhi Assembly bomb action was a similar action by the French anarchist Auguste Vaillant (1861–94) in December 1893[17] (Habib 2007). Valliant had hurled a bomb at the French Chamber of Deputies. Bhagat Singh had read about Vaillant and his courtroom speech in Upton Sinclair's anthology *A Cry for Justice: An Anthology of Literature of Social Protest* (1915). The bomb that Vaillant threw was a crude homemade device not meant to kill but to injure and make noise. Following his trial, he was hanged two months later. Valliant's act inspired fellow anarchists to stab to death the French President. An anarchist Emile Henry threw a bomb at Cafe terminus Hotel killing two people and injuring many others. The series of revolutionary actions climaxed in the passing of an anti-anarchist bill for the trial and imprisonment of several anarchists. Bhagat Singh was particularly impressed by a sentence in Vaillant's court statement – 'it takes a loud voice to make the deaf hear' – that he used in his testimony while being tried for throwing a bomb in the Delhi Assembly[18]

On revolution and peasants

Bhagat Singh's political ideas were an eclectic mix drawn from a broad cross-section of authors and theorists. As most people are wont to do, Bhagat Singh read the different theorists in his context, cherry-picked ideas and adapted them to his situation. In his writings, he does not display a nuanced understanding of the differences between the writings of Marx, Bakunin, Lavrov, Kropotkin and Lenin. For instance, Bhagat Singh simultaneously drew on Marx and Bakunin oblivious to the difference between them on the question of revolution, state and the role of the proletariat. For instance, Marx believed in an organised revolution led by trained cadres of the disciplined class-conscious proletariat. Bakunin, on the other hand, considered, notwithstanding the strong vanguardist undercurrent in his writing, an idea of a revolution that would take the form of 'a peasant *jacquerie* or the spontaneous uprising of an infuriated town mob.'

How did Bhagat envision revolution? Bhagat was at pains to explain that for him the idea of revolution went beyond being just 'an upheaval or sanguinary strife.' According to him, the term Revolution referred to a programme of 'systematic reconstruction of society' following the complete destruction of the existing order.[19] The point he was seeking to drive home was not to restrict the definition of revolution to destruction but the construction of the new order.[20]

> Revolution means action. It means change brought about deliberately by an organised and systematic work, as opposed to sudden and unorganised or spontaneous change or breakdown. The political revolution does not involve the transfer of state (or more crudely, the power) from the hands of the British to the Indians, but to those Indians who are at one with us as to the final goal, or to be more precise, the power to be transferred to the revolutionary party through popular support. After that, to proceed in right earnest is to organize the reconstruction of the whole society on the socialist basis.
> (Yadav and Singh 2006: 58–59)

The revolutionary vanguard was key to Bhagat Singh's view for taking power, leading the masses and the reconstruction of the society. He used the term so dear to Lenin – the 'professional revolutionaries' for the whole-time workers who had no other ambitions or life-work except the revolution. The greater the number of such workers organised into a party, the higher the chances of their success.[21] The young revolutionaries were to be recruited and trained through study circles, lectures and publication of leaflets, books, pamphlets and periodicals.[22] This party of professional revolutionaries was to be prepared to fight to obtain power: 'We, the revolutionaries, are striving to capture power in our hands and to organise a revolutionary government.'[23] Bhagat Singh and his cohort believed that either the revolutionary vanguard should prepare and bring about the revolution or ought to be equipped with weapons and have enough widespread support to harness the spontaneity of a popular rebellion for bringing about a revolution if an opportunity such as the Revolt of 1857 or the First World War appeared again in history.

Bhagat Singh comfortably meshed his belief in Leninist vanguardism with Kropotkin's deep commitment to peasant mobilisation and propaganda work as actualised by the Russian *Narodniks* belonging to the Zemya I Volya group (Party of Land and Freedom) [xvii]and later by anarchists across the world. The time that the young Indian revolutionaries spent waiting and preparing for revolution was devoted to spreading awareness, bringing about youth awakening and carrying out propaganda amongst the masses. For the latter purpose, the revolutionaries employed various modes: oral, written and, most importantly, through action. Following Kropotkin, 'action' included political assassinations, bombings, court trials and hunger strikes – different 'deeds' aimed at spreading propaganda and awareness about the revolutionaries, their programme and vision before a full-scale revolution could take place.[24]

The belief in the proletariat's revolutionary potential set Bakunin and Kropotkin – the anarchists – apart from Marx and Engels who saw the peasantry as a conservative historical force. Classical Marxism theorised for industrial Europe where the proletariat was to lead the socialist revolution. It was expected that the vanguard party would lead the peasants if they predominated in a particular country (Van der Waltand Schmidt 2009: 57–58). Bakunin, on the other hand, saw the peasantry as a revolutionary class and a natural affiliate of the working class. It wasn't romanticism that propelled Bakunin to believe in peasantry's potential. He had a clear-eyed view of the difficulties that inhered in mobilising the peasantry: paternalism, absorption of the individual by the *mir* and confidence in the Tsar (Bakunin 1971: 346). He was less sanguine about the revolutionary youth's ability to play an essential role in mobilising the peasantry. They could do so only if they were willing to 'share their (i.e. peasants') life, their poverty, their cause, and their desperate revolt' (Bakunin 1971: 350). Bhagat Singh echoed Bakunin's sentiments regarding the youth while speculating if the Indian youth were willing to sacrifice their city lives for villages as the *Narodniks* did: 'How many persons will be there who can give up their city life to live in village-like unwashed peasants?'[25]

The pre-occupation with peasant revolts and the mounting frustration regarding not being able to start a revolution in the face of brutal government repression were the two locomotives driving the expansion of propaganda by deed as a revolutionary political strategy in Europe and Russia in the second half of the nineteenth century (and later in the colonised world) (Cahm 1989: 85–86). The challenge was to endear the revolutionary cause to the masses while living in a repressive political autocracy. Zasulich's shooting of General Trepov was one such act amongst several others that took place during the 1870s that evoked considerable public attention and sympathy. Individual acts of terrorism that included shooting at the Tsar in 1879, the bombing of Tsar's carriage in 1880 and finally the assassination of the Russian Tsar in 1881 followed. Similar was the case of German revolutionaries who took to political terrorism in the 1880s as a response to severe government despotism.[26]

HSRA's espousal of propaganda by deed was a response to analogous impulse – what they saw as the bourgeois leadership's, especially Gandhi's,[27] and the earlier generation of revolutionaries' (HRA and Ghadar specifically)[28] failure to mobilise the peasantry coupled with government's brutal repression of the revolutionaries. Bhagat Singh yearned and hoped to endear the Indian revolutionary struggle to the masses (in this case the peasantry). He felt without the peasantry's support and participation the revolutionary vision would remain unfulfilled. Bhagat Singh firmly held that 'the real revolutionary armies are in the villages and factories, the peasantry and the labourers.'[29] Be it a national or a socialist revolution; neither could be accomplished without the participation of the masses:

> But if you say you are for the national revolution and the aims of your struggle is an Indian republic of the type of the United States of America, then I ask you to please let me know on what forces you rely that will help you bring about that revolution.

The only effects on which you can depend to bring about any revolution, whether national or the socialists, are the peasantry and the labour.[30]

He and his mates observed that the masses appreciated the revolutionaries but not their political actions. In the Kakori trial when the HRA revolutionaries were accused of robbing a train carrying government moneybags, young and old would come from villages and cities and catch hold of revolutionaries' hand and identify them as participants in the *dacoities* not knowing what the revolutionaries stood for.[31] Winning over the masses to the revolutionary cause in Bhagat Singh's view required changing the earlier strategy of committing *dacoities* for collecting funds and assassinating moles. The *dacoities* made the revolutionaries appear like common criminals and turned the people away from the revolutionary cause. He felt that revolutionary political actions that inspired the masses and nudged them towards the larger vision of independence were the need of the hour.[32] As Bhagat Singh stated in one of his essays:

> There is no use of killing any one individual. These actions have their political significance in as much as they serve to create a mentality and an atmosphere which shall be very necessary to the final struggle. That is all. Individual actions are to win the moral support of the people. We sometimes designate them as the 'propaganda through deed.'[33]

Bhagat Singh had wholly soaked up Kropotkin whom he read alongside Lenin and Trotsky. It is unclear, however, whether Bhagat Singh understood Lenin's and Trotsky's discomfort with the idea of propaganda by deed. Or for that matter if Bhagat Singh was cognisant of Kropotkin's discomfiture with and studious avoidance of the use of the term 'propaganda by deed'; or whether Bhagat Singh grasped Kropotkin's rejection of isolated individual acts of terrorism because he believed that the repression that followed these actions cancelled out their positive impact if any.[34] Kropotkin was discomfited by the narrow political nature of Russian terrorism, where violence was primarily directed against people associated with the government.[35] He felt that revolutionary action should complement the revolutionary struggle of the peasantry because without the latter one could not carry out a successful revolution.

While smidgens of Bakunin and Kropotkian ideas can be discerned floating around in Bhagat Singh's writings, his inclination towards vanguardism made him closer to Leninist belief in the dictatorship of the proletariat as an indispensable historical phase preceding the historical fading away of the state. It is difficult to establish whether Bhagat Singh appreciated the anarchist disdain of the efficacy of the intermediate stage of a dictatorship of the proletariat.[36] In Bakunin's view, the idea of proletarian dictatorship failed to take into account that military and bureaucratic centralisation was the essence of the state system and that no state could exist without them. Therefore, it was impossible for any form of state organisation to provide a solution to the peasant and working-class aspirations unless it was built bottom upwards.[37] Bhagat Singh unproblematically blended the two creeds. He held that the organisation of peasantry and labour was an essential precondition for bringing the socialist revolution to fruition, but at the same time, he anticipated the revolutionary party playing a significant role before and after the revolution.

Undoing spatial scales: anti-statist nationalism and internationalism

Bhagat Singh's revolutionism was an anti-statist creed. The ultimate goal of the revolution was to establish a stateless society. In Bhagat Singh's view, 'As a matter of fact, the state, the government machinery is just a weapon in the hands of the ruling class to further and safeguard its interest.'[38] And 'all forms of government rest on violence.'[39] Statism, in the Marxist-anarchist conception, was the locus of violence – structural violence. If elimination of structural violence was the aim, then the state as a form of human governance had to be done away with. The post-revolutionary society was to be one of absolute individual freedom: a society created, maintained and experienced collectively, and where military or bureaucracy was no longer needed.[40] If everything is shared commonly, there would be no greed. All will work together. There will be no fear of thievery, *dacoity*, etc. The police, jails, courts, armies will not be needed. The pot-bellied exploiters will also work. There will be more yield and lesser work. Everyone will be able to read and write. There will be peace and prosperity.[41]

Bhagat Singh even came out against democracy as a political system falling short of achieving the ultimate aim of human freedom: 'We do not want democracy or any other form of government. They say, "Undermine the whole conception of the State and then only we have liberty worth having."[42] He cited the example of Austrian, American and French democracies where certain sections of the population remained in a wretched condition. He questioned Rousseau's social contract:

> Is that deal serving its purpose? God and the government conspired after gaining political power and told the people that God had sent them to rule over them. People became fearful of God, and the rulers did whatever atrocities they liked to the people. The examples of Czar (Russia) and Louis (France) expose this fraud very well because their conspiracy could not remain concealed for a longer time.[43]

Nothing compared to the dazzling vision of a stateless communist society. Notwithstanding their difference on the efficacy and relevance of the dictatorship of the proletariat, all shades of Marxists and anarchists were in agreement that complete freedom could be experienced only in a stateless society.

The revolutionary aspiration and utopia for absolute freedom, political and human, was captured in Bhagat Singh's use of the term *Poorna Swaraj* – complete freedom from structural violence of the state, church and private property – the utopian space of 'aviolence' for one's nation. This was a conception of the nation that was more inclusive than the boundaries of the state. In this case, as Rebecca Karl rightly states, the 'scope of nationalism exceeded the scope of statism.'[44] In Bhagat Singh's case, the revolutionary struggle was at the same time a nationalist struggle because he was contending with colonialism as the foe. *Poorna Swaraj* as a telos also bared the entangling of nationalist and internationalist scales of resistance. Bhagat Singh discursively conceptualised, located and defined the adversary as transnational and not just local but the actual site of resistance was just that – national, local and immediate. He kept in sight the broader spatiality of domination while articulating and carving out the space of and for resistance within British India. What laid the grounds for this scalar entanglement were the books that Bhagat Singh was reading, the intertextuality of life and literature. Books that helped him imagine and dream of the revolution and to live a vibrant life waiting, planning and moving towards revolution, books that enabled him to transcend his immediate context and yet taught him how to struggle for its liberation.[45]

Nationalist consciousness in Bhagat Singh's generation was unfolding in a unique historical context. The late nineteenth and twentieth centuries saw an emergence of the first modern globalised world with new modes of communication and travel, mass migrations, intimate and parasitical transnational economic networks and the pandiculating high noon of European imperialism. A world with more considerable knowledge of itself as a more connected entity. The new connectivities fed, nourished and sustained new cultural and social formations and even newer forms of exploitation and violence. An unmistakable fallout was the circulation of subversive antiauthoritarian ideas clanking and straining against the chains of bondage and oppression finding expression in the Russian Revolution and the Easter Rising. It was also a world where nationalism was demonstrably becoming a weapon in global conflict.[46] While Colonialism as a transnational entity was the premise for anti-colonial nationalisms it was not the only impulse that generated them. The impulse also lay with the colonised as they sought to define themselves in a global arena. This undid the spatial scales of the two isms, nationalism and internationalism, in the interwar period. An awareness of one's struggle's in the global geography of colonial domination instinctively created metaphysically and imagined affinities with similarly structurally disadvantaged countries/nations. The struggle was undoubtedly national/local, but it was articulating itself and against a translocal structural and material entity. One of the modes that this resistance adopted was to link up discursively and materially with similar resistance movements in other parts of the globe or to imagine itself as an inheritor and bearer of similar historical struggles.

Bhagat Singh, in this case, was heavily drawing on anarchism, which was inherently internationalist in its conception. Bakunin believed that all states, governments and ruling classes practice class solidarity to protect their interests. Therefore, it behoved the popular classes to create solidarity across racial and national divisions (Van der Walt and Schmidt 2009:61). However, this did not imply that Bakunin was not in favour of anti-imperialist movements. While he gave unequivocal support to decolonisation, looking into the future of the nationalist struggle he also prophesised that they would become 'retrogressive, disastrous' if the sole aim were to bring about a political revolution and set up a powerful state (Van der Walt and Schmidt 2009:61). The leaders of the liberation movement would become the new ruling elite and use the ideas of national freedom and solidarity to harangue the working classes into submission. The struggles for national liberation, in Bakunin's view, had to entail social and economic revolution and link themselves to the larger international struggle. Nationalism, for it not to be reactionary had to link 'its aspirations and forces' with those of other countries (Bakunin 1971: 341–43).

As was with nationalism, internationalism also held a different meaning for Bhagat Singh. Internationalism primarily occupied an imaginative and discursive space premised on an empathetic response to the material conditions of oppression. It was a relational transnational identity of solidarity against oppression. The transnational solidarity that espoused was an imagined 'structure of feeling' against a mutual experience of oppression. International network (in the form of literature and arms that were flowing into British India from Germany and Afghanistan) did exist but did not drive the actions locally on the ground. There were no international leagues or networks that Bhagat Singh and his mates were feeding. They weren't plotting and planning a revolution across Asia or Europe.[47] In fact, notwithstanding the ideological affinities, the differences over strategy made the HSRA members distance themselves from the Indian communists such as Shaukat Usmani and Muzaffar Ahmad. Bhagat Singh and his cohort wished to focus on 'mobilizing the educated youth whom they wished to use as a vehicle of spreading awareness.' They firmly believed in the idea of using brave and demonstrative 'actions' to bring about a revolution in thinking in India. Durga Das Khanna, a member of NBS and an associate of Bhagat Singh recalls him as saying, 'Let us first try to do whatever we can in our own country and then we shall think of other countries of the world.'[48]

Conclusion: reconfiguring internationalism in a worldly world

If one were to ask how unique was Bhagat Singh's location in the national-international dialectics, we would see that he wasn't the first or the only one engaging in varying scales of resistance. The Indian revolutionaries since the early twentieth century were engaging with European anarchist writings and the methods of Russians revolutionaries. Historian Maia Ramnath has analysed the echoes and intersections between Russian anarchism and Indian nationalism and rightly argues that 'the urban intellectual Swadesh lists resembled the Russian Slavophiles,'[49] in their idolisation of the peasantry and a form of romanticised stateless socialism based on village economy. Several Bengal revolutionaries had travelled to Russia to learn bomb-making.[50] In 1907, Lala Hardayal had openly advocated adopting the Russian methods as the 'only methods' that could bring the English to their senses. In fact, Hardayal possessed a more sophisticated understanding of the European writers and anarchist philosophies than the young Bhagat Singh and a deeper commitment to international social revolution'(Brown 1975: 107, 112). He founded the Bakunin Institute in Oakland, the USA as a hermitage for wandering lecturers (Ramnath 2011: 95). There were other maverick nationalists such as Dhan Gopal Mukerji (1890–1936), M.P.T. Acharya (1887–1951) who were also moving transnationally, participating in international anti-imperialist movements (Ramnath 2011: 110–45) and who espoused an eclectic mix of anarchist and socialist ideas. What set Bhagat Singh and HSRA apart was the direct application of anarchist ideas in their political actions and the ideology they espoused.

In some ways, Indian nationalism at least the middle-class variant had always been worldly in a way that displayed an awareness of unfolding in a world connected through ideas and material ties. From the 1820s, the Indian reformers and thinkers associated with the 'Bengal Renaissance' exhibited a consciousness that was in dialectics with the world beyond the spatial confines of British India. The foremost litterateur, Bankim Chandra Chatterjee had a profound impact on nationalist imagination engaged and interacted with the world. He had read a great deal of contemporary social theory (Mill, Comte, Spencer, Hegel and French philosophers).[51] One can trace similar strains in most nationalist leaders. Internationalism was a value that all espoused. Even Gandhi was intellectually informed by the world but puts it aside when starts participating in the nationalist movement. Tagore went a step further and critiqued the nationalist while theorising importance of internationalism.

In part, the location of Bhagat Singh and HSRA in the global frame is as much historical as historiographical. While reading the anarchist and Marxist writers connected Bhagat to a wider transnational idea of revolution, it did not necessarily bring with it a concomitant awareness of and solidarity with the contemporary anarchists active outside Western Europe in the Caribbean, Peru, Argentina, South Africa, Egypt, Korea, China, Japan and Ukraine. Bhagat Singh and his friends remained unaware of the concurrently unfolding history of anarchism and Marxism in the non-European world and the European colonies.[52] This belies Erez Manela's argument regarding Wilson's international overtures leading to coming together of Asian nationalisms. Rebecca Karl rightly argues that for the most part the stories of Asian nationalisms matured and played themselves out independently of each other through the twentieth century. There were only a few ephemeral moments when they displayed cognisance of and acknowledged each other (Karl 1998: 1096–118). Focused on finding solutions to India's problem of political subjection and given his youth, in Bhagat Singh's case theoretical eclecticism and praxis predominated ideological refinement. The primary objective was to raise consciousness through actions. His and HSRA's trajectory is similar to the *Narodnik* activities that led up to the assassination of the Russian czar in 1881 and to that of the IRA's (Irish Republican Army) plots to kill Margret Thatcher in 1984. In anarchism and Marxism, Bhagat Singh not only found the solution to India's political subjugation but also to the social and economic problems of the Indian society.

Through an exploration of Bhagat Singh's location within a global framework, this chapter engages the broader issue of the relationship between political identity and the spatiality of resistance. It argues that the political geography of resistance – imagined and physical – plays a significant role in constituting political identities of those involved in the struggle. Here the crucial variable is the spatial scale of resistance – local, grassroots, provincial, national, international and so on. However, determining a fixed spatial scale to study a political identity is an intractable problem because, first, oppression and resistance to it not only involve multiple layers of experiences but also have an intertwined and dialectical character (then merely oppositional).[53] This means that the knowledge of both may not have a singular and stable meaning. The spatial scales of resistance can thus shift, reconstitute and acquire new and different significances during and after the struggle. As a consequence, political identities also continue to shift scales and gain new meaning. This problem acquires even greater immediacy in a globalised world where the separation between local (national) and global (international) may be a convenient heuristic device but nonetheless runs the risk of being an insufficient analytical lens. This chapter makes a case for discarding the local-global binary where the two are perceived as neatly and 'authentically' distinguishable from each other,[54] and instead examine the dialectics and interpenetration between the two frames. In doing so it questions the use of simplistic identity labels such as internationalist or nationalist, as if being one cancels out the other, to understand the lives of historical actors; and thereby enliven us to the limitations of historical categories, labels and frameworks that historians use to analyse the past which may be those of historians than of historical actors.

Notes

1 Maia Ramnath, *Decolonizing Anarchism: An Antiauthoritarian History of India's Liberation Struggle*, California: A. K Press and the Institute for Anarchist Studies, 2011, p. 20.
2 The word 'International' made its way into the popular lexicon in the mid-nineteenth century with the First International in 1864. Formed by Karl Marx, The First International was the first transnational organisation of the workingmen.
3 Harald Fischer-Tiné, "Indian Nationalism and the 'world forces': Transnational and Diasporic Dimensions of the Indian Freedom Movement on the Eve of the First World War," *Journal of Global History* 2 (2007), pp. 325–44; Thomas G. Fraser, "Germany and Indian Revolution, 1914–18," *Journal of Contemporary History* 12 (1977), pp. 255–72; L. P. Mathur, *Indian Revolutionary Movement in the United States of America*, New Delhi: S.Chand, 1970; Alan Raucher, "American Anti-Imperialists and the Pro-India Movement, 1900–1932," *The Pacific Historical Review* 43 (1) (1974), pp. 83–110; G. L. Dmitriev, *Indian Revolutionaries in Central Asia*, Kolkata: Maulana Abul Kalam Azad Institute of Asian Studies, 2002; Tilak Raj Sareen, *Indian Revolutionary Movement Abroad, 1905–1921*, New Delhi: Sterling Publishers, 1979; Kate O'Malley, *Ireland, India and Empire: Indo-Irish Radical Connections, 1919–64*, Manchester: Manchester University Press, 2010; Michael Silvestri, *Ireland and India: Nationalism, Empire and Memory*, Basingstoke: Palgrave Macmillan, 2007.
4 The HSRA comprised of Chandra Shekhar Azad, the surviving HRA members and the young revolutionaries who had been working to promote HRA in Punjab (Bhagat Singh, Sukhdev, Bhagwati Charan Vohra, Des Raj and Yashpal), United Provinces (Bijoy Kumar Sinha, Jaidev Kapur, Mahabir Singh, Batukeshwar Dutt, and Shiv Verma) along with Jatindranath Das, the bomb expert from Bengal and a few revolutionaries from Bihar, Phonindranath Ghosh and his associate Manmohan. See Dharmendra Gaud, S. N. Sharma, and Pandit Satyanarayan, *Krantiveer: Chandrashekhar Azad aur Unke do Gaddar Saathi*, New Delhi: Bhagat Singh Vichaar Manch, 2011, p. 69.
5 Shiv Varma, Oral History Transcript (OHT) no. 502, NMML, p. 43.
6 *Ibid.*, p. 42.
7 Suresh Salil, ed., *Ganesh Shankar Vidyarthi Aur Unka Yug*, Anamika, 2014.
8 Bombay Railway Strike involving 50,000 workers, the Girni Kamgar Union Strike in the Bombay city and other centres for 6 months

involving 25,000, G.I.P. Strike involving 50,000 workers in Nagpur and Bombay, andthe strike of 20,000 railway men of Lituah, Howrah, Oudal and Hsansa, in Sibnath Bannerjee Collections, List no. 236, Section III: Speeches and Writings of Sibnath Banerjee, No. 32 Meerut Conspiracy Case, NMML.
9 Varma, OHT, no. 502, NMML, p. 43.
10 Chand, Lala Feroze, Oral History Transcript, The Center of South Asia Studies, University of Cambridge (CSAS), pp. 24–25.
11 Yadav and Singh, *The Fragerance*, pp. 99, 101. I also found a copy of Oscar Wilde's play in the Dwarkadass Library (now housed in Chandigarh's Lajpat Bhawan) from where the HSRA were issuing and reading books.
12 A. J. Sack was the Director of the Russian Information Bureau in the United States at the time he wrote the book. The purpose of the book was to educate the American public about the efforts of the Russian Revolutionaries since the 1820s that eventually culminated in the Bolshevik Revolution of 1917.
13 Jaidev Kapur, OHT 431, NMML, p. 11, 104.
14 Ramnath, *Decolonizing Anarchism*, p. 272 (footnote 43).
15 Jaidev Kapur, OHT 431, p. 103.
16 Statement of Bhagat Singh and B.K. Dutt in the Delhi Assembly Bomb Case, in Yadav and Singh, *The Fragrance*, pp. 247–54.
17 Jaidev Kapur and Jaidev Gupta mention Bhagat Singh having read Sinclair's anthology. See Jaidev Kapur, 431, pp. 103–104; Jaidev Gupta, 346, p. 85.
18 Jaidev Gupta, 346, p. 85.
19 Bhagat Singh, "A Critique of the Indian Revolutionary Movement," in Yadav and Singh, *The Fragrance*, p. 44.
20 Bhagat Singh in his essay 'Anarchism' (in *Kirti*, May 1929) questioned the stereotype of the anarchists as 'cruel' and a 'blood sucker'; a person with no 'compassion in his heart' and one 'who relished destruction all around him,' in Yadav and Singh, *The Fragrance*, p. 78.
21 Singh, "Revolutionary Party," p. 61.
22 *Ibid*.
23 Singh, *A Critique*, p. 50.
24 Bhagat Singh' desire to surrender and be arrested after bombing the Delhi Assembly was part of the strategy to use the courts for the propaganda of their ideology. It was his idea to throw the bomb in the Assembly as a protest against the bills, in Shiv Varma, OHT 502, NMML, pp. 92–93; Communist leader Sibnath Banerjee talks about how communist and socialist propaganda was otherwise forbidden in British India but the Meerut Conspiracy Case gave these ideas wide publicity, in Sibnath Banerjee Collections, List no. 236, Section III: Speeches and Writings of Sibnath Banerjee, No. 32 Meerut Conspiracy Case, NMML, pp. 67–68.
25 Singh, "Russia's Nihilists," Yadav and Singh, *The Fragrance*, p. 97.
26 Cahm, *Kropotkin*, p. 91.
27 Singh, "Revolutionary Party," p. 55. Here Bhagat Singh critiques the Bardoli resolution of 1922. According to him the resolution 'clearly defines the horror the leaders felt when they saw the gigantic peasant

class rising to shake off not only the domination of an alien nation but also the yoke of the landlords.'
28 Singh, "Revolutionary Party," p. 62.
29 *Ibid.*, p. 54.
30 *Ibid.*, p. 59.
31 Jaidev Kapur, OHT 431, p. 51.
32 *Ibid.*, p. 52.
33 Letter on Hari Kishan's Case, published in *The People*, 14 July 1931, in Yadav and Singh, *The Fragrance*, p. 69.
34 Cahm, *Kropotkin*, p. 107.
35 *Ibid.*, p. 140.
36 Bakunin in 'Statism and Anarchy' completely debunked it: 'The differences between revolutionary dictatorship and statism are superficial. Fundamentally they both represent the same principle of minority rule over the majority in the name of the alleged "stupidity" of the latter and the alleged "intelligence" of the former.' In Dolgoff, *Bakunin*, p. 329.
37 Bakunin in 'Statism and Anarchy': 'No state, however democratic – not even the reddest republic – can ever give the people what they really want, ie, the free self-organization and administration of their own affairs from the bottom upward.' *Ibid.*, p. 338.
38 Singh, "Revolutionary Party", p. 56.
39 Bhagat Singh quoting Emma Goldman, in Yadav and Singh, *The Fragrance*, p. 79.
40 Lucien Van der Walt and Michael Schmidt, *Black Flame: The Revolutionary Class Politics of Anarchism and Syndicalism*, Edinburg: AK Press, pp. 53–54.
41 "Anarchism II," *Kirti*, June 1928, in Yadav and Singh, *The Fragrance*, p. 86.
42 Yadav and Singh, *The Fragrance*, p. 84.
43 "Anarchism," *Kirti*, June 1928, in Yadav and Singh, *The Fragrance*, pp. 83–84.
44 Rebecca Karl, *Staging the World: Chinese Nationalism at the Turn of the Twentieth Century*, Durham: Duke University Press, 2002.
45 The significance of European, Russian and American writers in the development of Bhagat's consciousness did not mean that his family and social background and the Indian authors had no impact on him. The Indian works such as Soham Swami's *Commonsense*, Sanyal's *Bandi Jivan*, Bankim's *Anandmath*, and Savarkar's *The First War of Independence* were equally inspirational and furnished Bhagat with historical details and empirical evidence of India's present condition.
46 Matthew E. Plowman, "Nationalism as a Weapon in Global Conflict: The Indo-Irish-German Conspiracy of World War I and the Anglo-American Response," paper presented in 19thAnnual Conference of the Association for the Study of *Ethnicity and Nationalism: Nationalism & Globalisation*, 31 March–2 April 2009, London Panel: "Nationalism and Global Political Conflict," 1 April 2009; Erez Manela, *Wilsonian Moment*, Cambridge: Harvard University Press, 2009; Maia Ramnath, *Haj to Utopia: How the Ghadar Movement Charted Global Radicalism and Attempted to Overthrow the British Empire*, Berkeley:

University of California Press, 2011; Kris Manjapara, M.N. Roy: *Marxism and Colonial Cosmopolitanism*, London: Routledge, 2010; Kama Maclean, *A Revolutionary History: Violence and Nationalism in Interwar India*, London: Hurst; "The History of a Legend: Accounting for Popular Histories of Revolutionary Nationalism in British India," *Modern Asian Studies* (2012), pp. 1–32; "The Portrait's Journey: The Image, Social Communication and Martyr-Making in Colonial India," *Journal of Asian Studies* (2011), pp. 1–32; A. G. Noorani, *Trial of Bhagat Singh: Politics of Justice*, New Delhi: Oxford University Press, 1996; Kuldip Nayar, *The Martyr: Bhagat Singh – Experiments in Revolution*,India: Har Anand, 2000 and *Without Fear: Life and Trial and Bhagat Singh*, India: Harper Collins, 2007; V. N. Datta, *Gandhi and Bhagat Singh*, India: Rupa, 2008; Malwinderjit Singh Waraich, Rajwanti Mann, and Harish Jain, eds., *Hanging of Bhagat Singh, Vol. I, II*, and III, Chandigarh: Unistar, 2010.

47 In case of the diasporic Indian revolutionaries such as the Gadarites, the London-based India House revolutionary groups or the ones in various parts of Europe and Asia, notwithstanding the transnational character of their activities, they also were no different in imagining the site of resistance as local. It was India's liberation that all of them were working towards.

48 Durga Das Khanna, OHT 294, NMML, p. 69.

49 Yadav, and Singh, *The Fragrance*, p. 71.

50 For details, please see Arun C. Bose, *Indian Revolutionaries Abroad, 1905–1922*, Patna: Bharti Bhavan, 1971.

51 Sudipta Kaviraj, *The Unhappy Consciousness: Bankimchandra Chattopadhyaya and the Formation of the Nationalist Discourse in India*, New York: Oxford University Press, 1995.

52 Benedict Anderson, "Preface," in Steven Hirsch, and Lucien van der Walt, eds., *Anarchism and Syndicalism in the Colonial and Postcolonial World, 1870–1940: The Praxis of National Liberation, Internationalism, and Social Revolution*, Brill, Leiden and Boston, 2010, pp. xiii–xx, p. xiii.

53 J. Sharp, P. Routledge, C. Philo, and R. Paddison, eds., *Entanglements of Power: Geographies of Domination/Resistance*, London: Routledge, 2000, pp. 1–42.

54 David Featherstone, "Spatialities of Transnational Resistance to Globalization: The Maps of Grievance of the Inter-Continental Caravan," *Transactions of the Institute of British Geographers* 28 (4) (December 2003), pp. 404–21.

References

Bakunin.1971. "Statism and Anarchy." In *Bakunin on Anarchy: Selected Works by the Activist-Founder of World Anarchism*, edited by Sam Dolgoff, 346. New York: Vintage Books.

Brown, Emily C. 1975. *Har Dayal: Hindu Revolutionary and Rationalist*. Tucson, AZ: University of Arizona Press.

Cahm, Caroline. 1989. *Kropotkin and the Rise of Revolutionary Anarchism 1872–1886*, 85–86. Cambridge: Cambridge University Press.
Chand, Lala Feroze Oral History Transcript, Center South Asia Studies, University of Cambridge (CSAS), 24–25.
Das, Ram Saran. 2007. *History of the Naujawan Bharat Sabha*, 14–15. Chandigarh: Unistar.
Dmitriev, G.L. 2002. *Indian Revolutionaries in Central Asia*. Kolkata: Maulana Abul Kalam Azad Institute of Asian Studies.
Fischer-Tinē, Harald. 2007. "Indian Nationalism and the 'world forces': Transnational and Diasporic Dimensions of the Indian Freedom Movement on the Eve of the First World War." *Journal of Global History* 2: 325–44.
Fraser, Thomas G. 1977. "Germany and Indian Revolution, 1914–18." *Journal of Contemporary History* 12: 255–72.
Gupta, Manmathnath. Jail Notebook, Acc. No. 1749, Nehru Memorial and Museum Library (NMML):297–98.
Habib, S. Irfan. 2007. *To Make the Deaf Hear: Ideology and Programme of Bhagat Singh and His Comrades*. India: Three Essays Collective.
Karl, Rebecca. 1998. "Creating Asia: China in the World at the Beginning of the Twentieth Century." *The American Historical Review* 103 (4): 1096–118.
Kaviraj, Sudipta. 1995. *The Unhappy Consciousness: Bankimchandra Chattopadhyay and the Formation of the Nationalist Discourse in India*. New York: Oxford University Press.
Mathur, L.P. 1970. *Indian Revolutionary Movement in the United States of America*. New Delhi: S. Chand.
O'Malley, Kate. 2010. *Ireland, India and Empire: Indo-Irish Radical Connections, 1919–64*. Manchester: Manchester University Press.
Prelooker, Jaakoff. 1908. *Heroes and Heroines of Russia: Builders of a New Commonwealth*. London: Simpkin, Marshall, Hamilton, Kent & Co., Ltd.
Ramnath, Mala. 2011. *Decolonizing Anarchism: An Antiauthoritarian History of India's Liberation Struggle*. California: A K Press and the Institute for Anarchist Studies.
Raucher, Alan. 1974. "American Anti-Imperialists and the Pro-India Movement, 1900–1932." *The Pacific Historical Review* 43 (1): 83–110.
Sack, A. J. 1918. *The Birth of Russian Democracy*. New York, NY: Russian Information Bureau, 51–52.
Salil, Suresh, ed. 2014. *Ganesh Shankar Vidyarthi Aur Unka Yug*. Anamika.
Sareen, Tilak Raj. 1979. *Indian Revolutionary Movement Abroad, 1905–1921*. New Delhi: Sterling Publishers.
Sharp, J., Routledge, P., Philo, C. and Paddison, R., eds. 2000. *Entanglements of Power: Geographies of Domination/Resistance*. London: Routledge.

Siljack, Anna. 2008. *Angel of Vengeance: The Girl Who Shot the Governor of St. Petersburg and Sparked the Age of Assassination*. New York, NY: St. Martin's Press.

Silvestri, Michael. 2007. *Ireland and India: Nationalism, Empire and Memory*. Basingstoke: Palgrave Macmillan.

Singh, Bhagat. 2006. "Why Am I an Atheist." In *The Fragrance of Freedom: Writings of Bhagat Singh*, edited by K. C. Yadav and Babar Singh, 25. Gurgaon: Hope India.

Sisir, Karmendu, ed. 2009. *Radhamohun Gokul Samagra*, 1, 2. New Delhi: Anamika.

Van der Walt, Lucien, and Michael Schmidt. 2009. *Black Flame: The Revolutionary Class Politics of Anarchism and Syndicalism*. Edinburg: AK Press.

Varma, Shiv. Oral History Transcript (OHT) no. 502, NMML,43.

Wilde, Oscar. 1908. *Vera; or, the Nihilists: A Drama in a Prologue and Four Acts*. London: Metheun & Co. Ltd.

Chapter 10

The languages of the Indian-English writer

Aruni Kashyap

Introduction

As an Indian-English writer, the question of audience is crucial to me. By 'audience' I don't mean readership. I mean the imaginary listener who shapes the text as I write it. It has nothing to do with who reads the books – stories are for any reader from any country of any race and gender. But for any writer, the audience is a dominant presence while 'telling' a story because it is conjoined with the idea of liberation, of freedom. The Indian-English writer doesn't have this freedom, unlike their counterparts in the Indian languages. And we need to work towards achieving this freedom. But the fundamental question is – how do we do it?

I can talk about myself: I am an Assamese, I am from the northeast and in many ways, I write about marginalised regions, themes, issues that I think are essential aspects of Indian reality that has been ignored. I have written one novel and some short stories, non-fiction and poetry. Often, I have been accused of writing only about Assam and Assamese life and not writing about, say, for example, people in Delhi (because I have lived in Delhi for little more than six years).

I am often surprised by this question: It is an innocuous question for the questioner. Why are you blowing it up, they would say, if I express dismay. But I don't think it is a legitimate question to ask an author. It is not a literary question. It has nothing to do with the literary imagination. It has little to do with the choices I make when I write fiction. It doesn't challenge the way I have depicted character or the way I have structured my novels. I couldn't ask for example, to Bangla writer, Ashapurna Debi, such a question when/what she is going to write about this or that.

The languages of the Indian-English writer 199

People don't understand how loaded such a question is and what kind of implicit prejudicial baggage such a question carries. To ask me when I am going to stop writing about Assam and write about Delhi or other places in India is to suggest that writing about Assam (or regional India) couldn't be a legitimate or high level of artistic endeavour for an Indian-English author; as though regional Indian life, Assamese life, has no meaning, depth and importance. As though it is very easy to write about life in the north-east. As if I have chosen to cook steamed rice instead of *kheer* for a meal.

I mentioned this because this is where the politics of audience (not readership and book buyers) comes in. I am an Assamese writer who writes mostly in English. My work is discussed in the media as stories from Northeast India because the general people of India do not have many stories of Northeast India in their minds because the term north-east is a convenient umbrella term to use to begin a discussion about this misunderstood, misrepresented and underrepresented region of India. It used to make me angry until I understood the reasons behind this – since I am an Indian-English writer from a marginalised space, I would always have to answer these questions until there are enough stories from the north-east published by the mainstream press (though I don't know how many stories would be enough). We have a long way to go. So I do not bother too much about these labels because they are here to go.

But I am also an English Indian writer. Historically, the Indian-English writer has been forced to accommodate the presence of a less aware Western reader from its inception. An Indian-English writer never had the privilege of speaking to the aware, sensitive, informed, industrious reader that a Marathi-Hindi-Tamil-Bangla author has been able to speak to for centuries. It is the kind of reader who deeply penetrates the text to participate in the meaning production. It is an ideal reader. The Indian-English writer never had this ideal reader because of the consequences of colonialism. When this body of work was developing, they wrote in a language that was considered the colonisers' language – the very act of writing in English was perceived as betrayal. In the place they wrote about, where their ideal reader inhabited, whose stories they told, they couldn't be read because this group who could read English was numerically weak. That is the reason, again and again, the relevance – if not rootedness – of the Indian-English writer, especially fiction has been questioned and debated for a long time now. The question of readership comes. The mobility and privilege that comes with writing in English is another aspect of the debate.

I have been curious for a long time how this affects the literary imagination of Indian authors who write in English. But things have changed a lot now. English has percolated like drops of water through layers of sand in a filter into varying strata of Indian society. The resident Indian-English writers do not have to write with this anxiety to accommodate the Western reader anymore, though we still have a long way to go to achieve this literary liberation because which Indian authors New York and London presses choose to publish exerts a great amount of influence in the Indian mind. (I must say, the non-English-speaking countries are ahead than their English-speaking Western counterparts in demonstrating curiosity to read diverse authors from India.)

This has troubled me ever since I was a student and wrestled with the politics of audience quite a bit. Who do I speak to when I write? If I try to write that elusive universal novel for a global readership, I would be producing water because of the general ignorance of the Western reader about complex Indian reality. If I write for a mainland-Indian readership, I stand the risk of reducing myself as an interpreter of the incomprehensible but colourful people of Northeast India who, according to most mainland-Indians, fight 'senseless,' 'contextless' wars trying to secede from India!

I couldn't liberate language and literary imagination if I tried to accommodate these two groups of readers, so I always keep only an Assamese person in mind when I write; or a person who would understand complex Indian realities, the layered nature of Indian experience, the metaphors that we use in everyday language unconsciously.

Much before I began to write, I read novels written in Indian languages. There, I found the parameters into which I could step in, postures I could pose in and write by assuming the centrality of my culture – Assamese culture. I wish it would be the same for every English writer in India one day – regardless of their first languages. As the global novel written in a language of broader communication raises its head, we need to think deeply about novels that address regional concerns, challenges local power structures.

Amongst the Indian-English writers, I found the most help in Amitav Ghosh's corpus whose novels, I think, as Sunil Ganguly quipped once, are Bengali novels written in English. In an interview with *Scroll.in*, Amitav Ghosh says,

> One of the greatest compliments I have ever received is from my friend and wonderful author, the late Sunil Gangopadhyay, who when releasing a novel of mine, said, 'E to dekchhibanglaboi, shudhuingrijitelekha! [But this is a Bengali book, only written in English!]' My narrative is very reminiscent of the Bengali novel of course. I think the Bengali novel talks to readers in a different way than the English one. It talks directly to the reader, it posits to the reader. When you read an English novel, it is a little like receiving a message in a bottle; the novel is not speaking directly to you.
> (31 January 2015, https://scroll.in/article/703385/five-thoughts-on-writing-and-a-post-script-from-amitav-ghosh)

R K Narayan's fiction too helped me write in the kind of liberated, sovereign language I wanted to write. But I learnt the most from Toni Morrison's novels who assumed the centrality of her race and its aesthetics while writing her fiction. In an interview with Charlie Rose, she says,

> In this country [the United States], many books, particularly then – 40s–50s – you could feel the address of the narrator, over my shoulder talking to somebody else. Talking to somebody white. I could tell because they were explaining things that didn't have to explain if they were talking to me.

The parallels between the situation of the Indian-English writer and conventions of African-American writing that Morrison broke are unmistakable. The Indian-English writer, in general, has been "consumed and concerned" – to use Morrison's words – by this imaginary presence of the Western, global reader. Morrison wrote in a language without taking into consideration a white audience. She refused to be consumed by and be concerned with the expectations of that readership. Until Morrison's arrival, African-American writing spoke to a white audience so whenever an African-American person read the books, they would find the narrator talking to someone else, explaining cultural matters – that is obvious to an African-American reader – to another person. We could see the same tendency in Indian-English novels. If an Indian writer from any region, any state, were speaking to me, s/he wouldn't have to write, for example, 'I went to attend Diwali – the festival of lights.' S/he just would need to say, 'I love Diwali.' Because, I, as an Indian reader, would always understand it. A hilarious example of this tendency is seen in the opening paragraph of Jhumpa Lahiri's Namesake where lines after lines are used to describe Ashima making 'jhaalmuri.' Would you write,'I made tea,' or

> When the water began to boil, I lifted the kettle from the burner and poured it into the cup. I threw a tea-bag into it and watched as the brown colour spread out. I poured some sugar into and a little milk. A few minutes passed. I squeezed the tea-bag and threw it into the bin?

Did Hemingway explain Thanksgiving to me? I didn't ask Nadine Gordimer to teach me history, and she didn't. But generations of Indian-English fiction writers (except a few) mostly until, perhaps the last half-a-decade, have been doing that for a long time. It has produced the Global Indian-English novel, along with a strange irony: The authors critically acclaimed in the Indian press, authors most loved by Indian readers (and I am not talking about Durjoy Dutta or Chetan Bhagat here), are not embraced by other centres of English writing such as Toronto, London or New York.

True liberation of Indian-English writing would happen only when we start writing in a language that would refuse to accommodate this global gaze (often Western); books that would be written in a sovereign Indian English and yet be embraced around the world. My attempt to arrive at a language that is free of the dominant Western gaze has nothing to do with the readership; it has got to do with having an independent literary imagination. I also come from a region that has a fraught relationship with the narrative of the Indian state. I grew up in the shadow of the gun and bomb-blasts, amidst heated discussions of political sovereignty of Assam. As an artist, sovereignty for me is to be able to shape sovereign imaginative texts. To be able to mould cultural productions that aren't bogged down by the burden of a dominant global, Western and mainland-Indian gaze. Hence, I am bothered when someone asks me who I write for.

When I was writing my first novel, this presence bothered me a lot. In my first draft, I included numerous irrelevant details that explained the history of Assam, its bumpy relationship with the Indian state, the context for the insurgency against which the novel is set. But then, I ended up with a book that I didn't want to write. I ended up with a book that I didn't identify. I was surprised to find the bitterness in the book when I had always thought my writing emerged from taking immense delight in the Assamese culture, not disappointment. I was disappointed by the anger that drove the narrative chapter by chapter.

There are nine chapters in *The House with a Thousand Stories*. I deleted five and rewrote them to do away with the anger. I realised I was looking at Assam from Delhi or England or somewhere else but not anywhere from the banks of the Brahmaputra. I thought, in what kind of a language Indira Goswami would have written? And I found the answer: It was much more rewarding to look at the rest of India from Assam, from the margins, than looking at the margins from the centre. That lens is always a bit cloudy. I took out the anger and brought the human drama to the centre stage by pushing the violence and the stories of human rights violations by security forces and the insurgents to the backstage. I wanted the story to be free to of these anxieties of who is to blame, who is cruel and who is not. If I had to celebrate the resilience of the rural folk in Assam, I had to bring their stories to the foreground and leave the stories of the agents who disrupted peace and the anger of the author behind. It would have been a huge injustice to the many stories under which the novel's main message is buried if everything was about my anger and my agenda of starting a blame game. And it wasn't only Indira Goswami who gave me the answers: All the fiction I read by Assamese and Bengali authors who didn't have to explain things to anyone, who didn't have to bother about a global reader and presented the standards and parameters that I could step in, that I could emulate. In a review of my novel published in an Assamese literary magazine Satsori, the critic Debhabhushan Borah said, 'This is an Assamese book, just written in English.' I still think that was the most charming and satisfying thing I heard about my book.

I am not sure if my quest to write in a free language has been achieved, but, I guess, a step has been taken. Maybe one day, English Indian authors would be identified by their immediate context, and they would be happy to call themselves Bengali writers who write in English, Marathi writers who write in English and so on. This would probably lead to a lot of Indian Englishs, but that could only be a good thing for us. It would make us richer.

Printed in the United States
By Bookmasters